Pete

GOD &
His Sexy Body

RelentlessLOVE
publishing

God and His Sexy Body: The Story of Adam and His Bride
Copyright © 2016 by Peter Hiett.
Published by Relentless Love Publishing
ISBN: 978-1535353373

Cover Design: Chachi Hernandez
Editors: Kimberly Weynen and Nate Bullis
Interior Design: Michael Hanna

Printed by CreateSpace, An Amazon.com Company
First Edition

Thank You

- Kimberly Weynen for helping me write this book, trying to teach me what a semicolon is, and suggesting the title to this book.
- Nate Bullis for helping us edit and your general all around awesomeness.
- Michael Hanna for teaching us how to make books and music.
- Matt Kinner for making all of this happen.
- Chris and Ginger for letting me use the Refuge.
- Ben Sullivan for making DownsideUp films.
- Chris Fellure for dreaming big dreams.
- Chachi for a most excellent book cover.
- Caravaggio for painting *The Incredulity of Saint Thomas* at the start of the 17th century in preparation for the cover of this book.
- Mom!
- Alison Schofield, (basically, professor of *God and Sex* in a highly prestigious university), for your help and your endorsement.
- Steve and Karla and all who gave to me, and the church, to make these things happen.
- Board of the Sanctuary for your immense encouragement, granting me the resources to make this possible, and your faith that God is Good.
- Sanctuary, my church, for allowing me to do this. You may not be rich or very large, but Jesus thinks you're quite attractive, and yes . . . *sexy.*
- Susan Hiett, my bride of thirty-three years. There are no words sufficient to describe what God has given to me in you. Thank you for being to me, and for me, the sacramental representation of the ecstatic communion that comprises the consummate Kingdom of God . . . and your *sexy* body.
- Jonathan, Elizabeth, Rebekah and Coleman for the fact that you still love me, even though I just made reference to Mom's sexy body.

Thank you GOD that

You are better than we thought,

The Love of Jesus is deeper than we know,

And your Spirit is everywhere working the wonders of Mercy.

Table of Contents

A Note to the Reader

God and His Sexy Body: The Story of Adam and His Bride is a popular commentary on Genesis chapter two, in which I have tried to create a relatively easy read, while at the same time, addressing theological issues rather unfamiliar to most readers. In an effort to maintain the flow of thought, I have placed some of my "bunny trails" in footnotes. If I were to travel back in time and give advice to my twenty-year-old inquisitive self, I would say, "Read the footnotes" and "Stop listening to Lynyrd Skynyrd so loud." I would also say, "Read more Karl Barth, George MacDonald, and the Early Church Fathers."

Some of the ideas in this book may seem novel to you, but they have a rich tradition in Church history and theological discourse. Hopefully, the footnotes and quotes can open doors to some of that material. For some reason, I quote C. S. Lewis rather extensively. I suppose that's because he was a brilliant writer who channeled many of the thoughts of George MacDonald, and because he is something of a popular and evangelical saint—and that's the neighborhood in which I live, and the crowd to whom I usually speak. I am a pastor, having been ordained in two Presbyterian denominations, but now pastoring a non-denominational church based in Denver, Colorado.

My writing comes from my speaking. And so, I'm not a big fan of grammatical rules or conventional punctuation. Yet, those literary devices are meant to accomplish what I've become accustomed to accomplishing with my voice. Fortunately, my assistant, Kimberly, paid attention in English class. When and where punctuation, spacing, and grammar gets "creative," just go with it. When and where it's "correct," thank Kimberly!

One particularly confusing grammatical convention, with profound theological importance, is capitalization in reference to the Divine. In Greek and Hebrew (The primary languages of Scripture), there is no capitalization. Yet in English, we often capitalize names for God and pronouns referring to God. This is far more difficult than it might seem. Translators struggle tremendously with a word like "spirit" or "Spirit." God is Spirit, yet He breathes into us our spirit (or Spirit), and according to Paul, "... *he who is joined to the Lord becomes one spirit* (or Spirit) *with him*" (1 Cor. 6:17). See the problem?

Take a word like love or Love; "*God is love*" (1 John 4:8) . . . or should it be "God is Love"? This becomes a profoundly theological question when we ask,

"How it is that the commandment is fulfilled?" Did God mean, "You will love" or "You will Love"? In other words, is love something I can do? Or is *Love* something done in me; is *Love* doing me? In other words, am I saved by my own decision and work? Or am I saved by God's decision and work in me—His work that is the new me? And where do we draw the line? . . . Is there a line?

If my body were a person, would it be capitalized? Is the body of Christ, Christ—same person or different? Where's the line between God and His bBody; between Christ and the cChurch?" "*It is no longer I who live but Christ who lives in me*" (Gal. 2:20). Thanks a lot, Saint Paul! You just created an impossible grammatical conundrum in English literature two thousand years later.

Is it grace or Grace? Is it faith or Faith? It's my faith, but it's "my Faith" because Jesus gave His Faith to me . . . right? He is "*our wisdom, our righteousness and sanctification and redemption*" (1 Cor. 1:30 RSV). Or should it be, "Wisdom... Righteousness...Sanctification... and Redemption (PSV – Peter's Standard Version)"?

Jesus said, "...*I am the way, the truth, and the life...*" (John 14:6). Or did He say, "I am the *W*ay, the *T*ruth, and the *L*ife"? Which would mean that your life is actually His Life, for which you ought to be grateful?

Well, I hope you see that English convention forces a decision on the author writing in English, that was not forced upon the author writing in Hebrew or New Testament Greek. So, in places, I have capitalized words in order to remind you that we're speaking of God, but that doesn't mean that we aren't speaking of you. In other places I have not capitalized words, to remind you that we're speaking of you, but that doesn't mean that we're not speaking of God. And let me remind you, that whenever you pause and ask, "Should that be capitalized or not capitalized," you are asking a deeply profound question that may take a lifetime to ponder . . . but keep reading.

There are many places where you may feel the need to stop and ponder. Please ponder—I'm counting on that—then, keep reading.

And thank you for reading. It's my joy (or Joy) to share with you the Good News.

God is better than you thought.

The love of Jesus is deeper than you know.

And the Spirit is everywhere working the wonders of Mercy.

Time for a Sexy Body

Genesis 1:1–2:4

God and His Sexy Body is about God and His sexy Body. Of course, God doesn't have a "body;" *"God is Spirit"* (John 4:24).

And yet . . .

- *"In the beginning was the Word, and the Word was with God, and the Word was God...And the Word became flesh and dwelt among us."* (John 1:1,14a).
- The Word in flesh is Jesus (whom Paul refers to as the *Eschatos* Adam),[1] and Jesus has a Bride who turns out to be us.
- *"Then the man* [the *Adam*] *said, 'This is bone of my bones and flesh of my flesh...'"* (Gen. 2:23a).
- And then Scripture says, *"Therefore a man shall leave his father and his mother and hold fast to his wife, and they shall become one flesh"* (Gen. 2:24).
- *"And the man and his wife were both naked and unashamed"* (Gen. 2:25). That's sexy.

So *God and His Sexy Body* really *is* about God and His sexy Body, yet at first, it might not seem so sexy. Don't worry; we'll get to that in time, perhaps that's why God made time—that you might stand before Him naked and unashamed at the end of time. Whatever the case, we'll begin with God and then observe how He creates a Body made for intimate, ecstatic, and eternal communion with Himself.

That might sound extremely exciting (It is!) . . . or downright terrifying, and on some level, it *is*—for all of us. We have believed the lies of the evil one regarding our Lord's intentions. This is why God cares about your sex life. The evil one can corrupt it and then use it to lie to your heart about the intentions of your Lord so that in His presence and at His touch you'll shut down your heart and

---

[1] 1 Cor. 15:45. *Eschatos* can be translated "last," "ultimate," "least," or "extreme"

hide in shame. If that's you, I pray that you'd have enough faith to keep reading even when it gets sexy.

Our Lord has bound Himself to you in an Eternal Covenant in order that you might commune with Him in the sanctuary of that Covenant, infused with ecstatic joy in His presence and at His touch. He won't abuse you. He pursues you, for He is romancing you. He is romancing you with Grace, in order to create faith, in order that you would freely surrender to Him. He is Love. That's what the Bridegroom most desires from His Bride: faith in His Love. And that's what the Father most desires from His children: faith in His Love. He is Love.

So *God and His Sexy Body* really is about God and His sexy Body, but it's also a commentary. It's not simply what I think; it is a commentary on what God thinks. It's a commentary on Genesis chapter two.

God and His Sexy Body is also the second book in a three part series commenting on Genesis chapters one through three. The third book will be about the tree in the middle of the garden. The first book is already written and titled, *The History of Time and the Genesis of You*. My hope is that you would read that book before you read this book. Yet, I suppose it's not necessary, if you read this introduction.

This commentary is built on a rather remarkable foundation—the revelation that we are still living in the sixth day of creation, on the edge of a Seventh Day in which everything...is *"very good"* (Gen. 1:31). It means that the deepest story in Scripture is not the story of our failure but the story of God's success.

The deepest story is not that humanity sinned and now God is trying to fix it with the whole Jesus and His *cross thing*; the deepest story is that God is making us in His image, and He does that through the Jesus and His *tree* (Hebrew: *ets*—tree, timber, cross) *thing*. He is creating us: His children, His Bride and His Body. He is creating us, and He won't fail even though we have, and do fail.

In the first book we examined Genesis chapter one, which is the whole story—His story and history: day one through day seven. In this book we'll examine Genesis chapter two: the astounding thing that God does on the sixth day and what it means for the Seventh Day. So, before we begin with chapter one of this book, I'd like to summarize what I wrote in the last book. And I'd like to do so with a story.[2]

God is taking us all on the journey of our own creation. Jesus is creating faith within His Bride upon this journey. God the Father is creating faith within His children. God is creating a Body of joy.

When my children were little they dreamed of a kingdom of joy, a magic kingdom. They dreamed of a whole new world. They called it Disney World. As a young pastor with four children it seemed to be an impossible dream. But several years ago, a friend made an offer that I couldn't refuse. To me, and my family, he offered a week's stay at one of the Disney resorts in Orlando. All we had to do was get there. We couldn't afford to fly, but I figured we could drive; we had a mini van!

Our children were three, six, eight, and nine at the time. I came up with the idea of surprising them because I just cherished that moment of revelation: I'd say, "We're going to Disney World!" Then their faces would light up with joy, and they would dance with delight before the goodness that was their father. I cherished the "moment of revelation," AND I knew that if we told them too soon they'd drive us crazy, and they might just die from a combination of joy and longing called hope.

As this summer approached, they pressed for information about vacation. I didn't want to lie, so I planned our route and realized I could tell them the truth—just not all of it. I realized that we'd be driving through Junction City, Kansas—my birthplace. And so, one day, when they were pressing, I exclaimed,

"Kansas! We're going to Kansas!"

They all said, "Wow! . . . What's in Kansas?" And I said, "Stuff! All kinds of stuff: hotels, swimming pools, stuff, we'll see . . . stuff." And so they put their hope in Junction City, Kansas.

I remember taking them to Mc Donald's one day, during that time. Their Happy Meal toys were promotionals for Disney World. Elizabeth said, "Dad this

---

[2] The following became a *Downside Up* film titled, *Journey to the Magic Kingdom.* You can view the film at: www.downsideup.com

is so cool!" I said, "What is it?" Her eyes got big; she described it to me—this land . . . I said, "Where is it?" She said, "Orlando or something," and then, "Dad it's really far away, we could never go there." I was just bursting inside, but I forced myself to say something like, "Well Honey, we're gonna have a good vacation...trust me." (Faith is trust.)

Well, they dreamed of Junction City, Kansas. The day finally came: May 28, 1998, our fifteenth wedding anniversary. Early that morning, we set out on I-70 for Kansas. If you subtract four hours of potty breaks it's about a six-hour drive from Denver to Junction City. Then one hour more, (seven hours) to Kansas City, where we'd rest for the night and then go on to the Magic Kingdom.

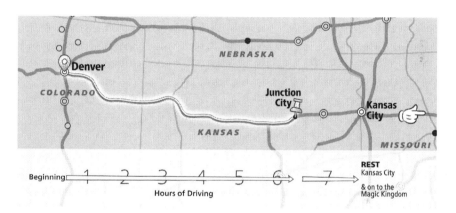

It was a long van ride for the kids, so when we exited I-70 for Junction City, they were pretty excited. John was looking for a motel with a swimming pool. They were all talking about seeing the place where Daddy was once a little boy. We drove past a beat up old bowling alley, and they all exclaimed, "Daddy, we could go bowling! We could go bowling!" And I said, "Maybe."

Soon, we arrived at the church my dad had pastored, right next to the beautiful old manse in which I had lived as a little boy. I'd called ahead, and now the current pastor, Dick Underhall-Pierce, was waiting to give us the grand tour.

My kids had disposable cameras which my mom and dad had given them to document our trip. As the pastor showed us around the church, the children kept saying, "I want to take a picture." And I'd say, "Well, you might want to save some film. There might be more stuff you'll want to take pictures of later on." They'd respond, "Like what?" And I'd reply, "Oh well, stuff . . . more stuff! Trust me."

Then, Pastor Underhall-Pierce took us next door and showed us the manse. After that, we all sat down on the front steps across from the park where I used to play. Coleman eyed the playground. I was video taping. Susan got the secret bag out of the van. Then I began the prearranged dialogue with Pastor Underhall-Pierce.

"So, what's to do here in Junction City?" I asked. He responded, "Well, gosh . . . you can go for a walk down at the lake." I said, "Well, we got a lake in Colorado." He said, "You could go to the bowling ally . . . and there's a miniature golf course." I said, "We've got that in Colorado." The kids were looking at me like I was nuts or evil or maybe both. "We've already seen the church and the manse," I mused. "It seems like there's really nothing else to do here. We might-as-well just go." The kids were confused and starting to protest, "But Daddy, No . . . I like bowling!"

Then I asked, "Hey what happens if you stay on that road, I-70, out there?" The pastor said, "Well, if you follow it long enough, and take a right, then head south you'd end up in Florida. Do you know anything that's in Florida?" They ventured a few guesses, then, Elizabeth said, "umm . . . Disney World?" I said, "Hey . . . LET'S GO TO DISNEY WORLD!!!"

Elizabeth said, "I'd rather stay here."
Jon said, "I'll think about it."
Coleman and Becky kept looking at the park.

Susan and I pulled out mouseketeer hats from the secret bag, threw them on everyone's head, including our own, and started dancing around singing: "We're going to Disney World, going to Disney World." Elizabeth said, "But what about Junction City?" I shut off the camera in frustration and said, "Get in the van."

Coleman said, "Shoot! I wanted to go to the park."
Then, Becky said, "I don't want to get in the van."
I think it was the most anti-climactic moment of my life.

I was embarrassed. Susan was embarrassed. We figured that Pastor Underh-all-Pierce must've thought our children to be the most spoiled children in the entire world.

I was walking them back to the van, *making* them get back into the van, trying to act cool in front of this pastor, thinking about the tongue lashing they were bound to get once the van door was slammed shut: "You disrespectful, ungrate-ful spoiled children. Do you realize how much this is costing me?" When all at once, a thought hit me—I think it was from God:

> "Hey Peter, now do you understand?"
> "This is what it's like to be your daddy."

You see, it's not that my children's hopes were too big, but too small. In the words of C.S Lewis: We are children content to play with "mud pies in a slum," when a "holiday at the sea" has been offered to us. "It would seem that our Lord finds our desires are not too strong, but too weak."[3]

And don't get me wrong: mud pies are fun—for a time. Junction City would be fun—for a time. But after three weeks of sitting in front of the Tasty Freeze, languishing in a hundred degree heat, Junction City would turn into Hell.

But you understand, don't you? Junction City was in their grasp. It was un-der their control. The Magic Kingdom was a painful van ride away. It looked like death. "Get in the van" sounded like, "Pick up a cross."

Well, you are aware that we have a Father in Heaven. And the Bible is full of journeys, and children confused and complaining on those journeys—Noah, Abraham, Moses and Israel, us. We're on a journey. Every week is a journey: day one to six, and then we rest on the Seventh Day, the Sabbath Day. Do you ever wonder, "What's the point of the journey?" God doesn't have to drive; He can fly. What's the point of this journey called "life," and our stop in this Junction City of a world?

---

[3] C. S. Lewis, *The Weight of Glory and Other Adresses* (New York: Macmillan, 1948) 3–4

Just like I mapped out our route from Denver to Junction City and on to the Magic Kingdom, I think our Father mapped out our route, from Beginning to now and on to the End. I think He even told us the route.

"In the beginning" is the start of Genesis chapter one. Then we read about six days of creation, kind of like six hours of driving. Toward the end of the sixth day man is made in God's image. And at the end of six hours of driving we came to a junction—Junction City.

On the Seventh Day God rests. And I knew that if we didn't get stuck in Junction city, but got on to Kansas City and a good night's rest, we'd be good for the Magic Kingdom.

On the Seventh Day of creation, according to Scripture, everything is finished: The End (*telos*); everything is Good. And in Genesis, the Prophets and the Revelation, that Seventh Day appears to be eternal. By "eternal," I mean bigger than all space and time, not an endless journey—not endless time, but all time filled with the End, (*telos aionion*) . . . a perfected, finished, and unfading eternal now. So on the sixth day God makes Adam; the name means "man" or "humankind." And on the Seventh Day, everything, everything, everything is very good—"It is finished."

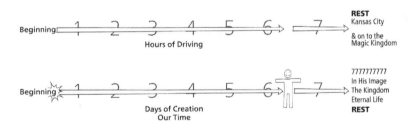

So here's a pertinent question: Where are we on this journey?

Well, are you "finished?" Is everything very good? Has God finished making humankind in His own image and likeness? You know the Bible describes the Seventh Day, when all has been made, and then goes back and describes how God makes man: "*The Lord God formed man...*" (Genesis 2:7). That's the sixth day. At what point is it *finished*? At what point is humanity *finished*, and we enter the rest of God's Seventh Day?

The Bible describes the Seventh Day and then describes the sixth day.

That's a rather critical observation, for most folks seem to think that the perfect Seventh Day came and went thousands or millions of years ago. They think everything was perfect until Adam and Eve messed it all up. Was everything perfect (*tetelestai*—"it is finished"), before Adam and Eve messed it all up?

- If everything had been perfectly good before Adam and Eve messed it all up, why was there a wall around the garden before they messed it all up?
- How do you explain that evil talking snake, and two naked people dumb enough and incomplete enough to listen to that evil talking snake?
- You know they didn't have the "knowledge of the good" and so couldn't have had faith in the One who *is* good. And surely that's not good.
- God even said, "It's *not* good that the Adam should be alone" (Gen. 2:7), BEFORE the Adam (man and woman) messed up and chose the *not* good.

Everything was not yet good in that garden. And man was not yet finished in the image and likeness of God in that garden. So, when is God's Seventh Day of rest? And when is Adam finally finished in the image of God?

If you take your cues from the meaning of the text, rather than our antiquated modern notions of time, it seems pretty clear that Genesis chapter one is like the *History* of all time . . . And that, for most of us, we still "live" in the sixth day of creation.

A few years ago physicist Gerald Schroeder wrote a couple of books elucidating the fact that, according to Einstein's theory of relativity, the age of the Universe is entirely dependent on the standpoint of the observer.[4] And now, remember that there is no earth to stand on "in the beginning."

---

[4] Gerald Schroeder, *The Science of God* (Broadway: NY, 1998)
Gerald Schroeder, *Genesis and the Big Bang* (Bantam: NY, 1990)

Schroeder calculates that if the creation is about fifteen billion years old from the standpoint of the earth, it must be about six days old from the standpoint of the Big Bang—or at least the moment that matter first forms and light is first emitted, just after the Big Bang.

Whether or not he got the physics exactly right, it's clear that arguing about the age of the earth—old or young—is just silly . . . and even more importantly, not metaphorically but actually, and scientifically, we really could be "living" in the sixth day of creation on the edge of an eternal Seventh Day.

The Seventh Day doesn't start until Jesus, the perfect image and likeness of God, hangs on a tree in a garden on the sixth day of creation, on the sixth day of the week, at the sixth hour, and cries, *"It is finished:" tetelestai* (John 19:30). It's at that tree that we are given eternal life (*zoen aionion*)—Seventh Day life, the Life of the age to come.

And that means the big story is not that God made everything good, we messed it up, and now He's trying to fix it with the Jesus thing. It means the big story is that He's making us in His image with His Word, who is Jesus, and He won't fail. It means our Father is taking us on a journey, and we will all arrive at our destination, but on the sixth day we all find ourselves at a junction.

It's a place where we make a choice. Or should I say the Father creates a choice in us. It's the place where His choice becomes our choice, and we choose to "get in the van." Jesus is the van. Jesus is the Way. Jesus is the Beginning (*arche*) and the End (*telos*). Jesus is the Plot. Jesus is the Grace of God. Jesus is the Judgment of God. Jesus is the Father's choice. Our choice surrendered to the Father's choice is called salvation. The Father's choice in us is called faith.

You know, it just about killed my kids to get in the van . . . and yet they finally did get in the van. Maybe they saw that it killed me that it was killing them; they knew that their pain was my pain and so my pleasure was their pleasure. My love for them created just enough *faith in me*, within *them* . . . to get in the van.

But what if they hadn't gotten in the van? Would I have left them forever in Junction City or consigned them to endless torment? No! . . . because that wouldn't make me happy! Their pleasure is my pleasure. You know, I hate Disneyworld without my kids. It's their happiness that makes the Magic Kingdom magic for me.

If they hadn't gotten in the van, I wouldn't have consigned them to endless torment. However, I might have allowed their bad choice for a time . . . so that my good choice might become their choice . . . in time.

Maybe that's why God made time. In other words, I might have said, "Fine you can just stay in Junction City!" But I would've stayed with them; I would've descended into that hell with them. Then after three weeks of sitting in front of the Tasty Freeze or wandering through Wal-Mart bored as hell, I'd say, "Now, let's get in the van!"

Think about it: Until we'd had our crisis[5] in Junction City, the Magic Kingdom was only my choice, but as I shut the van door . . . *my* choice became *our* choice. Granted it was only the size of a mustard seed, but the seed grew . . . and became a kingdom. And that's how we got the hell out of Junction City.

So, why stop in Junction City at all? Why does God allow this fallen world at all? Is there a point to the suffering in the sixth day? Well, I don't think I can fully answer that question in every detail, but I do know that stopping in Junction City made the Magic Kingdom that much more magic. Over and over again it happened:

> We'd be standing in line for one more ride on Space Mountain...
> Or eating those giant turkey legs that they call alien legs...
> Or walking on the beach late at night under the moon looking for sea turtles laying their eggs in the sand...
> And one of the kids would just stop me, and their eyes would get huge as they would exclaim,
> "Oh daddy!
I can't believe I wanted to stay in Junction City!
I love you!"

It means, "I trust you!" And that's called "faith." You know, all sorts of folks visit the Magic Kingdom or Disneyworld and just have one hell of a time—I mean it feels like hell. It feels like Hell, and maybe it is Hell *because* they don't have faith in Love.

---

[5] Crisis comes from the Greek word *krisis*, translated "judgment" in English Bibles.

Understand? Faith in Love—who is our Father— is what makes the Magic Kingdom magic for us. And that means the magic starts in the van. It's the Seventh Day, on the sixth day, in the van . . . when we have faith. He said, *"The kingdom of heaven is at hand"* (Matt. 4:17).

We got the hell out of Junction City, in Junction City, because it was already Heaven in the van.

My kids are young adults now, and they love to reminisce about family vacations. And this is the crazy thing: what they seem to miss most is our time in the van. Don't misunderstand: They still love the Magic Kingdom. It's just that now they know—the thing that makes the Magic Kingdom magic is the thing that grows on the journey, in the van. It grows in the van and lasts forever— faith in Love. God is Love. So, "Get in the van!"

Well, that's a summary of the first book, *The History of Time and the Genesis of You*. And it's an introduction to the second book, *God and His Sexy Body: The Story of Adam and His Bride*.

I know it seems wrong to introduce a book that contains the word "sexy" with a story about a father and his kids. And it certainly would be wrong if I applied that word to my children and me, their father. But, I hope you see that God is not only a Father that wants His children to trust Him and surrender to His Love. God is also a Great Bridegroom[6] who wants His Bride to trust Him and surrender to His Love—He is Love, in flesh, Jesus.

Just as I took my kids on a journey and earned their trust, so I took my wife (then girlfriend) on a journey and earned her trust. I dated her for four years, and we were engaged for one-and-a-half years—that was too long. But for the sake of my illustration, imagine that we dated seven years and were engaged that

---

[6] Isaiah 54:5, "For your Maker is your husband."

last year. Well, that journey would be critical for creating trust, for that journey doesn't end in a theme park but a bedroom, where two become one flesh.

If a father makes his kids go to a theme park against their will, it wouldn't be fun ... but no one would call the police. However, if a man makes a woman go on a honeymoon against her will it's called rape, and the "honeymoon" doesn't feel like Heaven, but Hell.

You see? I'm suggesting that God is preparing all of us for such intimate communion that if we don't have faith in Love (and God is Love), if His choice does not become our choice, Heaven will feel like Hell. The Good News is that all creation, all space and time, is the setting for our journey—a journey on which God in Christ Jesus is creating faith in Love in us.

The Seventh Day, the finished creation, the Kingdom of Heaven is a Magic Kingdom of unspeakable ecstasy and delight, but the ticket to enter is faith. Faith is not *your* creation; it's *God's* creation created in you by Grace. The LORD is the Great Bridegroom. He is romancing you (John 12:32) from a tree that we call the cross. He is the Word who upholds all things. He is romancing you, and He arranges all things to do so.

- Well, the main point of the first book is that God is making "everything... very good," and everything is good on the Seventh Day.
- Now we'll be reading about how He makes us good on the sixth day. "It's not good that the Adam should be alone."

We're reading the story of Adam and his bride, which is, according to Paul, a reference to "*Christ and His Church*,"[7] which is God and His sexy Body.

We'll get to *sexy* ... but the story begins with dust.

---

[7] Ephesians 5:32 I'm not making this up!

I-Contact

Genesis 2:4–7

Genesis 2:7 KJV *And the LORD God formed man of the dust of the ground, and breathed into his nostrils the breath of life; and man became a living soul.*

"Ashes to ashes and dust to dust." Dust and ashes are basically the same thing. This is a picture of my father's ashes, in a bag, in my hand:

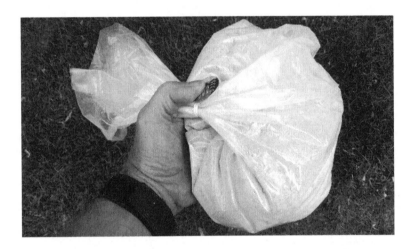

My father was a pastor. When I was a child, I was routinely used as an illustration in his sermons. So, I'm sure he wouldn't mind being used as an illustration in one of my books. But those ashes aren't him, right? They are just his ashes—or *were* his ashes—I doubt he still wants them.

When I'm not using them as an illustration, they sit in a box on my mother's breakfront in the TV room. We're not quite sure what to do with them. We've thought about spreading them somewhere up in the mountains but haven't decided yet.

I've read that the chemicals in a bag of human ash are worth anything from about $4.50 to $160. Whatever the case, is that what Dad was worth? Is that what you're worth? Is that all you are? Chemicals?

If we added some water and waited a bit, a bag of dust and ashes would turn back into something like clay—human clay. You may remember how prophets like Isaiah and Jeremiah taught that God was the potter and we are the clay. Through Jeremiah, God says that Jerusalem will be broken like a potter's vessel in the valley of Gehenna—yet, in the end, Jerusalem descends new from Heaven adorned as a bride prepared for her groom, the Potter. Perhaps you also remember how Judas hung himself, fell, and was broken, in the Potter's Field, in the valley of Gehenna, and how the blood of Jesus purchased that field.[1] In his letters, Paul refers to us as clay or "earthen vessels." In other words, clay containers. "Clay is fashioned into vessels; but it is on their empty hollowness, that their use depends."[2] Do you ever feel empty or hollow? Maybe that's not so bad . . . or at least better than being full of yourself . . . And maybe you'll be filled with more than yourself.

The English word *Adam* sounds like the Hebrew word *adamah*, which means *ground*. Adam is "formed" of *adamah*. In Genesis 2:7, the word translated "formed" is commonly used of a potter forming clay. The Hebrew is a bit confusing here, so some translations include the article before the English word "man" as if it were referring to one man, while others do not—as if it were referring to all men or humankind.

It seems Scripture is referring to both one man and all people, for *Adam* means man, humankind or humanity. Yet *Adam* is also one man—the first man and also the last man: Jesus (1 Cor. 15:45). Well, we'll ponder that much more, but for now, just notice: "Earthlings" are made of "earth." So, is that what we are? Is that what *I am*—dust and ashes? Simply an earthen vessel? $4.50 to $160 worth of chemicals full of nothing?

Perhaps you've heard that every cell in your body is replaced every seven years. I did a little research and discovered that's kind of true. Skin cells are replaced

[1] Jer. 7:31–31, 18:1 – 19:15, 31:28–40; Matt. 27:3–10; Acts 1:17–18; Rev. 21:2 — The study of these verses opens a remarkable window upon the events surrounding the death of Judas, hope for all humanity and the ability of God, the Potter. *Gehenna* is sometimes translated "Hell" in modern translations—it's rather instructive to note that *Gehenna* is the location of the Potter's Field and that God is a remarkably skilled Potter.

every few weeks, fat cells about every ten years, and some neurons in the brain appear to last your whole life. Whatever the case, your dust *now* is almost entirely different than your dust seven or ten years ago.

Well, if God uses our old dust to raise us from the dead, I'm pretty sure that Dad wouldn't want the bag of dust on the breakfront.[2] That's the dust from his weak and wrinkly, eighty-four-year-old body. I bet he'd want the dust from his twenty-five-year-old body—the body I never met. And yet I knew Dad . . . same Dad, different dust!

So, where *is* that dust from his twenty-five-year-old body? I don't know. Perhaps some of it's scattered in fields, mountain streams, and garbage dumps. Perhaps some of it's in me. And who gets it in the new creation? Some of Dad's old dust is now my dust, so are we going to have to wrestle for it on Resurrection Day?

Some of Dad's dust was definitely chicken dust, beef dust, pig dust. Who gets it in the new creation? Are we going to have to wrestle pigs and chickens on Easter morning?

> Am I dust and ashes? Am I this body?
> Am I these thoughts that I'm thinking... or just thought?

You know, some of my dad's dust was used to form electrical circuits in a supercomputer called his brain. But was he just a brain? Just the dust that formed the neural pathways in his brain? Am I just a brain? Just a computer? Am I my thoughts? Am I my feelings? You know, some of my dad's dust was once hormones, neural peptides, and a fair amount of caffeine.

> Am I my thoughts?
> Am I my feelings?
> Am I my accomplishments?

---

[2] You know God seems to have used Jesus' old dust when He raised Him from the dead. I mean, there was no body in the tomb on Easter morning. I don't know if that dust was significant or if God was just showing off. Whatever the case, it wouldn't have been the same dust that Jesus consisted of when He was thirteen.

Some folks will have a bigger bag of dust and ashes than others because they accomplished more eating. Some ancient societies thought you could take stuff with you (like houses, cars, and bank accounts). Yet, even if you took the whole earth, it would still be dust and ashes.

According to Scripture (Zeph. 3:8–9, 2 Pet. 3:8–19), this whole earth is going to be judged by fire. The whole thing will be *cremated*, if you will. But is *that* who I am? Dust and ashes?

One day, my kids will be holding my bag of dust or visiting a grave that contains my dust. Think of your own dust. Can you picture your dust?

Now ask yourself:

Who am I?

How can I be the dust that I am thinking about?

What am I?

Think about the "I," your "I"[3] ... Did you do it?

I can think about my dust, my body, my thoughts, my feelings, my accomplishments ... But how can I think about my "I?"

If I think some thoughts, I can't be the thoughts I think.

If I feel some feelings, I can't be the feelings I feel.

If I accomplish something, I can't be my own accomplishment.

If I will an action, I can't be the action that I will.

If I observe me, I can't be the "me" that I observe.

Do you see? As soon as I observe "I," it's no longer "I" but "me."

Now, I'm not just messing with you, and this isn't just semantics. It's a huge problem for philosophy, psychology, sociology, ethics, and even robotics. How can I be self-aware and conscious? What is a person? What is (or am) "I"?

Recently, it's even become a problem for physics, for it's become abundantly clear that an "observer" collapses the state of subatomic particles, which are the

---

[3] I am putting this "I" in quotation marks, not because this "I" is untrue, but to point out that we are speaking of "I" in this special way. This "I" is profoundly true— maybe it's actually "the Truth." Whatever the case, when I use quotation marks, I am highlighting the fact that we are speaking of something in a special way.

building blocks of all matter—which is all dust. In other words, for the physicist, the most confusing thing in all creation is what "I" am... not "me," but the "I" that observes me.

"Phenomenology is a school of philosophy and psychology based on the work of George Herbert Mead.[4] It argues that a person is best understood as consisting of three parts:

✓ First is the body. It's objective. It's an object: dust and ashes.

✓ Second is the stream of consciousness that Phenomenology would call "me" or "self." When someone says, "Tell me about yourself," we tend to describe our thoughts, our feelings, our accomplishments . . . "me" as an object in this world. Surprisingly, that stream of thoughts and feelings may be pretty much dust and ashes as well. If they cut out part of your brain (dust), you may lose some memories and even feelings; you may lose part of your "me," but not your "I" that forgot some of your "me."

✓ The third part of the person is the "I" that is aware of "me," the "I" that observes "me." In fact, the "me" is like the footprint left by the "I" in the dust of this earth—the footprint I leave in the past or hope to produce in the future. "Me" is a footprint formed by "I" in space and time. Perhaps you could think of the "I" as a seed—an eternal seed—dropped into a pot of dust and ashes that turns into a plant called "me." The "me" changes over time and may turn back into dust and ashes, but "I" go on. "Me" is produced by "I" interacting with dust in space and time. However, "I" do not really belong in space and time. I don't feel at home in space and time—my own dust and ashes.

---

[4] Anthony Campolo, *A Reasonable Faith, Responding to Secularism* (Word Books: Waco TX, 1983) 121–128. I'm very indebted to Tony Campolo for his marvelous discussion of Phenomenology, as well as many other fascinating topics, in this marvelous book.

C. S. Lewis wrote:

> ...We are so little reconciled to time that we are even aston-
> ished at it. "How he's grown!" we exclaim, "How time flies!"
> as though the universal form of our experience were again
> and again a novelty. It is as strange as if a fish were repeatedly
> surprised at the wetness of water. And that would be strange
> indeed; unless of course the fish were destined to become, one
> day, a land animal.[5]

In the same way, I swim in space and time, yet I'm constantly amazed at it. You are, too. You say things like:

"I can't believe I'm in Denver. To think I was just on the beach in Hawaii!"
...Amazed at space.
"I can't believe I'm fifty-three! Only yesterday I was twenty-one!"
...Amazed at time.
"Just think! I was there and then, and yet, I am here and now."

I will always be here and now, for as soon as here and now becomes there and then, I am no longer there and then but here and now. "I" am here and now. "I" do not really exist in space or time. "I" don't take up space. "I" can't observe "I" in space. And "I" don't really exist in time. But maybe I touch time. "I" cre-ate memories in time—my past. And "I" have hopes for the future—a time to come. But "I" am now: here and now.

- Tony Campolo writes, "Now is the non-existent point that separates past from the future. I can't describe now because by the time I say 'now' it is already past. Nevertheless, I know that now exists because it is where 'I am.'"[6]

---

[5] C. S. Lewis, *Reflections on the Psalms* (New York: Harcourt, Brace and Company, 1958) 138.

[6] Campolo, 127.

- St. Augustine wrote, "There is nothing I know better than now. It is more real to me than any other time, and yet when I reflect upon it, it doesn't exist at all."[7]
- C. S. Lewis wrote, "For the Present [Now] is the point at which time touches eternity."[8]
- Paul Tillich wrote, "It is the eternal 'now' which provides for us a temporal 'now.'"[9]
- Albert Einstein revealed that at the speed of light ("God is light"), all time is present in an eternal now.

Whatever the case, I exist *now*, here and now, perhaps *in* space and time but certainly not *of* space and time. So, I am not simply an object in this world. I cannot be known objectively. You can know all about "me," "myself," "my dust"—me in the past or the hope for me in the future, yet I can remain totally unknown to you. I can only be known by I-contact. That is, "I" can only be known by subjective encounter, personal relationship.[10] That's why my children can know me in a way that the FBI, CIA and American Medical Association can't know me.

The FBI can know all about me, but only a person–another "I" who chooses to be with me–can truly know me. I can only be known in the present—here and now—for I am.

> God said to Moses, "I am who I am." And he said, "Say this to
> the people of Israel, 'I am has sent me to you.'" God also said to
> Moses, "Say this to the people of Israel, 'The LORD [Yahweh], the
> God of your fathers, the God of Abraham, the God of Isaac, and

---

[7] Augustine, *The Confessions*, trans. Edward B. Pusey (New York: Pocket Books, 1951) XI, p.14 cited in Campolo, 127.

[8] C.S. Lewis, *The Screwtape Letters* (New York: Macmillan, 1961), 68.

[9] Paul Tillich, *The Eternal Now* (New York: Charles Scribner's Sons, 1963), 131.

[10] What exactly I-contact is, I can't tell you. Yet we will spend the rest of the book discussing it. I think the best word for it may be Love. No one can explain Love. Love explains all things; God is Love.

the God of Jacob, has sent me to you.' This is my name forever,
and thus I am to be remembered throughout all generations."
—Exodus 3:14–15

God is "I AM." His proper name is *Yahweh*. It appears to be a play on the Hebrew verb "to be"—*ha-yah*. So, *Yahweh* probably means I AM or "being-ness."
So, the definition of is, is God. He is the ground of all being, all space, and all
time. He is the Light, and His Word is the Light of the world. Jesus said, "*God
is Spirit*." "Spirit" (*pneuma* in Greek) is also translated as wind or breath. It is
something intangible, not of this world. "I AM" is Spirit—*Yahweh*. The name
Yahweh appears for the first time in Scripture in Genesis 2:4b.

> ... *in the day that the Lord God made the earth and the heav-*
> *ens, when no plant of the field was yet in the earth and no herb of*
> *the field had yet sprung up—for the Lord God had not caused it*
> *to rain upon the earth, and there was no man to till the ground;*
> *but a mist went up from the earth and watered the whole face of*
> *the ground—then the Lord God formed man of dust from the*
> *ground, and breathed into his nostrils the breath of life; and*
> *man became a living being* (In the KJV: "*a living soul.*")
> —Genesis 2:4b–7

I AM took dust and breathed (spirited) into that dust His own breath (Spirit).

I AM breathed eternity into an earthen vessel.

I AM kissed the dust, and Adam became a living soul. That's who I am.

"*And this is eternal life*," said Jesus, "*that they know you the only true God, and
Jesus Christ whom you have sent*" (John 17:3). Leo Tolstoy wrote, "To know
God and to live are one. God is life."[11] Martin Buber wrote, "All actual life is
encounter."[12]

---

[11] Leo Tolstoy, *My Confession* (New York: Thomas Y. Crowell, 1887), 103–108. *Cited in* Diogenes Allen, *Spiritual Theology* (Boston: Cowley, 1997), 53.

[12] *Cited in* Anne Lamott, *Traveling Mercies* (New York: Anchor Books, 1999), 115.

Henri Nouwen writes:

> ...Real life takes place in the here and the now. God is a God of the present. God is always in the moment, be that moment hard or easy, joyful or painful. When Jesus spoke about God, he always spoke about God as being where and when we are. God is not someone who was or will be, but the One who is, and who is for me in the present moment. That's why Jesus came to wipe away the burden of the past and the worries for the future. He wants us to discover God right where we are, here and now.[13]

Paul wrote:

> *When we cry, "Abba! Father!" it is the Spirit himself bearing witness with our spirit that we are children of God, and if children, then heirs, heirs of God and fellow heirs with Christ, provided we suffer with him in order that we may also be glorified with him.*
>
> —Romans 8:15b–17 RSV

When you cry, "Abba Father," you experience I-contact with the Spirit of I AM.

> I can't tell you exactly what "I AM" is, for "I AM" defines all that is...
> Yet, I believe that "I AM" has revealed Himself in Jesus.

> I can't tell you exactly what "I AM" is... or what "I" am.
> Yet, I can tell you that "I" will be like Jesus.

John wrote:

> *Beloved, we are God's children now, and what we will be has not yet appeared; but we know that when he appears we shall be like him, because we shall see him as he is.*
>
> —1 John 3:2 ESV

---

[13] Henri Nouwen, *Here and Now* (New York: Crossroad, 1994), 18

What I'm trying to say is that even though I can't tell you exactly what "I" is, just by asking, "Who am I?" you reveal that you are a profound wonder and treasure made (or being made) in the image of God.

As I argued in the first book in this little series, *The History of Time and the Genesis of You*, we are being made in the sixth day of creation on the verge of an eternal Seventh Day, where everything is good.

In the text we just read (Gen. 2:4b), Genesis refers to the six days in which God made the heavens and the earth as "*the* day"—a single day—revealing that these days are not your normal calendar days. In verse 5, the text reads, "*When no bush of the field was yet in the earth...*" That would seem to be the third day of creation. And perhaps God started arranging our dust on that third day? Biologically speaking, we come from quite a lineage of dust.

Whatever the case, it's on the sixth day that God created "*man...male and female, he created them*" (Gen. 1:27). And as we learned: On the Seventh Day, "*It is finished*," and everything is "*very good*." And so, God is still making people; isn't He? I was privileged enough to see Him make four . . . and of course, I'm watching as He makes millions more. I mean, God is still breathing into dust and ashes, breathing into clay.

Genesis 1 indicates that God spoke creation into existence. And if He spoke, or speaks, us into existence, He speaks a Word. That Word is Jesus. On Easter, He appeared to His disciples and breathed on them saying, "*Receive the Holy Spirit*—Holy *Pneuma*" (John 21:22). God is still breathing into clay.

So, I can't tell you exactly what "I" is. Theologians and Philosophers have debated that for thousands of years. Yet it seems that your "I" is somehow analogous to "I AM." It's the breath of "I AM," or a piece of "I AM" or the Word of "I AM." It's what makes you human and what finishes making you human in the image of God. It's the Spirit placed in you— even in your mother's womb— and the Spirit that falls on the church at Pentecost.

I don't know—and theologians and philosophers don't know—how to parse all of that out. But it clearly means that every person who wonders, "Who am I?" ends up revealing, just by the wondering, that they themselves are a great wonder and a priceless treasure. They contain the breath of God. They have the capacity to know God. They have the capacity to love Love. God is Love. They have a capacity for I-contact. That's what makes a person "holy." Holy means wholly other," not of this world.

The Jewish theologian and philosopher Martin Buber taught that there are two types of relationships in our world: "I–it" relationships and "I–thou" relationships.[14] "I–it" describes our relationships to things, and we often relate to people as things. "I-thou" describes one "I" connecting with another "I," not as an object to be manipulated and used but as a person to be known and loved.

We'll speak about this much more when we study the two trees in the middle of the garden in our next book, but there is a way to relate to people that produces death and a way to relate to people that produces life and *is* Life. Life is I-contact. Murder is turning an "I" into an "it." Crucifixion is doing so on a tree. Well . . . for now, just note that an "I" is a marvelous and holy "thing," for "I" am capable of I-contact. I can be loved and love. I can know another "I."

So, I can't tell you exactly what "I" is—yet I bet you know. I mean you don't know *what* it is, but you know *who* it is, or who one is. I bet you know at least one *who*; and often times the *who* you know best has very little *what*. I mean they're often a spirit with very little "earthen vessel" like a tired old man or a little girl.

See?

✓   I suspect that the Bible might refer to what phenomenologists call the "I" as the spirit. (Hebrew: *neshamah* or *ruach*, Greek: *pneuma*)[15]

✓   And refer to that which phenomenologists call the "me," as the "life or the "soul" (in Hebrew: *nephesh* and in Greek, *psuche*).

✓   And the body as dust.

---

[14] "To man the world is twofold, in accordance with his twofold attitude. The attitude of man is twofold, in accordance with the twofold nature of the primary words which he speaks. The primary words are not isolated words, but combined words. The one primary word is the combination I-Thou. The other primary word is the combination I-It…"
Martin Buber *I and Thou: Second Edition* (New York: Charles Scribner's Sons, 1958) 3.

[15] Genesis 2:7 has *neshamah*. Genesis 1:2 has *ruach*. *Ruach* is far more common, but both refer to spirit and breath. Texts like Job 4:9 and Isaiah 42:5 seem to hold them in something of an interchangeable relationship.

In the beginning God breathes His Spirit into some dust creating a soul and then that soul begins to create itself, its "life"—more soul, more knowledge, more accomplishments, diplomas, successes and failures, more ego, more pride, more earthen vessel, more *what* to hide the *who*. The *what* is actually dirt and the *who* is divine.[16]

Old men, like my dad, have lost most of their earthen vessel. I mean by the time my dad died, he had gone from 180 pounds down to about 90, but more importantly he had learned to surrender his ego, look people in the eye, and make I-contact. My dad loved Love, and loved to love Love, and for him that was Life. Jesus said, "*You must lose your life (psuche* or psyche—earthen vessel) *to find it.*"

Old men, like my dad, have lost most of their earthen vessel and little children haven't had time to manufacture much of one for themselves . . . or as themselves. Jesus taught that we must become like little children to enter His kingdom.

So, we may not know what an "I" is, but every person has one. Every person is priceless treasure hidden in an earthen vessel. We tend to value earthen vessels, promote earthen vessels, use earthen vessels and forget what they contain. But watching your father die, having children of your own, or just giving a cup of cold water to the "least of these" can change that.

Soon after my children were born, I was surprised at the passions that rose in me. My children had no resume to impress me. They were born with only a few pounds of earthen vessel—earthen vessel that seemed to constantly leak, spit

---

[16] We will discuss this in much more detail when we get to chapter 3, but it appears that my "I" creates a "me" in space and time. Yet, I did not create my "I." If I assume that "I" am my own (which we all do), and I assume that "I" must create a "me" in the image of God by taking knowledge of Good and evil from the tree (law) and applying that knowledge to myself in the strength of my own flesh ("me"), I build a "me" upon a lie—that lie is that I am my own creator. I must lose that self to become my true self. My true self is built on the truth that God is my Creator.

When I am proud of my self (my "me"), I live in an illusion that must be destroyed. When I am grateful for my self (my "me"), I live in the truth—the truth that "I" am a gift of grace and "me," the life of "I," is also a gift of grace. I live in the truth that my "righteousness" is imputed to me, that it is a gift to me. It is Christ's life, Christ's "me" given to me. Therefore, I don't hang on to "me" as a possession, but I receive "me" and offer "me," I live "me" in freedom. I lose my life and find it.

up, cry and demand attention. Yet I'd look in their eyes and make I-contact. They knew me, and I knew them. They had what I called "a-moral value." I mean they didn't know the good or accomplish some good to make themselves valuable to me. They were good for nothing . . . just good.

Even today, twenty years later, when their big old earthen vessels cause me a world of pain and sometimes sorrow, I remember that they're still good for nothing, just good. In fact, if I'm honest, when they seem especially good for something, I often lose sight of that indescribable "good for nothing—just good." So, sometimes when their earthen vessels break and they come wandering down the road like a prodigal returning home, I see them as they are; and something in me wants to party. I-contact makes me want to party . . . Maybe it is *the* party.

> While an "I" trapped alone in an earthen vessel is hell,
> I think God our Father hates that kind of hell.
> It's "not good" for Adam to be alone.

One day when my daughter Elizabeth was about two, I took her to the park where she learned to slide down the slide. She'd stand on top of the slide and say, "See, I do it! See, I do it!" and I'd say, "Yeah, you're awesome. You're amazing!" After a time, I sat down and just watched her, mesmerized by the beauty and wonder of her mere existence—not simply the fact that she could slide down the slide, but that she knew me and loved me, that she was a piece of me calling out to me—a breath of God in clay.

Soon, a woman arrived with her two-year-old daughter and her daughter also started sliding down the slide, and she'd say to her daughter, "You're awesome. You're amazing!" But when my daughter slid down the slide she said nothing. Before long, Elizabeth was standing on top of the slide screaming at this woman: "See me! See I do it; I do it; see me!" And this woman wouldn't even look.

Maybe you've felt like little Elizabeth: "See me; see me!" And no one sees. Well, the Father sees. And I saw. I saw the breath of God calling out for recognition and love, and there was no answer. I saw, and I grew furious.

People say they don't understand the wrath of God the Father. Well, I'm a father, and I saw, and I grew furious. In fact, I remember fantasizing about picking up a 2x4 and smacking the woman in the head while screaming, "Look at my daughter! She's the greatest slide slider in this whole God-damned world!"

I was just about to get up when this thought, or voice, or Word entered my head and said something like this:

> "Hey Peter,
>
> *What if* that woman is my daughter and you don't see her?
>
> *What if* I see her and feel her pain . . . just as you see and feel for Elizabeth?
>
> *What if* each and every child in those cardboard shacks, in Tijuana just to the south of here, is my child, and they cry: 'See me! See me, feed me, feed me!' and Peter you just don't see them?
>
> *What if* I'm the Father of the last and the least of these?
>
> *What if* I'm the Father of all?
>
> Perhaps you should drop to your knees in gratitude Peter, that I have taken your stripes and born your chastisement, that I have turned my wrath upon myself, for you see Peter . . . you are my child as well!"

Do you understand? What do I do when my son Jon doesn't see Elizabeth or Elizabeth doesn't see Jon? What do I do with the anger? What does the good Father do with all the passion—all the wrath?

What does God the Father do:
  When one daughter won't feed another daughter?
  When one son murders another son?
  When each traps their own heart and the other's heart in a lonely prison of fear and shame, and when all the children seek to take His own Life, the Father's Life, the Life of Love?
What does the good Father do?

He lets them (*aphiemi* in Greek). In other words He forgives them—*aphiemi*.

And when they see it, when they see Him, when they see "I AM" nailed to a tree, when they hear Him cry, *"Father forgive,"* when they see the Word of I Am deliver up His Spirit, His breath, His *nephesh* . . . it changes them.

We can't begin to fathom all that happened on the cross, but it was I-contact. And the fact that He suffered and died for all (for God was in Christ reconciling the world to Himself, 2 Cor. 5:19) shows that we each are holy.

Who am I? The one for whom I AM suffered and died—the beloved.

It's the "I" in me. It's the breath in me that makes me holy. And this is what believers mean by the "Sanctity of Human Life."

- No one may see the old man suffering alone in a nursing home, but God sees. He contains the breath. So, *"deep calls to deep."* I AM— jealously yearns over the spirit He has made to dwell in that man.
- No one may want the baby in the womb, but God sees and God wants. It appears that even an unborn baby contains the breath, so John the Baptist leapt in Elizabeth's womb in the presence of Jesus in Mary's womb.
- And now, no one may see you or want you, but God sees, and God wants you. Perhaps you feel abandoned by your children. Perhaps you've had an abortion and now feel buried in shame. Perhaps you think that God has damned you to Hell, and you feel totally alone. Listen closely: you are an absolute treasure and unspeakable wonder— you contain the breath. And "I AM" has done, and is doing, literally everything to make contact with you. It is not good for Adam to be alone.

I think it's wonderful that Christians care about the sanctity of human life. And yet it's tragic that we seem to care so little. Unborn babies contain the breath; unwanted elderly poor contain the breath; ISIS militants contain the breath; and if there are "living souls," that is *nephesh* in Hell (however you define that), they contain the breath. I mean if it takes the breath of God to make a person a person, then how could we abandon persons to an endless Hell? I don't think God does.

For Christ also suffered once for sins, the righteous for the un-righteous, that he might bring us to God, being put to death in the flesh but made alive in the spirit, in which he went and pro-claimed to the spirits in prison, because they formerly did not obey, when God's patience waited in the days of Noah, while the ark was being prepared, in which a few, that is, eight persons, were brought safely through water... For this is why the gospel was preached even to those who are dead, that though judged in the flesh the way people are, they might live in the spirit the way God does.

—1 Peter 3:18–20, 4:6

As I said, we can't begin to fathom all that happened on the cross, but it was I-contact.[17] It was the Creator kissing the dust and causing us to live. As a new father, I couldn't stop kissing my kids. Each kiss was like a breath filled with meaning, and the meaning was a Word: "I love you." We are created with the kiss and are still being created with that kiss.

Eleven years ago my father died. Eight years ago I was publicly tried and de-frocked for not publicly confessing that it was impossible for some people to be saved. For fifteen years I had followed in my father's footsteps and built a thriv-ing church of several thousand people from just a handful. All at once it came tumbling down, for I believed that the Word of God descended even into the depths (Eph. 4:9, Ps. 22:29) of the earth and that all who died in Adam would be made alive—really alive—in Christ (1 Cor. 15:22, Rom. 5:19).

It's a long story, but suffice it to say, I felt like my psyche, my life, my ego—and that of my family—had been reduced to dust and ashes. A fraction of my church asked if we could start a new church about a half hour away in down-town Denver. I agreed, but didn't feel like worshiping. For the first seven months I didn't preach. I could barely breathe.

One Sunday evening, as I sat in our rented space downtown, I felt this puff of air, and looked to see who was puffing on me. No one was there. The next week,

---

[17] We will discuss this much more thoroughly in this book and the next, but none of our explanations will exhaust the meaning of the atonement. The atonement is the judgment of God, and God's judgments are "unsearchable... and how inscrutable his ways" (Rom 11:33)!

I did preach—I had made myself begin again—I quoted the Song of Solomon in my sermon and learned that a literal translation of the text meant, "*The Lord puffs on his garden*"[18]

Over the next several months, it kept happening: puffing in my hair, on my face, on my lips, my hands, even my notes (One night I saw my notes move). I ran out of scientific explanations, and I remember thinking, "God, thanks for this, whatever it is . . . but I want to know why this whole thing happened, why did You reduce my kingdom to dust and ashes? Thanks for this puffing, but what the hell are You doing?"

Sometimes it was strong, and sometimes it was weak; sometimes others felt it too. When I didn't feel it, I'd worry that I'd messed up somehow. We had moved into our current building when one particular Sunday night in October, it was nuts; the puffing thing was just crazy—all over my body. It was so bizarre and so strong I just couldn't help but laugh!

I looked over at Susan. She was writing furiously. My wife, Susan, has a fascinating spiritual gift. Sometimes God will speak to her in words and sentences that she hears in her mind. Well, I knew the Lord had just told her something. She handed this paper to me.

Oct 2009

Peter

I have never stopped kissing you. Sometimes my kisses are sweet. Sometimes they burn but believe this my kisses never stop. I love you

---

[18] Song of Solomon 4:16

It reads, "October 2009, Peter, I have never stopped kissing you. Sometimes my kisses are sweet. Sometimes they burn. But, believe this, my kisses never stop. I love you."

You know, the enemy tells us that this life is all about convincing the Lord to kiss us, that it's about earning the love of God, the blessing of God, the breath of God. But Life is all about believing that He *has* kissed us, and He won't stop kissing us. It wasn't long after that October night that I stopped feeling the puffing, but I know I must not stop believing in the kisses.

Sometimes, the bigger the earthen vessel, the harder it is to feel the kisses, the harder it is to make I-contact. Little children like kisses. Perhaps at times, God helps us lose our lives, our earthen vessels, our psyches so we might find them . . . not old, but forever new. Eternal life is I-contact.

You have an "I."

> *For it is the God who said, "Let light shine out of darkness," who has shone in our hearts to give the light of the knowledge of the glory of God in the face of Christ. But we have this treasure in earthen vessels...*
>
> —2 Corinthians 4:6–7 RSV

You have an "I." You were made and are being made for I-contact. One glorious day you will have a body and will *be* a body made for I- contact, made for Love.

> *For we know that if the earthly tent we live in is destroyed, we have a building from God, a house not made with hands, eternal in the heavens. Here indeed we groan, and long to put on our heavenly dwelling, so that by putting it on we may not be found naked. For while we are still in this tent, we sigh with anxiety; not that we would be unclothed, but that we would be further clothed, so that what is mortal may be swallowed up by life.*
>
> —2 Corinthians 5:1–4 RSV

All actual life is encounter. —*Martin Buber*

To know God and to live are one. God is life. —*Leo Tolstoy*

Can I know what "I" is? Some of these mystics reply, "Can the knife cut itself? Can the tooth bite itself? Can the eye see itself? Can the 'I' know itself?"
                                                            —*Anthony Demello, <u>Awareness</u>*

"My name is not I WAS, nor is it I WILL BE, but I AM. To really know Me, you must know Me in the present. You cannot know Me as I AM unless you come to Me every day. You cannot know Me as I AM unless you abide in Me."
                                                            —*Rick Joyner, <u>The Call</u>*

Breathe

Genesis 2:7

Genesis 2:7 KJV *And the LORD God formed man of the dust of the ground, and breathed into his nostrils the breath of life; and man became a living soul.*

This is a picture of my father and me a short time before he died. He suffered from a disease that slowly took his breath. Dad was the last of a family of fifteen. He used to tell me of how he missed them, and of a dream he had where everyone was back together. Dad was also a twin. Dan Hiett, my dad, shared the womb with Don Hiett, my uncle. However, Don Hiett died in infancy.

When my other uncles were angry with my dad they'd say, "You're not Dan, you're Don; Dan died," and my dad would go crying to my grandma, "Am I Dan or Don . . . alive or dead?"

My sister once gave him a book about twins who lost their twin brother or sister. I remember my dad saying, "Peter, this is it; this explains me: all my life I've felt like someone so close to me was missing." The temporary presence of

Don Hiett created an absence in Dan Hiett that made Dan long for the lasting presence of his brother Don.

So, my dad just always wanted to be with people. He called me "dear" and always wanted a kiss, and that was embarrassing in junior high. For a month or so, the year before he died, he had to stay in a nursing home. He was miserable; he so missed his family and home. And I'd complain to God saying, "Why are you putting him through this? He not only has to slowly surrender his breath, he has to slowly surrender the desires of his heart."

Dad was able to die at home, but one desperate wish remained unfulfilled. He wanted to come back to church. That had confused me for about twenty-three years. My dad was a pastor and had wonderful experiences with church, but in the last twenty years of ministry he experienced tremendous pain from church, yet, he still so longed for more church: I-contact.

It's hard to watch someone die. It's hard to witness the unfulfilled longings. We all have unfulfilled longings, and we're all dying. Perhaps you've had to die to a business this year, or a dream or desire. Perhaps you've recently watched someone die—a parent, a spouse, a child—and so you died, a bit.

My dad loved the mountains and he loved horses. He used to tell me how his horse died, and I still remember how his hiking legs gave out. We took him for a hike, and he fell over on my daughter Elizabeth. He was so embarrassed and confused. It was his lungs: he was beginning to yield his breath and the desires of his heart.

I would complain, "God, why can't you do it quickly? Why do you only seem to nurture these painful longings?" In the end, my dad looked like a pile of dry bones. And in the end, more than any other tangible thing, I think my dad longed for breath. His eyes would grow big and he'd try to gasp for breath. Dr. Paul Brand writes, "I know of no human experience that produces such a spasm of uncontrolled panic as does breathlessness." [1]

In the end, he had no breath, and he expired.

In the beginning of my children's lives they inspired, and I got to watch.
It's hard to watch someone expire, but it's a thrill to watch someone inspire.

---

[1] Dr. Paul Brand and Philip Yancey, *In His Image* (Grand Rapids, MI: Zondervan, 1984) 169.

"In the beginning..." God *in*spired Adamah.[2]
"In the beginning..." God *ex*pired . . . to *in*spire Adam*ah*, making Adam.
"In the beginning..." God breathed His breath into dust, and man became a living soul.

It's as if God created the soul by blowing a place of emptiness into the dust with His own breath, as if God blew lungs into the clay with a Word–a breath. (A Word is breath full of meaning.) The Hebrew words *neshamah* and *ruach* are each translated as "breath" or "spirit." In Greek, *pneo* is "breathe" or "spirit," as a verb. *Pneuma* is "breath" or "spirit," as a noun, and *pneumon* is lungs. The English word "spirit" comes from the Latin *spiritus*, which translated literally is "breath."

So, we *ex*pire, which means "breathe out."
And we *in*spire, which means "breathe in."

In Greek *ekpneo* is "expire, breathe out."
And *empneo* is "inspire, in spirit, breathe in."

Well, in the beginning, God *in*spired Adam–breathed into Him, like a kiss. (Mouth-to-mouth resuscitation, without fear, is a kiss). God expired to inspire Adam. And yet, that first Adam sinned.

That first Adam and Eve didn't trust God, and they didn't trust that God's Word was good, and so they tried to take knowledge of the good; they tried to take life from a tree as their own possession; they tried to take life and hang on to life and refused to surrender that life, which was now death. They refused to surrender—as if they inhaled and would not exhale. We'll talk about this much more when we get to Genesis chapter three, but it certainly appears that they *inspired*, or were *inspired*, and then refused to *expire*.

That's like a body part that receives blood, but won't bleed blood. And you know, "...*The Spirit is life*...." (Rom. 8:10), and "...*The life of the flesh is in the blood*..." (Lev. 17:11) The Spirit, the breath, the oxygen is in the blood.

---

[2] OK, this could get confusing. I don't mean that God inhaled dust, but that He exhaled spirit into dust. He in "spirited" the dust and Adam was inspired. God is entirely inspirational!

Well, they held their breath, *the* breath—the Spirit. They held their spirit and death reigned.

In the Old Testament people have "spirits," but it's like they're trapped in death. If you don't expire, you can't inspire; there is no respiration.

In the Old Testament it appears that everyone descends into *Sheol* (Psalm 89:48, Eccles. 9:10) . . . yet in a way they're already there. "*The cords of Sheol entangled me; the snares of death confronted me,*" writes David in Psalm 18:5. *Sheol* (that's *Hades* in Greek) is the realm of the dead; the realm of spirits trapped in earthen tombs. Paul writes, We were "*dead in our trespasses and the un-circumcision of our flesh*" (Col. 2:13). We were dead in the "un-cutoff-edness" of our earthen vessel; like a spirit trapped in a stone tomb, an earthen vessel; like a breath unable to be breathed.

And as we'll discuss in much greater detail, God did say, "*The day you eat of it you will die*" (Gen. 2:17b). That's the sixth day . . . and as we've mentioned, it's still the sixth day for most folks that you bump into on a regular basis. So, maybe most folks are dead or dying—like a person that's inhaled, but cannot exhale their *pneuma*.

Perhaps life is love, and love is surrendering your *pneuma*, your spirit. [3]

We say, "God is Father, Son, and Holy Spirit (Holy Breath)."
    The Spirit emanates from Father and Son.
        Father and Son breathe the same breath–like a kiss.
        Love is like a kiss.

To love is to offer your spirit . . . like a sacrifice.

"*This is love: not that we loved God, but that he loved us and sent his Son as an atoning sacrifice for our sins*" (1 John 4:10 NIV).

---

[3] In his book *Release of the Spirit*, Watchman Nee writes, "The Alabaster box must be broken." ... "If the alabaster box is not broken, the pure spikenard will not flow forth. Strange to say, many are still treasuring the alabaster box thinking its treasure exceeds that of the ointment." Nee is saying that our pride, our ego, even our soul must be broken so our spirit can flow out and commune with God – the Sprit that is God. God is Love.

God is Love. Love given to us is Jesus. The Life is in His Blood.

"This is love:" God *expired* so we would be *inspired*.

God breathes life into us . . .
  But we hold our breath . . .
    We hold our lives.

Sometimes spoiled children do that trying to gain control. Sometimes children—actually about five percent of children under six—hold their breath until they pass out. Overwhelmed with anxiety and fear, they hold their breath. In asthmatics, the parent has to calm the child and hold the child saying, "Relax. Breathe out, breathe in."

We all hold our breath under stress: the chest tightens and the breath grows shallow. Doctors and counselors give us "breathing exercises" to battle the anxiety and the fear.

 So, try it:
 Take a deep breath.
 Breathe out . . . breathe in . . . That's life.
 Breathe out . . . breathe in . . . Now . . . hold it...hold it... hold it...

Sometimes that's the way we live our lives. Isn't it? Afraid to expire–afraid to die. And yet, we're already dead . . . or good as dead.

Fear of losing your life is death.

And how weird is that? We're each surrounded by Life, by Wind, by Spirit . . .
  But if you hold it in you're dead.

 In fear, I think: "I better not lose my life; I better save my life."
 So, I suck life out of everything and everyone.
  I suck life and hold it in. And so I'm dead.

Richard Rohr points out that some scholars think the name of God, *Yahweh*, originally described the sound of breathing. *Yah*-inhale. *Weh*-exhale.[4]

In Jesus' day, and still to this day, many Jews were so afraid of saying the name in vain that they made a law that you couldn't say it at all, even though the prophet said, *"Everyone who calls on the name of the Lord (Yahweh) shall be saved"* (Joel 2:32). *Yah*-inhale. *Weh*-exhale.

You must breathe to be saved.

> You must *expire* to *inspire*.
>
> > You must lose your life to find it.

Maybe sin is like holding your breath. It's holding the spirit, holding the life, refusing to surrender, refusing to love, refusing to breathe . . . God.

> *"God is Spirit."* (John 4:24)
>
> *"...'In Him we live and move and have our being'"* (Acts 17:28).

And so, what's our problem, Adam (and by that I mean humanity)?
What's our problem? We must be holding our breath—the Breath.

A few years ago, I noticed something in all four gospels that I think we may easily miss. In all four gospels, the last thing Jesus does on the cross is surrender His Spirit–His breath.

> ✓ *And Jesus cried out again with a loud voice and yielded up his spirit (pneuma).*
>
> —Matthew 27:50

"Yielded up" translates the Greek word *aphiemi*, normally translated "forgive."

> ✓ *And Jesus uttered a loud cry and breathed his last (ekpneo-expired). And the curtain of the temple was torn in two, from top to bottom. And when the centurion, who stood facing him, saw*

---

[4] Richard Rohr, *The Naked Now* (New York: Crossroad, 2006), 25.

that in this way he breathed his last (ekpneo-expired), he said, "Truly this man was the Son of God!"

—Mark 15:37–39

Crucifixion literally takes a man's breath on a tree. The crucified can inhale, but not exhale. Yet Jesus must've pushed Himself up on the nails to exhale His last breath. We took it, yet He *gave it*–He *for*gave it. The centurion saw that and said, "This man was the Son of God."

✓ *Then Jesus, calling out with a loud voice, said, "Father, into your hands I commit my spirit (pneuma)." And having said this he breathed his last (ekpneo).*

—Luke 23:46

✓ *When Jesus had received the sour wine, he said, "It is finished," and he bowed his head and gave up (paradidomi–He delivered up) his spirit (pneuma).*

—John 19:30

Using my computer, I searched the Old Testament and couldn't find any place—in all the Old Testament—where a man (an *adam*) was said to "give up his spirit."[5]

So, get the picture?

God breathed into Adam, and Adam held his breath–his spirit:

In Ecclesiastes, Solomon writes, *"All go to one place. All are from the dust, and to dust all return"* (Eccles. 3:20). In the Old Testament upon the death of the body, the spirit appears to be trapped in the earth like a ghost trapped in a grave. Hell (that is, *Sheol/Hades*) is holding your breath–your spirit.

---

[5] Except maybe Psalm 31:5 where David "commited his spirit" or "yielded," and there he's a picture of Christ. And surely he held his spirit—he held his breath when he violated Bathsheba and murdered her husband.

Remember what Peter wrote? Jesus *"proclaimed to the spirits in prison"* who *"did not obey in the days of Noah..."* He *"preached even to those who are dead..."* (1 Pet. 3:20, 4:6).

Isaiah had prophesied, *"Your dead shall live; their bodies shall rise. You who dwell in the dust, awake and sing for joy! For your dew is a dew of light, and the earth will give birth to the dead* (Hebrew: *raphaim*—'the ghosts')" (Isa. 26:19).

In Matthew, right after it says that Jesus *"yielded up his spirit,"* it says, *"the curtain of the temple was torn in two."* [Remember that Christ's body is a temple and our bodies are temples— clay temples.] Jesus *"yielded up his spirit. And behold the curtain of the temple was torn in two, from top to bottom. And the earth shook, and the rocks were split. The tombs also were opened. And many bodies of the saints [holy ones] who had fallen asleep were raised, and coming out of the tombs after his resurrection they went into the holy city* [New Jerusalem?] *and appeared to many"* (27:50–53).

In Ezekiel 37, God calls Ezekiel "Son of man," which as you know is what Jesus called Himself. He says,

> *"Prophesy to the breath; prophesy, son of man, and say to the breath, Thus says the Lord God: Come from the four winds, O breath, and breathe on these slain, that they may live."* Ezekiel *does and watches as they come to life.* Then the Lord says, *"Son of man, these bones are the whole house of Israel. Behold, they say, 'Our bones are dried up, and our hope is lost; we are indeed cut off.' Therefore prophesy, and say to them, Thus says the Lord God: Behold, I will open your graves and raise you from your graves, O my people."*
> —Ezekiel 37: 9–12

Well, I hope those scriptures fire your imagination and fill you with an outrageous hope that redemption reaches into the depths of the grave, the pit of *Sheol*, but for now . . .

God breathed into Adam, and Adam held his breath . . .
  Until the last Adam surrendered His breath;
    Until Jesus expired.

It's extremely important to remember that Scripture refers to Jesus as "*the last Adam*" (1 Cor. 15:45), that is "the *Eschatos* Adam," which means "the uttermost Adam," which could mean "the least Adam" and the "ultimate Adam," that is "the super man." Imagine a man who is least of all, yet greatest of all . . .

Well, Jesus was the first to expire and the first to inspire in the finished creation. Jesus is "*the firstborn of all creation... the firstborn from the dead*" (Col. 1:15,8).

"The firstborn." And what does that say about us?

Paul writes, "*The whole creation has been groaning together in the pains of childbirth until now. And not only the creation, but we ourselves...*" (Rom. 8:22). This is because "creation waits with eager longing for the revealing of the sons of God" (Rom. 8:29), all so that Christ Jesus "*might be firstborn among many brethren*" (Rom. 8:29).

Jesus told us that we "*must be born again*" (John 3:3). An even more accurate translation would be that we "must be born from above." Jesus made it clear to Nicodemus that He wasn't talking about a birth that Nicodemus had already experienced.

If Jesus was the first born of all creation and first born from the dead, and He said this before He died, then He said it to people that hadn't truly been born, but would need to be born, like Jesus would be born. And doesn't that mean that on Good Friday, in the midst of the worst trauma and travail, we watched the birth of our big brother, Jesus the Christ, from inside the womb? That would be like Dan Hiett watching Don Hiett born first from inside the womb, then feeling his absence and longing for his presence—as if someone very important was missing, like an empty place in Dan longing for Don, longing for I-contact.

Well, on Good Friday we watched the birth of our big brother Jesus from inside the womb—the womb, that is, this world.

Watching the death of Jesus or one of his brethren is watching a birth from inside the womb—the womb we call this world. It's hard to watch a death. It's a thrill to watch a birth!

Have you ever chewed on that idea: that all space and time... is a womb? If it is, what's outside the womb? What's beyond, outside, before and after the Big Bang? Of course we know that none of those prepositions (beyond, outside, before and after) actually work, for they all assume space and time; and the Big Bang is the beginning of all space and time. Well, given that mystery, if the Big Bang is the very creation of space and time, if the Big Bang is the very creation of all natural law, that is, all nature, then "outside" all nature must be the super-natural . . . by definition.

As we mentioned in the last chapter, the two biggest mysteries in modern physics are:

✓ What (or who) is "outside" or "before" the Big Bang. AND

✓ What (or who) am "I?" . . . "The observer."

    [Remember "The observer" that can collapse the quantum
    state of subatomic particles, which are the building blocks of
    all matter, all "nature"?]

See, it's like all nature is a womb in the belly of the supernatural, the belly of God. And within "me," in that womb, is the breath of God, which makes me who "I" am.

It's like creation is a womb in the belly of eternity. And within my earthen vessel is implanted an eternal seed.

It's like I am fertilized with eternity. "[God] *has put eternity into man's heart, yet so that he cannot find out what God has done from the beginning to the end*" (Eccl. 3:11), writes Solomon. It's like, eternity longing for eternity, from within us. Why the painful longings in this world, why the hunger in my soul, why the taste of something eternal and then its absence? Why hope?

Martin Luther used to say, "Imagine if a baby could reason inside the womb, surely it would wonder: 'What are these hands for, these feet for? What is this mouth for? What is this empty place in my chest for?'"[6]

If you were that baby, the best evidence for another world might be yourself, and things within yourself . . . like your lungs. What's the purpose of lungs in a womb? The baby receives all of his or her oxygen through the body of the mother, and then the umbilical cord. Life (spirit, oxygen) from outside the womb, and outside the mother, is mediated to the baby through blood in the umbilical cord. And that's good, by the way, for if the undeveloped baby were exposed directly to air, the baby would be burned–oxidized.

And if, right now, we were exposed directly to God, who is Spirit, and eternal . . . we just might get burned–oxidized . . . That's fire–Holy Eternal Fire.

So, life is first "breathed" into the baby through the blood in the cord, which is very much a part of that womb world. To the baby it might seem to be the most important thing in that womb world.

But, what about the lungs? What's the purpose of lungs for a baby in a womb world? There's no air to breathe in a womb . . . and yet, as early as ten weeks gestation, doctors detect breathing movement in the baby. By twenty-eight weeks, the baby will breathe amniotic fluid. It will breathe the fluid in his or her world, as if sustained by that world, even though sustained by oxygen from another world. So, of course the baby isn't really breathing because it's not breathing breath; the baby isn't really breathing but only preparing to breathe.

Maybe, (perhaps most of the time) we don't really love, but are preparing to love. To really love, would be to love Love . . . like you breathe breath. It would be to surrender your spirit and receive the Spirit, not because you have to, but because you want to. It's become your nature.

Well, imagine if you were a baby in the womb and you had a skeptical twin with you in that womb. He might say,

> Why the breathing?
> There's no point in breathing.
> Just hang on to that cord! Hang on to your life!

[6]   Rev. Richard Wurmbrand, *In God's Under-ground* (Glendale, CA: Diane Books Publishing Co., 1976), 204.

That's kind of like saying:

> Why the loving? The hoping? And the faithing—the trusting?
> There's no point in Faith, Hope, and Love.
> Just hang on to this life!
>> Love too much, and you might lose your life!
>> Perhaps it's best not to love at all—
>> Love hiking . . . and your legs will one day give out.
>> Love a horse . . . and it will die.
>> Love your family . . . and they'll break your heart.
>> Love a church . . . and you'll get crucified.
>> Love anything, and you'll be disappointed.
>> Love God? There is no God. There is no love.
> So, take one big breath, suck in as much as you can.
> Then stop breathing. Stop hoping. Stop trusting.
> Just hold your breath and hang on to that cord!

Did you know that birth is profoundly traumatic for a baby? It is. But the trauma, the birth pains, the contractions have a purpose: they expire the baby. I learned this from the doctors when my first son was being born. Susan and Jonathan experienced twenty-four hours of labor. Those contractions literally squeeze the amniotic fluid out of the baby's lungs. The pressure is so intense that the baby can no longer inspire amniotic fluid, but only expire the fluid.

The baby had been inspired with "spirit" through the dust of its world, through the body of the mother and the blood in that cord. But now, through birth, the baby is expired of his or her entire world.

Imagine how that feels to the baby. The world that had been such an inspiration begins to press in from every side; the baby experiences tribulation and travail. It grows so intense that the baby must expire his world—all the fluid in his lungs. He must expire that which would seem to be his "life," even as he is expelled from his world.

There is a blinding light, probably a rude smack on a naked behind and then he takes a tremendous breath; he inspires, and then expires a scream. Then he inspires. Then he expires, inspires, expires, sees with his eyes, runs with his feet, eats pizza with his mouth, feels the arms of his mom and dad; the baby lives; the baby is home.

The baby is expired; for in a moment, in the "twinkling of an eye," the baby will be inspired by a whole new creation. The end is the beginning. The death is a birth. And all that remains of that umbilical cord, all that remains of that which seemed most important, all that remains . . . is a wound, a scar that we call a belly button.

At funerals, I often tell people to lift their shirts and gaze at their navels. Feel free to do so now. Gaze at your navel; take a big breath and then speak a word–make a declaration: "Umbilical cord, you used to be everything to me. You were my breath, my life, but I was made for another world. Thank you, but I don't need you anymore; I'm free!"

Then, look up at this world, or look in the mirror at your old wrinkly dried up umbilical cord of a body and say, "You used to be everything to me, but I'm being made for another world. Thank you, but you're not necessary anymore; I'm free!"

There are only three belly button verses in the Bible:

- ✓ Ezekiel prophecies that when God found us our navel cord was uncut. We were dependent upon, and tethered to, this world (Ezek. 16:4).

- ✓ Proverbs 3:5,8 translated literally says, "*Trust in the Lord with all your heart and... it will be health for your navel.*" That is: "trust in the Lord, and it will be health for your relationship with this world." You won't be addicted to this world, constantly sucking the life out of this world.

- ✓ In Song of Solomon 7:2, to the Bride, the Lord says, "*Your navel is a rounded bowl that never lacks mixed wine.*" That sounds kinda sexy, huh? We'll learn more about that in chapters to come.

Well, we were just saying that watching the death of Jesus (or one of His brethren) would be like watching a birth from inside the womb. There'd be travail, pain, and then absence. And if you wondered: "Is there life after birth?" Well, the best evidence would be the longing within you, the empty places in your own chest.

C.S. Lewis wrote: "If I find in myself desires which nothing in this world can satisfy, the only logical explanation is that I was made for another world."[7]

Perhaps those desires are like the unsatisfied places, the empty places in your chest, and perhaps those places are unique in all creation. Perhaps those desires are formed by the life that God has breathed into you in this world–the life that you must expire to inspire.

Lewis continues the thought in another place:

> The mold in which a key is made would be a strange thing, ...a strange thing if you had never seen a key: and the key itself a strange thing if you had never seen a lock. Your soul has a curious shape because it is a hollow made to fit a particular swelling in the infinite contours of the divine substance...For it is not humanity in the abstract that is to be saved, but you– the individual.[8]

You must lose your life to "find it" (Matt. 16:25); expire it, to inspire it... But it is "it." I mean the thing you find is "your life"—"your life," but filled with God, and God is Love, and God is Spirit.

You expire your emptiness and inspire God—your unique experience of God, who fills the uniquely empty experiences of your life.

You expire your life and inspire God.

And maybe that's living! Not hanging on to life, but breathing life, breathing Spirit, breathing God. That's living your Life. And maybe we can begin to live that eternal life, even in this womb of a world.

---

[7] C. S. Lewis, *Mere Christianity* (New York: Macmillan, 1943), 120.

[8] C. S. Lewis, *The Problem of Pain* (New York: Macmilllan, 1962), 147

Have you ever noticed how each resurrection experience is individual and unique?

- ✓ Doubting Thomas gets to put his hand in Jesus' side; Jesus fills his doubt with Himself.

- ✓ Coward Peter is reinstated as the rock.

- ✓ Confused disciples on the way to Emmaus get all of Scripture explained to them.

- ✓ John, the son of thunder, receives the Revelation and becomes the Apostle of Love.

- ✓ The last of all, Mary, becomes first of all . . . to see Him. It seems that Mary was a harlot, and she (and we) become the Bride.

When you breathe Him in, you will know Him as no other person ever has or will. Your empty longings become His unique presence. Your old empty self becomes the fullness of God (Eph. 1:23). Your expiration becomes your inspiration.

If you don't hold your breath.

So, how do we get the courage?

How do we get the faith to not hold our breath, but to surrender our spirit?

> *On the evening of that day, the first day of the week, the doors being locked where the disciples were, for fear of the Jews, Jesus came and stood among them and said to them, "Peace be with you." When he had said this, he showed them his hands and his side. Then the disciples were glad when they saw the Lord. Jesus said to them again, "Peace be with you. As the Father has sent me, even so I am sending you." And when he had said this, he*

breathed on them and said to them, "Receive the Holy Spirit."
–the Holy *Pneuma*–My breath.

—John 20:19–22

The disciples are locked down in fear, holding their breath, afraid to exhale. And Jesus appears in that room; He appears in that womb–to His former womb mates. And He shows them His scars–that place on His body where He had been cut away from this world. He showed them His eternal belly button and said, "Have peace," as if to say, "When the birth pains start, remember me, your brother, firstborn from the dead, firstborn of many brethren."

But He didn't just show them, He breathed on them. He *inspired* them. To some degree, they had already been *expired* at His cross. His crucifixion knocked the air right out of them, knocked the arrogance and ego (the illusion that they could create themselves and save their own lives) right out of them.

Jesus had said, "*I go to prepare a place for you...in my Father's house...*" (John 14:2). We are the Father's house–His temple. So, maybe "the place prepared" is the place prepared by His presence, then absence, which makes us long for more presence–the eternal presence. He is the breath of God in flesh. His appearance, and then His absence, makes us long for His abiding presence.

Well, at the cross, Jesus *expired* them . . . (they died with Him.)
Jesus *expired* them . . . and now He *inspires* them.

"*Thus it is written, 'The first man Adam became a living being* (soul); *the last Adam became a life-giving spirit* (a life-giving *pneuma*–the Holy Breath)" —1 Cor. 15:45.

I cannot adequately explain this, but I hope you see. Life is communicated to all of us through the dust of this world: through biology, sex, fertilization, food, and shelter . . . and Jesus is "The Life." Jesus is the Word of the Father that upholds all things, "the light that enlightens all men" (John 1:9). And He is the life that we took on the tree and the life that God gave on the same tree.

Now, in this womb of a world, eternal life is communicated to us directly through Jesus Christ crucified and risen from the dead—like mouth-to-mouth resuscitation, like a blood transfusion through broken body. Eternal Life comes through the gift of the Spirit on Pentecost, and the communion table is like an umbilical cord.

> *"The life... is in the blood"* (Lev. 17:11).

> *"...God has sent the Spirit* (the breath) *of his Son into our hearts, crying, 'Abba Father'"* (Gal. 4:6).

> *"That... he may grant you to be strengthened with power through his Spirit in your inner being, so that Christ may dwell in your hearts through faith..."* (Eph. 3:16–17).

> *"Faith is the substance of things hoped for..."* (Heb. 11:1 NKJV).

Faith in you is the Spirit of Christ in you, Christ's courage to die, and rise, in you, Christ living eternally in you, Christ breathing in you.

> When we exercise faith, we die with Him and rise with Him.
> We surrender the Spirit and receive the Spirit.
> We begin to breathe.

> You know He didn't come to simply die for us . . . He came to die *with* us;
> He came to help us expire, for you can't inspire until you expire.
> You can't rise with Him, if you haven't died with Him.

It was twelve years ago March 8th that my father died. The last thing he ate was a piece of broken bread. The last thing he drank was a drop of wine. The last thing he said to me was, "Thank you," after I said, "This is His body given to you. This is His blood shed for you." I didn't know he was going to die in a few minutes, but I knew he was close. Everyone else had left the room, and we had a few minutes alone.

He could no longer speak. I rested my head on the bed by his chest. He was like a valley of dry bones, and I could hear his old breath crackling and popping as his lungs filled with fluid from the pneumonia.

I said, "Dad, I want to pray for you." I prayed something like this: "Father in heaven, it must be terrifying not knowing if you can catch your next breath. Please help my dad to know deep down inside that he no longer needs to breathe air . . . because, Father, he can breathe your Spirit. God, help dad to relax and breathe you. In Jesus' name, Amen."

I kissed my dad on the head and said, "I'm going home to get my stuff, and I'll come back to spend the night." When I returned, he had just breathed his last . . . and first.

My sister said he started to slide as soon as I left. He'd inspire and expire, then stop. Then inspire and expire, then stop longer . . . like he was testing the water, testing the air, testing the atmosphere in another world. He inspired and expired one last time. He expired carbon dioxide and inspired the Spirit of God.

He was home.

We had witnessed my father's birth from inside the womb. And maybe I had even prophesied (or the Son of Man, in me, had prophesied) to the dry bones. And now my dad, Dan Hiett, breathes God. Maybe that first breath was terrifying. Expiring the dead life of this world must be terrifying, but breathing God must be ecstasy. Every breath is Easter. Every empty longing is fully filled with the eternal presence of God. But that presence isn't static. It's dynamic.

I doubt it's like breathing in this world. He doesn't have to expire life, be emptied of life, before he then inspires life. No! I think he experiences a river of life. Because he no longer holds his breath, he is a river of breath. It flows through him like blood flows through arteries in a body. He is that body, the Body of Christ.

A friend told me that she saw my Dad after he died. She was hiking in the woods on a mountain, praying. She said she looked up and saw him riding a beautiful horse, laughing, smiling, and he said, "Lorie, have hope."

He loved mountains, hiking, and horses, but he had to expire his desire to inspire the full-fillment of his desire.

He longed for family, but had to expire that desire. And now he has his family back forever . . . God's family and his family. Dad longed for his brother in the womb; now he's got his big Brother Jesus and his other brother Don.

And Dad longed to come back to church, and I think he did come back to church. Seven and a half years ago, three and a half years after Dad expired, I was about to go through that most challenging time of my relatively pain-free life. I was about to be tried, defrocked, and branded as a heretic. It's a rather amazing story, but as a young man I had seen my father go through basically the same thing and had always been terrified that it would happen to me.

I had just given communion and people were coming forward to receive the body and blood when my wife, Susan, grabbed my arm and said, "Peter, I just saw your dad!" Her eyes were huge, and she was shaking: "Peter he was standing right in front of us. He was so excited and so full of life. (Not the eighty-pound bag of dry bones, dust and ashes that he was when we saw him last.) His eyes were like fire," she said. "He had a bowl in his hand, and he leaned forward and said, 'Susan and Peter, do not be afraid to drink from the cup the Lord has for you,' and then he vanished."

I think I know what it meant. I had seen my dad hurt, and I was terrified of being hurt in the same way. I was holding my breath (and I still hold my breath). But my dad was saying, "Peter . . . breathe. Breathe out your fear, anxiety, sin, and control. You must surrender control. And breathe in God's Grace. Breathe out your life, and breathe in Christ's life. Live His life. Live Faith, Hope, and Love. You are His Body."[9]

On the night that Jesus was delivered up, He took bread and broke it saying, "This is my body given to you; take and eat." And He took the cup saying, "This is the covenant in my blood, poured out for the forgiveness of sins; drink of it, all of you."

> The life is in the blood.
> Don't be afraid to drink the cup that the Lord has for you.
>> Expire your sin, and inspire God's Mercy.
>> Expire your control, and inspire Freedom.
>> Expire your judgment, and inspire God's Judgment.
>> Expire your flesh, and inspire the Spirit.
>> Expire your ego, and inspire Love.
>> Expire your life, and inspire God's Life.
>> Expire your self, your soul, and inspire Jesus.

---

[9] Several years ago, a friend shared with me the following, "Peter, I don't know what it means, but the Lord told me your calling is to be filled and then emptied, filled and then emptied, filled and then emptied. Don't be afraid to be emptied because you'll always be filled." Preaching does feel like that. It can terrify me, but I'm still just learning to breathe.

> Expire and inspire: love and be loved, and love and be loved, and love, and be loved; expire and inspire . . . even now. Eternal life is now.

By Faith, we can even begin to breathe now. We can expire and be inspired now. For faith in us is Christ dying and rising in us. And now I hope you see one more reason that the expiration of Jesus, the death of Jesus, brings us life. He didn't just die His own death. He died Adam's death. He died humankind's death. He causes Adam to breathe. He is Adam breathing.

Eve and that first Adam took the fruit from the tree and held their breath; they hid themselves in fig leaves and self-righteousness. God had told them, "*The day you eat of it you will die.*" That was the sixth day of creation.

Jesus delivers us from the curse, but would He do that by making God a liar? Would He do that, by making it so that we could eat of it and not die? Or would He do it by giving us the courage to die, with Him?

As long as "I" refuse to die, as long as "I" hold my breath, "I" remain trapped in this "body of flesh," this "earthen vessel," this womb, this tomb. Do you see? This body, this world is the womb in which the Seed begins to grow. But this womb turns into a tomb if I refuse to be born and refuse to breathe.

And this tomb is more than a physical body. This tomb is an ego, a self that becomes self-righteous, an independence and self-sufficiency that turns into Hell. And by Hell, I mean *Sheol* or *Hades*, the outer darkness where men weep and gnash their teeth. If one refuses to die to self, before their body dies, they still must die. That's why suicide isn't death, but a self trapped in death; it's not the death of self, but a final assertion of self.

Bill Maher once said, "Suicide is our way of saying to God, 'You can't fire me, I quit.'" And that's true. The problem with suicide is that it doesn't work. It's not surrendering control. It's seizing control; it's holding your breath; it's refusing to expire; it's taking "your life," when true Life is giving life and receiving life. Life is a river that flows through you like blood in an artery. When we dam the flow we damn ourselves.

A damned self hasn't died to its self. So, like I said, if one refuses to die before the body dies, they remain in *Sheol*; they sink into *Sheol*; they remain trapped in dust; they sink back into the womb that is this world. But all is not lost.

King David writes:

Where shall I go from your Spirit (Breath)?
Or where shall I flee from your presence?
If I ascend to heaven, you are there!
If I make my bed in Sheol, you are there!
...If I say, "Surely the darkness shall cover me,
and the light about me be night,"
even the darkness is not dark to you;
the night is bright as the day,
for darkness is as light with you.
For you formed my inward parts;
you knitted me together in my mother's womb.
I praise you, for I am fearfully and wonderfully made.
Wonderful are your works;
my soul knows it very well.
My frame was not hidden from you,
when I was being made in secret,
intricately woven in the depths of the earth.

—Psalm 139:7–8, 11–15

Jesus said, "The son of man (Adam) came to seek and save the lost (*apololos*) – also translated "the perished," "the destroyed" (Luke 19:10). The *Eschatos* Adam came to save the lost, and I see no biblical reason to think that He stops doing so on the day your body dies. Indeed, Scripture is clear that He descends into *Sheol* preaching gospel: "lose your life, for my sake and the kingdom, and you will find it... Breathe!"

But what if they don't breathe? Will *Hades* win? Can death win?

In Revelation 20, John sees "the dead" standing before the throne. They are judged by the things written in the books, judged *"according to what they had done"* (Rev. 20:13). That means their ego, their pride, their arrogance, their shame and fear, their self-righteousness is exposed to the burning grace of God—Divinity.

Theos is the Greek noun for God, and *theios* or *theion* is the Greek adjective for "God-ness" or Divine. *Theion* can be used as a substantive adjective meaning "Divinity." This is clearly how Paul uses the word in Acts 17:27,29.

Theion is also translated "brimstone" or "sulfur." To the ancients brimstone meant "Godstone." In Isaiah 30:33 it's pictured as coming from the mouth of God and setting *Gehenna* on fire: *"For Tophet (Gehenna) is ordained of old... the breath of the LORD, like a stream of brimstone, doth kindle it"* (Isa. 30:33 KJV). Did you catch that? Did you catch that? The *neshamah* of *Yahweh*, the breath of the Lord is like a stream of *Theion*! *"Is not my Word like fire, says the Lord..."* (Jer. 23:29). Is not Jesus, the Adam that stands on the mount of transfiguration, burning brighter that the sun? Is He not the breath of God, and the meaning of God, in new and eternal flesh? Yes. He is.

Jesus is the Judgment of God.

And why am I telling you this? Well, in Revelation 20:13, after John sees "Death and *Hades*" give up "the dead" that were in them, after he sees them stand before the throne, he writes,

> *Then Death and Hades were thrown into the lake of fire. This is the second death, the lake of fire. And if anyone's name was not found written in the book of life, he was thrown into the lake of fire.*
> —Revelation 20:14–15

Now we can't explain all of that, but this much seems clear:

✓ You cannot hold your breath forever without end. Jesus said, *"I am... the end"* (Rev. 22:13). In the end, all who hold their breath will be thrown into the Lake of God's Burning Breath, "Fire" and *Theion* (Rev. 21:8). "Fire that is Divinity." God is Spirit, and God is Love. Love wins.

✓ That lake is the death of death. It is the second death. As Paul puts it: Apart from Christ, we are all "dead in our trespasses and the *un-cut-off-edness* of our flesh" (Eph. 2:5). We are all dead in our arrogance and self-righteousness. We all hold our breath, refusing to expire. Expiration is the death of death and that's life. Life is the death of death. Life is the second death.

If your name is written in the Lamb's Book of Life, you won't be thrown into the Lake of Life (Fire).[10] In some amazing way, perhaps you're already there. Remember what happened to the disciples on Pentecost? Tongues of Fire! They had expired, and on Pentecost they inspired the breath of God and expired praise—that for which Adam is made (Eph. 1:6,11).

✓ Jesus is the death of death. Jesus is "the Life." *"If we have been united with him in a death like his, we shall certainly be united with him in a resurrection like his"* (Rom. 6:5). Perhaps that offer is eternal. Whatever the case, it is now. When we come to Christ, or Christ comes to us, we surrender our selves to be crucified with Him, and our *"body of sin"* (Rom. 6:6) is *"brought to nothing."* We expire with Him. And we are inspired with Him. The alabaster flask is broken, perfume spills out and the aroma fills the entire house with praise (Matt. 26:7). To the unredeemed this appears to be foolishness and a waste. But it is love, and God is Love, and Adam is in His image.

The author of Hebrews writes:

> *Since therefore the children share in flesh and blood, he himself likewise partook of the same things, that through death he might destroy the one who has the power of death, that is, the devil, and deliver all those who through fear of death were subject to lifelong slavery.*
>
> —Hebrews 2:14–15

The fear of death is the fear of expiration, but without expiration there is no inspiration. Jesus came to give us the faith necessary to expire, to "deliver up our spirit," to breathe.

---

[10] Perhaps "the dead," who hold their breath and whose names aren't written in the Lamb's Book of Life, are thrown into the Lake of Fire and Divinity so that their names would be written in the Lamb's Book of Life. Perhaps even these die so they can live, for "death is no more." "'Death is swallowed up in victory.' 'O death, where is your victory? O death, where is your sting'" (1 Cor. 15:54–55)? Perhaps it's time that we who call ourselves "the Church" stop giving death the victory and announce that Jesus wins.

In the Gospel of John Jesus says:

> *The Father loves the Son and has given all things into his hand.*
> *Whoever believes (has faith) in the Son has eternal life; whoever*
> *does not obey the Son shall not see life, but the wrath of God*
> *remains on him.*
>
> —John 3:35–36

Why does the wrath of God remain on him? Well, maybe the Father wants His children to breathe.

Jesus continues:

> *Truly, truly, I say to you, whoever hears my word and believes*
> *(has faith in and through) him who sent me has eternal life. He*
> *does not come into judgment, but has passed from death to life.*
> *Truly, truly, I say to you, an hour is coming, and is now here,*
> *when the dead will hear the voice of the Son of God, and those*
> *who hear will live.*
>
> —John 5:24–25

Jesus came to give us the courage to expire ourselves—to sacrifice ourselves—that we might be inspired by God, that we might live.

> *About the sixth hour, on the sixth day of the week, on the sixth*
> *day of creation "there was darkness over the whole lad until the*
> *ninth hour, while the sun's light failed. And the curtain in the*
> *temple was torn in two. Then Jesus calling out with a loud voice,*
> *said, "Father, into your hands I commit my spirit!" And having*
> *said this he breathed his last.*
>
> —Luke 23:44–46

The stone temple was broken; Christ's body was broken; the earthen vessel was broken and the Spirit got out. It was "finished." That was the end of the sixth day, the day in which Adam is made in the image of God.

It was the end of the sixth day and the beginning of an eternal Sabbath Day, when and where everything is "very good." God alone is good. God is Spirit. God is Love. And, through Christ, God will fill all things . . . especially Adam.

Well, the "day we eat of it," we *do* die. And on the Seventh Day, we live. God's Judgment is death and resurrection. God's judgment is Jesus. God's Judgment is Grace.

For some reason people say that Jesus died so we don't have to. But Jesus died so we wouldn't stay dead. Jesus died so that we would die and live. Jesus expired so that we would expire and inspire, so that we would surrender our spirit and receive God's Spirit, so that we would become a vessel that channels His Spirit—not a vessel that damns the Spirit. We are destined to channel His Spirit like a body part bleeds out and bleeds in, channeling a river of life in a living body. If we're cut off from that Body, "bleeding" looks like death, but if we're connected to that Body, that "bleeding,"—that expiration and inspiration—that respiration is Life. And life is Love. Adam is predestined for Love.

C. S. Lewis said it this way:

> ...in self-giving, if anywhere, we touch a rhythm not only of all creation but of all being. For the Eternal Word also gives Himself in sacrifice; and that not only on Calvary. For when He was crucified He "did that in the wild weather of His outlying provinces which He had done at home in glory and gladness" [George Macdonald]. From before the foundation of the world He surrenders begotten Deity back to begetting Deity in obedience. And as the Son glorifies the Father, so also the Father glorifies the Son.... From the highest to the lowest, self exists to be abdicated and, by that abdication, becomes the more truly self, to be thereupon yet the more abdicated, and so forever. This is not a heavenly law which we can escape by remaining earthly, nor an earthly law which we can escape by being saved. What is outside the system of self-giving is not earth, nor nature, nor "ordinary life," but simply and solely Hell. . . .The golden apple of selfhood, thrown among the false gods, became an apple of discord because they scrambled for it. They did not know the first rule of the holy game,

which is that every player must by all means touch the ball and then immediately pass it on. To be found with it in your hands is a fault: to cling to it, death. But when it flies to and fro among the players too swift for eye to follow, and the great master Himself leads the revelry, giving Himself eternally to His creatures in the generation, and back to Himself in the sacrifice, of the Word, then indeed the eternal dance "makes heaven drowsy with harmony." All pains and pleasures we have known on earth are early initiations in the movements of that dance: but the dance itself is strictly incomparable with the sufferings of this present time. As we draw nearer to its uncreated rhythm, pain and pleasure sink almost out of sight. There is joy in the dance, but it does not exist for the sake of joy. It does not even exist for the sake of good, or of love. It is Love Himself, and Good Himself, and therefore happy.[11]

Jesus delivers us from the curse by helping us die . . . that we might live. So, my dad breathed his last and breathed his first. He did not descend into *Sheol*. He is not dust and ashes. He is not a bag of dry bones. He is the eternally dancing and happy Body of Christ—the *Eschatos* Adam.

Say: "Father, in Jesus' name, into your hands I surrender my spirit. Amen."

---

[11]   C. S. Lewis *The Problem of Pain* (New York: Macmillan, 1962) 152–153.

The whole kingdom of God – the catholic, actual mystery that, come fair response or foul, is irremovably mixed into creation – operates by *warm breath*. It takes its origin from a Father's breathed-forth *Word* who spoken once for all eternity brings the world out of nothing into being. It marches through its history under the guidance of a *Spirit* – a *ruach*, a *pneuma*, a wind, a breath – who, proceeding from the Father's speaking of the Word, confirms that Word with signs following. And the imagery grows more and more complex. Jesus breathes out the Spirit upon his disciples after his resurrection. After he has ascended, he sends that same Spirit upon the church as a rushing mighty wind. And finally, when the church goes forth to announce the leavening of the world by all this Trinitarian heavy breathing, it is by yet more warm breath – even by hot air – that the proclamation is made: "For after . . . the world by wisdom knew not God, it please God *by the foolishness of preaching* to save them that believe" (KJV, emphasis mine).

—*Robert Capon, <u>Kingdom, Grace, Judgment</u>*

For at that time he showed our frailty and our fallings, our discouragements, our abasements, our humiliations and our outcastings; all the woe which it seemed to me could possibly befall us in this life. And with this he showed his blessed power, his blessed wisdom, his blessed love, in which he protects us at such times as tenderly and as sweetly for his own glory and as safely for our salvation as he does when we enjoy most pleasure and comfort; and with this he raises us in spirit right up to heaven, and turns everything to his glory and our joy everlastingly; for his love never allows our time to be lost.

—*Julian of Norwich, <u>Revelations of Divine Love</u>*

CHAPTER 3

The Missing Link

Genesis 2:4–7

In 1831, Charles Darwin set out on his famous journey aboard the HMS *Beagle*. On that trip to the southern seas of South America he would begin to formulate his theory of evolution. In 1832 the *Beagle* arrived in Tierra Del Fuego in what is now Argentina. It was there that Darwin encountered what was later referred to as "the missing link,"—a group of what he characterized as cannibals. Later in *The Descent of Man*, Darwin wrote, "We thus learn that man is descended from a hairy, tailed quadruped..."[1] He goes on to describe the residents of Tierra del Fuego,

> The astonishment which I felt on first seeing a party of Fuegians on a wild and broken shore will never be forgotten by me, for the reflection at once rushed into my mind—such were our ancestors. These men were absolutely naked and bedaubed with paint, their long hair was tangled, their mouths frothed with excitement, and their expression was wild, startled, and distrustful.[2]

Darwin concluded that the Fuegians were "the lowest of human forms yet discovered."[3] Here is an actual photo of what many in Darwin's day concluded to be the missing link:

---

[1] Darwin, C., *The Descent of Man: part 2*, American Home Library Company, New York, 1902, p. 784

[2] Ibid. p. 796

[3] Bergman, Jerry, *The Darwin Effect* (Master Books, Green Forest AZ, 2014) p. 170

According to Darwin's theory, it might take thousands or millions of years for natural selection and chance mutations ("the survival of the fittest") to produce a modern human from an intermediate form. Well, I'm not a Darwin hater; and as I mentioned in our study of Genesis 1, I do believe that Darwin was on to something—there is a "natural selection;" I just don't buy the idea that it's responsible for life, so much as death. I don't know exactly what Darwin expected from the Fuegians, but it appears that by the end of Darwin's life something changed his mind regarding the status of the Fuegians in our family tree.

Well, no matter what you think of Darwin, he does raise fascinating questions: "Where do we come from?" As well as, "Where are we going?" If there's a missing link to our past, there must also be a missing link to our future. If we evolved from something, we must also be evolving into something.

Friedrich Nietzsche was one of the first to postulate our missing link with the future. He argued that the next evolutionary step would be the "super-man," the "uber-man."[4] Adolph Hitler was a huge fan of Nietzsche. He believed that the next evolutionary step was the Aryan race. Karl Marx believed that the next evolutionary step was the Communist State. People are still postulating the next evolutionary step. Maybe it's the X-men: Dr. Xavier, Magneto, Storm, Mystique and all their mutant friends. Maybe not. Whatever the case, the populatirty of these movies reveals that we all want to know where we're from and

---

[4] See Friedrich Niezsche *Thus Spoke Zarathustra*.

where we're going. We all want to know the *alpha* and the *omega*, the first and the last, the beginning and the end of Adam (humankind). We all want to know the missing link that tells us who we are.

> **Genesis 2:4-7** *These are the generations of the heavens and the earth when they were created, in the day that the Lord God made the earth and the heavens. When no bush of the field was yet in the land and no small plant of the field had yet sprung up—for the Lord God had not caused it to rain on the land, and there was no man to work the ground, and a mist was going up from the land and was watering the whole face of the ground—then the Lord God formed the man of dust from the ground and breathed into his nostrils the breath of life, and the man (Adam) became a living* [nephesh: soul, person, life, creature].

That tells us where we're from and maybe where we're going. There is a first Adam and a last Adam, beginning and end. We'll get to where we're going in a few pages, but now let's discuss where we're from.

"When no plant of the field was yet in the earth." That appears to have been the third day of creation, which would imply that God formed man's body—man's dust—over three days. Three is a pretty significant number in Scripture . . . especially for the body of Christ. You might just remember that for future reference. Maybe that has something to do with Jesus and His body rising from the dust.

Maybe it has something to do with space and time. If what we've postulated is true, the third day of creation was millions and millions of years ago, and now we live toward the end of the sixth day on the edge of an eternal Seventh Day. If that's the case, three of those days would indicate that God has been forming our bodies, out of dust, for millions of years. So, perhaps a fish body, a lizard body and an ape body were part of the design process.

Does that offend you? Is your body that much better than an eagle's, or a tiger's, or an apes? Is it really an opposable thumb or a big brain that makes you human (that is *Adam*). Personally, I'd be rather honored to know that I'm a biological cousin to a big old silverback mountain gorilla. But you see? It's not my body that makes me *Adam*.

So, perhaps God has been forming Adam's dust for millions of years, but on the sixth day He breathed into that dust and made a *nephesh*—a living soul named Adam.

Genesis one already described it in this way:

> **Genesis 1:1,26,27,31** *In the beginning, God... Then God said, "Let us make man in our image, after our likeness.... So God created man in his own image, in the image of God he created him; male and female he created them.... And God saw everything that he had made, and behold, it was very good. And there was evening and there was morning, the sixth day.*

In Genesis 2:5, God is called *Yahweh*, which, as you remember, basically means, "I am." And you remember that He gives me an "I" that makes me who I am.

Yet, in Genesis one, the Hebrew word translated God is *Elohim*. *Elohim* is a fascinating word, for it isn't singular, but plural. Both *El* and *Eloah* are singular words translated "God," while *Elohim* is clearly plural. That's a mystery for Jews, which they attempt to explain in a variety of ways. It's also a mystery for Christians. It's just that Christians have a name for the mystery and have built a couple thousand years of theology around that mystery. Of course that name is "Trinity."

It's important to understand that the word "Trinity" doesn't appear in Scripture and as a doctrine it wasn't well defined until after the Council of Nicea in 325 AD. And yet the idea that God is one, yet somehow plural, has been present from the very start. In the early church, some argued that God is two persons: Father and Son—while the Spirit describes the relationship between them. The view which won the day, having been classically refined and defined by Athanasius of Antioch, is that God is three persons and one substance—the Trinity. Three persons, co-equal, co-eternal and consubstantial that exist in *perichoresis*, which means something like "mutual indwelling." And this *perichoresis* is not static but dynamic as each offers up the self for the other, glorifying the other. Of course all our human words and concepts fall short of the reality that is God, yet nonetheless they help us speak of that to which Scripture testifies and our hearts bear witness: "God is Love."

I don't mean to bury you in C. S. Lewis quotes, but he does seem to say it best:

> All sorts of people are fond of repeating the Christian state-
> ment that "God is love." But they seem not to notice that the
> words "God is love" have no real meaning unless God con-
> tains at least two Persons. Love is something that one person
> has for another person. If God was a single person, then be-
> fore the world was made, He was not love.... And that, by the
> way, is perhaps the most important difference between Chris-
> tianity and all other religions: that in Christianity God is not
> a static thing—not even a person—but a dynamic, pulsating
> activity, a life, almost a kind of drama. Almost, if you will not
> think me irreverent, a kind of dance.... And now, what does
> it all matter? It matters more than anything else in the world.
> The whole dance, or drama, or pattern of this three-Personal
> life is to be played out in each one of us: or (putting it the
> other way round) each one of us has got to enter that pattern,
> take his place in that dance.[5]

As he states, for God to be love there must be at least two persons in the dance.
Perhaps He made you a person, that you would join the dance.

Now read it again:

> *Then God [Elohim - plural] said, "Let us [plural] make man
> [singular] in our image [plural]." ...So God created man in his
> own image, in the image of God he created him [singular], male
> and female [plural] he created them [plural].*
> —Genesis 1:26,27

God is a plurality in a singularity we call the Trinity. And a man (or woman) is a
singularity called to live in a plurality—a plurality called a *marriage* or a *family*.
And it's more than just a family; it's a community.

---

[5] C. S. Lewis, *Mere Christianity*, 152–153.

So, God is Love, and Love is Life. We are called to live in love. But how do we love if we're only made of dirt?

> **Genesis 2: 7** *...then the LORD [Yahweh – "I AM"] God formed man of dust from the ground, and breathed into his nostrils the breath of life; and man (Adam) became a living [nephesh].*

Don't make too much of this, but once upon a time someone showed me a picture that looked something like this:

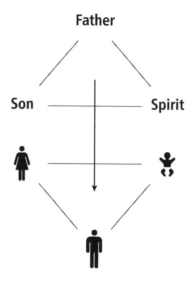

God is a Trinity of love. And He makes us a Trinity of love, but more than a trinity, a *qua*ternity, a *quin*ternity (I invented those words), a big family, and a community. That is, you certainly don't need to be married and have kids. That just expresses on the biological level what is true on much deeper levels for all of us. "It is not good for Adam to be alone." You don't need to get married or have kids, but to express the image of God you must learn to love in community. Life is love in community.

Love is offering up your spirit. Life is spirit (breath) circulating in a body. Life is respiration.

> *In this is love, not that we have loved God but that he loved us*
> *and sent his Son to be the propitiation* [sacrificial offering] *for*
> *our sins.*
>
> —1 John 4:10

At the cross we refused to love, and Love would not stop loving. Love, in flesh, expired. Jesus lifted His head and delivered up His Spirit (His Breath). That's the Spirit that Christ breathed on His disciples when He rose on the third day. That's the Spirit that fell on the new community we call the church as they began to love God and love each other in His image. That was the birth of the living breathing Body of Christ in this world.

God the Father glorified the Son in the bodies of those dejected and ragtag disciples as He raised them from the dead with Christ. And God the Son glorified God the Father as He worshipped Him in His new Body, His Sanctuary. And it was all done in the power of the Spirit.

And as they moved out into the world, the Body grew as Christ in them ministered to Christ in "the last and least." And so God the Father ministered to God the Son, and God the Son glorified God the Father as the Spirit animated the dirt that is our selves and returned to the Father as praise—the Spirit that continues to fall on us, fill us, and animate us. Life is respiration; life is the movement of the Spirit between members of a Body or persons in a Trinity; life is the dance of Love.

It's utterly shocking when you reflect on it! But God is calling us into the dance that is Himself. God is loving God through us. My friend Baxter Kruger says it like this:

> The Father himself set his love upon you before the founda-
> tion of the world and predestined you to be adopted into the
> very Trinitarian life of God. And his own beloved Son, Je-
> sus Christ, has come and accomplished his Father's dreams
> for you and the human race. And even now the Holy Spirit
> is bearing witness with your spirit that this is the truth[6]...The

---

[6] I received this in an e-mail... not sure where it came from

gospel is not the news that we can receive Jesus into our lives.
The gospel is the news that Jesus has received us into his."[7]

Words fail me at this point, yet I hope you can recognize the Truth, who is the Word:

- On the sixth day of creation God speaks a Word that makes us in His Image. Jesus is that Word.
- On the sixth day of creation, God breathes His meaning into dust, and "I AM" makes me who I am—a person capable of I-contact.
- On the sixth day of creation, God in Christ Jesus delivers up His Spirit that fills His Body, Bride, and Temple, and we begin to expire and inspire; we begin to live Love in the image of God.

This is the sixth day of creation and how that happens on the sixth day of creation is what the remainder of these books on Genesis chapters two and three are about. How that looks in the course of a person's lifetime in this sixth day world may be unique to each person and certainly remains a mystery, but perhaps it's something like this:

God breathes His Spirit as a Word—a breath with meaning (*logos*)—into a mound of clay in a woman's womb saying, "Let there be Peter and there was Peter."

The Breath creates an empty space that's felt as a longing, and Peter breathes the breath back in the form of a question, "Is there a God, and does He love me?"

His father and mother speak the Meaning full Breath, the Word, back into his life saying, "Yes, God adores you and longs for you."

Peter seeks the Word because the Word is seeking Him. He's inspired and expires. He tastes Beauty, Truth, and Love, and then he longs for Beauty, Truth and Love. The Word is Beauty, Truth, and Love. The Word is present, then felt as absent, which makes him long for more presence. The expiration makes him long for inspiration.

---

[7] Baxter Kruger, *The Shack Revisited* (Faith Words, NY. 2012) p. 142

It's the Word that chooses him to choose the Word at camp one evening. He thinks it's his decision even though it's God's decision finding His place in Peter. The Word is God's Decision, His Judgment.

The Spirit returns to God as Peter sings songs at youth group, inspired . . . to expire the Breath.

The Breath returns to Peter in manifold and untold ways—a sunset, a kind word, a "miracle," a moment of inspiration as he reads the Scriptures.

Peter expires the Breath as faith, hope, and love, even as a kiss on the forehead of his earthly father as he exhales carbon dioxide and inhales the Kingdom.

The Word inspires Peter, even as a kiss in a worship service when Peter feels utterly rejected and alone. God still breathes on the *Adamah* in His Garden.

Peter holds the Breath in anxiety, shame and fear; He takes the Life trying to control his life; He crucifies the Word of God; he sins. In infinite mercy, God breaks his earthen vessel; Peter expires confession . . .

And God inspires Him with Grace. Free Love is Grace. God is Grace. Jesus is the Word of Grace. The Breath is the Spirit of Grace. Peter doesn't *own* Love. He *lives* Love. And that's the eternal dance of Grace.

At the end of the sixth day, Peter will fully sacrifice his *nephesh* and deliver up his spirit as an offering of love. He will die.

And he will live. He will be inspired with the breath of the Father and clothed with the Life of Christ, the Righteousness of Christ. He is the body of Christ, risen from the dead. Peter will inspire and expire the breath of God without fear, for he will know his Lord will never stop kissing him, never stop inspiring him; He will know God is Good; He will choose the Good in freedom; He will love and be loved as the image of God in an eternal Seventh Day: expiration and inspiration, respiration, *perichoresis*, the eternal dance of Love, all because of what God has done in Christ Jesus our Lord.

Jesus is the missing link to our origins.
Jesus is the missing link between God and me.
Jesus is the missing link between you and me.
Jesus is the missing link to what we will become.

It's utterly shocking when you reflect on it! But God is calling us into the dance that is Himself. And God is calling us to be the visible image of that dance, even now, in this world—the dancing Body of Christ.

Listen to Jesus' prayer in John 17

> "I...ask...that they may all be one, just as you, Father, are in me, and I in you, that they also may be in us, so that the world may believe that you have sent me. The glory that you have given me I have given to them, that they may be one even as we are one, I in them and you in me, that they may become perfectly one, so that the world may know that you sent me and loved them even as you loved me."
>
> —John 17:20–23

In 1839, in his research journal, Charles Darwin wrote that the "Fuegians hardly seem to be fellow creatures and inhabitants of the same world."[8] They seemed to be excellent candidates for designation as "the missing link." Sadly, it was that designation in the minds of Europeans that appears to have led to something of a genocide in Tierra Del Fuego. It wasn't Fuegian cannibals (as Darwin had mistakenly labeled them), who committed the atrocities. It was Western settlers, who seemed to believe that they were most fit to survive[9]—that they were the next evolutionary step.

But is that the way to where we're going? Is that the next evolutionary step: the survival of the fittest? Or is it the sacrifice of the fittest?

Before European settlers arrived in Tierra Del Fuego claiming their "manifest destiny," missionaries, having read reports of the Fuegian people, arrived speaking the Word. Converted British naval officer, Captain Allen Gardin-

---

[8] Bergman, p.171

[9] Ibid. p. 171–2

er, and a team of six other missionaries arrived from England on December 17th 1850. Gardiner founded the Patagonian Missionary Society, which was renamed the South American Missionary Society in 1864. Having experienced the Grace of God he breathed the Grace of God, as worship and as a witness. His journal can still be read online.[10] It was found near his body and the bodies of their companions. Due to the hostility of the Fuegian people and the late arrival of a supply ship, Allen Gardiner and his fellow missionaries all sacrificed their lives speaking the Word to the people of Tierra Del Fuego. Eight other missionaries were massacred in 1859. Then in 1862 Wait Hockin Stirling established contact, I-contact. By 1869 over four hundred residents of Tierra Del Fuego had been baptized.[11] They were baptized into a body in the name of the Father, Son, and Holy Spirit. When news of this new community—characterized by sacrificial love—reached Darwin, He was so impressed that he changed his view of the residents of Tierra Del Fuego and became a financial supporter of the South American Missionary Society.[12]

Perhaps the next "evolutionary step"—that is, the thing that man is predestined to become—the Super Man—is not fine Aryan stock, like Hitler and many Europeans assumed. Nor is it Marx's communist state. Nor is it the X-men. Instead, it's all sorts of unique and strange people living in a community animated entirely by love.

Perhaps it's not achieved through the survival of the fittest, but the *sacrifice* of the fittest; it's not achieved through conquest—but cooperation. Perhaps it's not competition—but communion.

As I mentioned in the last book, and as any biologist can tell you: Life is not competition, but *cooperation*. It's one cell sacrificing it's will to another cell; it's one body part sacrificing for another body part; it's one man who expires so another can inspire. Life is respiration. Competition explains the limits of life—that is death, but only love explains life. So, sacrificial love must be the

[10] Project Canterbury, excerpts from Captain Gardiner's journal, accessed in 2015, http://anglicanhistory.org/sa/gardiner/marsh/05.html

[11] Creation.Com, accessed in 2015, http://creation.com/darwin-and-the-fuegians

[12] Bergman p. 172

origin of life and ecstatic love the end and goal of life. *"In him was life, and the life was the light of* (adam) *men"* (John 1:4).

> Jesus is the missing link to our origins.
> Jesus is the missing link between God and me.
> Jesus is the missing link between you and me.
> Jesus is the missing link to what we will become.

> Jesus is who we most truly are.
> He is the Super Man.

To be imago Dei means designation to a common, shared humanity. According to Genesis 1:26, Adam, human being, is a singular who corresponds to a divine plural. According to Genesis 1:27, men and women are a plural that corresponds to a divine singular. This grammatical shift between singular and plural is intentional and important.... Sexual difference and community belong to the very image of God itself, they are not merely related to human fertility. So this community already corresponds to God, because in this community God finds his own correspondence. It represents God on earth, and God 'appears' on earth in this male-female image. Likeness to God cannot be lived in isolation. It can be lived only in human community.

—*Jurgen Moltmann, God in Creation*

We believe in one God the Father Almighty, Maker of heaven and earth, and of all things visible and invisible; And in one Lord Jesus Christ, the only-begotten Son of God, begotten of the Father before all worlds, God of God, Light of Light, Very God of Very God, begotten, not made, being of one substance with the Father by whom all things were made.... And we believe in the Holy Spirit, the Lord and Giver of Life, who proceedeth from the Father and the Son, who with the Father and the Son together is worshipped and glorified, who spoke by the prophets.

—*The Nicene Creed*

In order for charity to be true, it demands a plurality of persons; in order for charity to be perfected, it requires a trinity of persons.

—*Richard of St. Victor, De Trinitate*

CHAPTER 4

The Super Man

Genesis 2:4–7

In 1998, Muhammad Ali was a passenger on a flight from Chicago to Vegas. At one point, he was confronted by a lowly flight attendant who told him to fasten his seatbelt. Ali replied, "Superman don't need no seat belt!" To which this flight attendant replied sweetly, "Superman don't need no airplane."

I suppose we'd all like to be Superman, but we look in the mirror and see Clark Kent.

> **Genesis 2:5–7** *When no bush of the field was yet in the land and no small plant of the field had yet sprung up—for the Lord God had not caused it to rain on the land, and there was no man to work the ground, and a mist was going up from the land and was watering the whole face of the ground—then the Lord God formed the man of dust from the ground and breathed into his nostrils the breath of life, and the man became a living* [nephesh: soul, person, life, creature].

> *"...and the man became a living soul"*
> or
> *"...and man became living soul"*

Either translation is accurate. The article, "a," before "soul" is supplied by the translators and the article, "the," before "man" is a Hebrew letter that some translate and most leave un-translated. And all that makes some sense when we consider that *Adam* means "man," as in humankind. Yet, in just a few verses Adam is going to get up and start walking around. It's like he's one . . . but many. We know that he's at least two; for in a few more verses God will divide him in two making male and female. So, you see, at this point, the Adam is a "he-she," and Adam is a "you and me."

I don't have a problem with the idea that there was a person named Adam in a garden long ago, but you see this Adam is more than just one person . . . He's like all persons and still seems to be one person, one super person—a super man.

THE SUPER MAN | 79

How do we make sense of that? Well, if we believe Scripture is inspired by God (which I hope we do), then, we believe Scripture interprets Scripture, and we probably also believe that later texts interpret earlier texts and that Jesus gives meaning to them all.

According to the New Testament, Jesus makes sense of Adam in every possible way. The Gospel of John goes out of its way to point out that on the sixth day, at the sixth hour, Jesus was crucified on a tree in a garden and buried in that garden and that, when He rose, Mary mistook Him for the gardener (John 19:4, 41, 20:15). And of course He is the Gardener—the ultimate Gardener.

Rabbi Paul, who wrote most of the New Testament, and had a thorough understanding of the Old, tells us a great deal about Adam in numerous places—he tells us things that very few seem to believe. In Romans Paul writes this:

> *...death reigned from Adam to Moses, even over those whose sinning was not like the transgression of Adam, who was a type of the one who was to come. But the free gift is not like the trespass. For if many died through one man's trespass, much more have the grace of God and the free gift by the grace of that one man Jesus Christ abounded for many.*
>
> —Romans 5:14–15

Paul teaches that Adam was a "type" of Jesus the Christ. The word is *tupos* in Greek. It's where we get our word "type," but it means more that our word, "type." *Tupos* is literally a reference to the mark left by a blow–an imprint. Imagine a field of soft clay (*adamah*).

If you were to take Jesus and press Him face down into the clay, the imprint left in the clay would be a *tupos* of Jesus. And, according to Paul, Adam is a *tupos* of Jesus. Adam is an earthen vessel fit to be perfectly filled with Jesus. In 1 Corinthians, Paul shares a similar thought:

> *For as by a man came death, by a man has come also the resurrection of the dead. For as in Adam all die, so also in Christ shall all be made alive... Thus it is written, "The first man Adam became a living being"; the last Adam became a life-giving spirit. But it is not the spiritual that is first but the natural, and then*

the spiritual. The first man was from the earth, a man of dust;
the second man is from heaven. As was the man of dust, so also
are those who are of the dust, and as is the man of heaven, so also
are those who are of heaven. Just as we have borne the image
of the man of dust, we shall also bear the image of the man of
heaven.

—1 Corinthians 15:21–22, 45–49

The creation of Adam is also the revelation of Christ. And just as you look like Adam, you will look like Christ. Indeed Christ is the "last Adam." That can mean "the least" like Clark Kent, and it can mean "the ultimate" like Superman. And of course it means both: You are the Clark Kent in which Superman is revealed. It's in your weakness that He is strong. And that's not to denigrate Clark Kent. Superman chooses to be Clark Kent and hopes Clark Kent would choose to be Superman.

Yet maybe we're less than Clark Kent, for we don't choose to be Superman, we even hate Superman. We can be anti-Superman and even anti-Christ, yet maybe that's the very glory of Christ. For as Paul writes, *"Where sin increased, Grace abounded all the more"* (Rom. 5:20). And you see, this is Paul's point, sin increased in Adam. That's bad news . . . and very good news, for *"where sin increased"* the "last Adam" is revealed, and Grace abounds all the more.

And I hope you also see: It's the last Adam that gives meaning to the first Adam. There is no *Adam* made of *adamah*, without a last *Adam* to leave His imprint in the *adamah*. It's like the last Adam is an Eternal Adam, and the first Adam is his first step, his first imprint, in the dust of space and time. He—the *Eschatos* Adam, Christ—is who you most truly are. Karl Barth says it this way:

Our relationship to Adam is a subordinate relationship, because the guilt and punishment we incur in Adam have no
independent reality of their own but are only the dark shad-
ows of the grace and life we have in Christ.... We have come
to Christ as believers and Christians, because we had already
come from Christ, so that there was nothing else for us to do

but believe in Him[1]....What is Christian is secretly but fundamentally identical with what is universally human....So it is Christ that reveals the true nature of man. Man's nature in Adam is not, as is usually assumed, his true and original nature; it is only truly human at all in so far as it reflects and corresponds to essential human nature as it is found in Christ.[2]

Most informed Protestants would argue that Karl Barth was the greatest theologian of the 20th century.

Karl Barth wrote for theologians; Vincent Donavan ministered to the Masai tribe in East Africa. He says the same thing in a different way:

> Man is not just like a fire sputtering for a few moments, then fizzling out, darkness before and after.... a thing without meaning among the many things of the earth. Man is God appearing in the universe, appearing visibly in the midst of all he created. That changes the meaning of man, doesn't it?
>
> I can see you Masai shaking your heads and saying, No! Man is not God. We know man, and he is filled with evil. He fights, he kills, he destroys, he does everything to separate others, and to separate himself from them.
>
> I say to you Masai; you have not known man, you have never seen a man. Creation is not yet finished. What you see is creation groaning and moaning even until now, yearning to be finished and completed, to be the body of God.
>
> But suppose the fullness of time had come and the work of God was perfect, and there appeared a man who was perfectly

---

[1] How it is that we come to believe in Him will be the main topic of our third book on Genesis: *The Tree in the Middle of the Garden.*

[2] Karl Barth, *Christ and Adam* (New York, New York: The Macmillan Company, 1956), p. 48, 111–112

a man, according to the plan of God, a man completely human. If, once upon a time, there was such a man who was so completely a man, so perfectly human, then there would be no other way to describe him than to say; this man is God–God appearing in the universe. Isn't that so? Jesus was that man.

Perhaps the really surprising thing that the man Jesus did in his lifetime was to show us, not only what God is, but what man is.[3]

Now I know this is incredible . . . and I sure don't want to make myself Jesus or God, yet Paul did write, *"It's no longer I who live, but Christ who lives in me"* (Gal. 2:20). He seemed to believe that his body of clay was like the imprint of Christ and that now, because of the death and resurrection of Christ, it was being filled with the substance of Christ.

I mean Paul *actually* believed that He was the body of Christ—the last, ultimate, super *Adam*. His identity was fully Christ, but not as if he alone were Christ and you were not Christ or Christ were no longer Christ, but as if all things were his and he was Christ's and Christ is God's.[4]

Well, if man is "God appearing in the universe," and Jesus is the first perfected man, *"firstborn among many brethren"* (Rom. 8:29 KJV), and we, the brethren, are his body . . . wouldn't that mean that Jesus, the head, was born into the new and finished creation on Easter Sunday and we, his body, will soon follow? So, watching the death of Jesus is not only like watching the birth of our big brother from inside the womb; it's witnessing the birth of our own head.

I know, from watching four births, that where the head goes, the body soon follows. And, speaking as a Father, I certainly wanted the body to follow. I wasn't content to leave the body inside the womb, so I doubt that God the Father is content leaving you in this womb of a world.

When Jesus was born He expired this world and inspired the atmosphere of the New Creation. Even now He sends that life to His body through His blood.

---

[3] Vincent J. Donovan, *Rediscovering Christianity*, p.57

[4] 1 Cor. 3:21–23 "So let no one boast in men. For all things are yours, whether Paul or Apollos or Cephas or the world or life or death or the present or the future—all are yours, and you are Christ's, and Christ is God's."

You know every part of your body receives breath—oxygen—from the head, through the trachea, lungs, and blood in your blood vessels. Each body part inspires breath and expires breath like a river, inspires life and expires life like a river of life—*"the life... is in the blood."* Bleeding is respiration, and respiration is life; *perichoresis* is life; the dance of love is life.

If a body part is attached to a body, bleeding feels like Life, and it *is* Life. Yet if a body part is not connected to a body or a body part is clogged (that is dammed or damned), if a body part refuses to lose its life and find its life, if a body part refuses to bleed . . . well, it's good as dead.

Now I know we just said more than we can comprehend, but I do believe that this much in true:

- The creation of Adam is the revelation of Jesus.
- Jesus is your true identity.
- The idea that you don't belong is a lie.
- Fear of losing your life is a trick.
- The new you is the Superman.
- And that matters, for as long as you believe otherwise, you will act like a pile of dirt and the entire Superman will suffer.

I don't hear many people speak about the biblical vision of the Superman–the *Eschatos* Adam. I suppose that for many it's just too fantastic to believe. It's often obscured by translators trying to make the text reasonable. But without Saint Paul's picture of the "new *Adam*," I don't know how anyone could understand much of Romans, 1 or 2 Corinthians, Colossians or Ephesians.

Let's take a look at Ephesians. In Ephesians 1, Paul says something absolutely incredible:

> *In him we have redemption through his blood, the forgiveness of our trespasses, according to the riches of his grace, which he lavished upon us, in all wisdom and insight making known to us the mystery of his will, according to his purpose, which he set forth in Christ as a plan for the fullness of time, to unite (anakephalaiomai) all things in him, things in heaven and things on earth.*

In him we have obtained an inheritance, having been pre-destined according to the purpose of him who works all things according to the counsel of his will, so that we who were the first to hope in Christ might be to the praise of his glory....And he put all things under his feet and gave him as head (kephale) over all things to the church, which is his body, the fullness of him who fills all in all.

—Ephesians 1:7–12, 22–23

The Greek verb translated "unite" is *anakephalaiomai*. *Kephale* means "head." *Kephalaioo* is a verb meaning "to wound a head" or "to recapitulate" or "to sum up." Put them all together and *anakephalaiomai* means something like "to sum up under one wounded head."

Paul writes that this is the plan for the fullness of time. Did you know there was a "fullness of time?" The plan is to sum up, recapitulate, unite, and bring to-gether all things under one wounded head. I'm not sure exactly what this means for rocks, trees, and bugs, but for us it means that we will become the healthy and functioning body of that head. Not "might become," but *"will"* become because He works all things according to "the council of his will." We will be *"redeemed through his blood"*—forgiveness.

In chapter four Paul continues his thought:

There is one body and one Spirit—just as you were called to the one hope that belongs to your call— one Lord, one faith, one baptism, one God and Father of all, who is over all and through all and in all. But grace was given to each one of us according to the measure of Christ's gift. Therefore it says,

"When he ascended on high he led a host of captives, and he gave gifts to men"

(In saying, "He ascended," what does it mean but that he had also descended into the lower regions, the earth? He who descended is the one who also ascended far above all the heavens, that he might fill all things.) And he gave the apostles, the prophets, the

evangelists, the shepherds and teachers, to equip the saints for the work of ministry, for building up the body of Christ, until we all attain 1. to the unity of the faith and of the knowledge of the Son of God, 2. to mature manhood [literally: to the finished man], 3. to the measure of the stature of the fullness of Christ, so that we may no longer be children, tossed to and fro by the waves and carried about by every wind of doctrine, by human cunning, by craftiness in deceitful schemes. Rather, speaking the truth in love, we are to grow up in every way into him who is the head [kephale], into Christ, from whom the whole body, joined and held together by every joint with which it is equipped, when each part is working properly, makes the body grow so that it builds itself up in love.

—Ephesians 4:4–16

There is one body, and one Spirit, and one *"Father of all"* (and Paul has been speaking about *"all the families of the earth"* (3:15). We have each been given grace according to the measure of Christ's gift, and Christ gave all—He gave His life, actually forgave His life, and the life is in the blood, a river of blood.

And He gave each of us gifts for serving:

1. Until we all *"attain a unity of* trust *(Faith)"* and knowledge that belongs to Christ;

2. Until we all *"come to the finished* (this is the word Christ used on the cross)... *man,"* "the perfected *Adam;"*

3. Until we all attain *"the measure of the stature of the fullness of Christ."*

Speaking the truth in love, we are to grow up into Him who is the head.

Many years ago, I took my children to see a kids' movie. I didn't expect much, but I think it changed my life. By the end of the movie I was sobbing in the theatre, and my kids were trying to figure out what was wrong. But nothing was wrong. I just realized that everything was right.

The *Iron Giant* is a about a giant alien robot, who has the power to destroy the earth (all judgment is in his hands), and a lonely fatherless boy named Hogarth. Hogarth and the Iron Giant become friends after the giant falls to earth in the woods behind Hogarth's house. The principalities and powers of this world, government officials, who've tracked the Iron Giant, are terrified of the Iron Giant. One of them launches a nuclear missile locked on to the location of the Iron Giant. But the Iron Giant is "with us—*Emmanuel.*" I mean, the Iron Giant has chosen to be with humanity, particularly Hogarth. So, to destroy the giant is to destroy all humanity.

The giant makes a decision—a judgment—and says to Hogarth, "No following." ("Where I am going, you cannot follow me now" [John 13:36]). Then the giant blasts off into the heavens aiming for the intercontinental ballistic missile. As he hones in on the missile, right before he offers his life for the sins of the world, he quotes Hogarth, saying to himself, "You are who you choose to be: Superman." And at that, he hits the ICBM. It ignites in the clouds of heaven such that every eye sees him (Rev. 1:7, Zech. 12:10), and they watch as the pieces of the Iron Giant rain down, like a shower of grace, all over the face of the earth.

Sitting there in the theater that day, having preached through Genesis, the Revelation, Ephesians, and the Gospels, I think I began to realize just how far and wide those pieces fall.

I hope you remember a picture like this from my first book on Genesis. Our world is created in six days, and on the Seventh Day everything is *"finished,"* everything is *"very good."*

THE SUPER MAN | 87

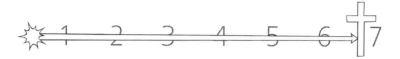

We realized that the cross (the tree) is the end of the sixth day and the beginning of the seventh. It's where we die with Christ and rise with Christ, where we receive "eternal life" from the Seventh Day. It's where Jesus cried, "*It is finished.*" Scripture teaches that this is the "*syntellia* of the ages" (Heb. 9:26, 1 Cor. 10:11). That means the end, the full perfection of the eons, the summation of all time.

Yet, check it out: You're still reading this book in time. You exist in the sixth day with a bit of the Seventh Day—eternity—in your heart. Jesus is "*the end*" of the ages, yet the End has made His home in your heart. And the End was revealed in time.

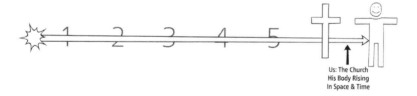

Us: The Church
His Body Rising
In Space & Time

And I think the End is still being revealed in time. In the words of Vincent Donavan: "Man is God appearing in the universe." Jesus is the head, and we are His body. He is "*the image of the invisible God*" (Col. 1:15). He said, "*If you've seen me, you've seen the Father*" (John 14:9). He gives us His body and His blood. And Paul writes that we are His body, being filled with His blood. Those that already submit to this judgment—this decision to be united under one "sacred head now wounded" are called "the Church," the *ecclesia*, the "called out."[5] Currently, this is few, but it may very well become all.

Whatever the case, Scripture is clear that the Church, who is the Bride and the New Jerusalem, consists of far more than just those that raised their hand at church camp sometime after 33 AD. It includes Moses and Elijah (They show up on the mountain with Jesus), and at least the twelve sons of Israel (the New Jerusalem is literally constructed with them), and according to the prophets it includes all Israel (Ez. 37:11-12), and it seems, all people (i.e. Is. 25:6, 26:19, 45:23, 66:23, Zeph. 3:9) . . . even those in *Sheol/Hades*, where men "weep and gnash their teeth" (Isa. 26:19, Ps. 22:29, not to mention all the New Testament texts).

Well, I'm just trying to point out that when the *Eschatos* Man was crucified for all to see, the pieces of His body seemed to fall far and wide. You acknowledge this whenever you come to the communion table and receive His Judgment: "*This is my body which is for you. . . This is my blood . . . .*"

When you ingest His Judgment you agree with His Judgment, and His judgment becomes your judgment. You see? None of us *chooses* to be the Superman. In the words of Scripture, "*None is righteous, no, not one; no one understands; no one seeks for God*" (Rom. 3:11). That means no one seeks love.

God is Love. But when we ingest Christ's body, we ingest God's judgment—He chooses to be the Superman; He chooses Love in freedom; He chooses to be Himself; He chooses to be Jesus—Jesus means "I AM is Salvation." Faith, Hope, and Love in you is Christ rising in you.

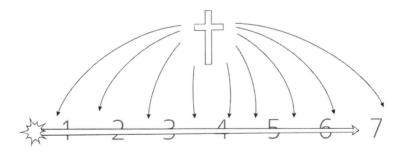

[5] Jesus said, "Many are called and few are chosen" (Matt. 22:14). In the context of the parable, after which Jesus says this, all are called and one is chosen. The friend of the king is chosen to be cast into outer darkness. I believe this is because He has given his wedding garment—His righteousness—to the "many."

He is "*the first and the last (eschatos), the beginning and the end*" (Rev. 22:13). He is the lamb that was "*slain from the foundation of the world*" (Rev. 13:8 KJV), and the pieces fall far and wide. I think the pieces fall throughout all space and time. Well, we are His Body now, and His Body is growing.

At the end of the *Iron Giant*, the pieces of the Iron Giant rain down all over the earth. Hogarth finds one little bolt, which he keeps in a special place in his bedroom. He does this in memory of the Iron Giant, his friend. Kind of like when you take the Body of Christ and place it in the depth of your being in memory of Jesus.

The movie ends, when Hogarth is suddenly wakened in the wee hours of the morning. The bolt under his bed is flashing; it's come to life and begun rolling toward the window. Hogarth looks as it rolls out the window and down the road. Suddenly, all over the world, pieces of the Iron Giant seem to come to life and begin to hop, crawl, and move toward something. Then we see what it is: On a glacier in Greenland sits the head of the Iron Giant. The eyes open: ANAKEPHALAIOMAI. All the members of the Iron Giant are being united, summed up and recapitulated under one sacred head now wounded.

So, I sat in the theater bawling, not because something was wrong, but because all that was wrong would be summed up in something, or some*one*, so right.

Immediately after Paul describes how the body of the Superman builds itself up in Love. He tells the Ephesians to no longer walk like unbelievers, futile in their thinking and "alienated," cut off, from the life of God due to ignorance and a hardness of heart. He writes:

> But that is not the way you learned Christ! — assuming that
> you have heard about him and were taught in him, as the
> truth is in Jesus, to put off your old self [literally: old man, old
> Adam], which belongs to your former manner of life and is cor-
> rupt through deceitful desires, and to be renewed in the spirit of
> your minds, and to put on the new self [literally: new man, new
> Adam], created after the likeness of God in true righteousness
> and holiness. Therefore, having put away falsehood [literally:
> the false, the false man] let each one of you speak the truth [Jesus

is "the Truth"] *with his neighbor, for we are members one of*
another.

—Ephesians 4:20–25

How do we put on the Superman?

Let's review:

- We are each an earthen vessel.
- We each contain a breath, or spirit, breathed into us by God.
- In faithlessness, fear and shame we hold our breath.
- If we hold our breath, we die. Life is respiration.
- We must expire to inspire; we must lose our lives to find them.
- We are being created in the image of God.
- God is Love, and Love is giving Spirit. Love is a dance.
- God is a Trinity: three persons and one substance—Love.
- We are to be a community, many persons and one substance—Love.
- We are the body of the Superman, the body of Christ.
- Christ's body died, but it is coming to life.

Each part of my body expires and inspires all at once. In a living body, circulation is respiration. Bleeding is life, a river life. "*The life (nephesh) of the flesh is in the blood*" (Lev. 17:11). The breath, the oxygen is in the blood. But if a body part refuses to bleed and holds the blood, it dies.

My body parts constantly "forgive" each other. *Aphiemi*, the Greek word most often translated "forgive," means to let or allow or to suffer.[6] Each body part constantly forgives blood, yet one thing is not forgiven. One sin is unforgiveable. It's blasphemy against the Spirit—the Breath—that's in the blood. In a body, un-forgiveness is the unforgiveable sin. Jesus said, "*If you do not forgive others their trespasses, neither will your Father forgive your trespasses...every sin and blasphemy will be forgiven people, but the blasphemy against the Spirit will not be forgiven*" (Matt. 6:15, 12:30-31). A refusal to forgive will not be tolerated in the Kingdom of God. You must expire to inspire.

---

[6] As we continue I hope you will remember this biblical definition. I will continue to use this word with the biblical definition in mind.

THE SUPER MAN | 91

"In him was life..." (John 1:4) writes John. And Jesus said, *"I am... the life"* (John 14:6). So, if you ever refer to "your life," as if you own it, aren't you admitting that you stole it . . . particularly, if you're a Christian and so claim to have surrendered it? It's not your life. So, in reality no one can "take your life." It's Christ's life.[7] And He already *for*gave His life. He did it on the tree, when He cried, *"Father forgive them"* (John 23:34) and delivered up His Spirit—His breath. He did it on the tree, but He did it, and has done it, and will always do it, for it is Love. God is Love. In the words of George MacDonald: "When he died on the cross, he did that, in the wild weather of his outlying provinces in the torture of the body of his revelation, which he had done at home in glory and gladness."[8]

> When one person forgives, it looks like a cross.
> When two people forgive, it looks like a marriage.
> When everyone forgives, it looks like a dancing body.

When we preached through Ephesians at my church a few years ago, I tried to explain it using some props at the communion table. One week, I demonstrated how we were each like the communion chalice (We use earthen vessels made by a potter.) We're each like the chalice, yet each a unique chalice. God wills to pour His breath, which is blood, which is wine into each of us.

"Clay is fashioned into vessels; but their use depends on their empty hollowness." If you're full of yourself, you can't be filled with God. You must die to

---

[7] In Psalm 51:4 David writes, "Against you, you only, have I sinned and done what is evil in your sight, so that you may be justified in your words and blameless in your judgment." "Against... you only," yet David had just murdered Uriah and basically raped Uriah's wife. David realized that it wasn't Uriah's life or wife that he took. It was His Lord's life and wife. He says it happened that God would be justified and blameless in His Judgment. His Judgment was to redeem David, and although a son of David would die, a son of David would be born. Jesus is the seed of David, born of his sin with Bathsheba. Jesus is the revelation of the Judgment of God—Grace.

[8] George MacDonald *Unspoken Sermons*, (Memphis, TN: Bottom of the Hill Publishing, 2012) 193

yourself—be emptied of self—to be filled with God. Yet that old self does have a purpose, for where sin increased grace abounds all the more.

The form of your sin, which will be revealed as "emptiness" (your decision to choose nothingness) becomes the form of God's Grace, which fills it. The unique form of your "old man" becomes the unique form of the "new man," which fills that empty illusion. The unique form of your false man is the imprint that's filled with the true man—the *Eschatos* Man. Where you have believed that "*you are salvation*," God will reveal "*Yahweh is salvation*," *Ye-ho-shua*, Jesus.

Well, one week we talked about the earthen vessels. A following week, I said, "What if the vessels were pipes? You know, with an opening at both ends. Well then, you wouldn't be filled and emptied, filled and emptied, but you could be constantly filled and constantly emptied, yet never empty of the river of life. I mean, what if each of you were a unique earthen vessel connected to other unique earthen vessels? Then you would each have a unique relationship with Christ and a unique way you receive and communicate the life of Christ. Yet each of you would receive all of Christ, according to 'the measure of his gift'— all of the life of Christ would flow through all of you and each of you."

Now, I wish I had earthen pipes, but all they had at Home Depot was PVC pipe. So during the message I constructed this:

We called him the PVC Frankenchrist. All I can make is a monster. But I hope you see God can make, and is making, a body:

> *Consequently, when Christ came into the world, he said, "Sacrifices and offerings you have not desired, but a body have you prepared for me; in burnt offerings and sin offerings you have taken no pleasure." Then I said, "Behold, I have come to do your will, O God..."*
>
> —Hebrews 10:5–7

Have you ever wondered what all the blood is about in that Old Testament temple? Well, if we inspired and refused to expire, if we took life and refused to give life, doesn't that mean we took Christ's blood and refused to surrender Christ's blood? Maybe every time we sin we take His life and refuse to surrender His life, for He is the Life.

So, why did God require that they offer all that blood in the temple? Well, maybe it was His blood that they took from the temple. And what's the temple? Jesus said that His body is the temple. So, Jesus forgives the blood taken from His temple And Jesus gives the blood offered in His temple. Jesus causes the blood to flow in His temple. And now Jesus reveals that we are His temple. Jesus forgives His blood that we all might live.[9] Jesus expires us and inspires us. Jesus is our respiration. Life is respiration.

When He alone forgives it looks very painful; it looks like a cross. When we all forgive we will be His dancing Body and that Body is happy.

So, how do we "put on" Christ? How do we put on the Superman?

---

[9] People often are upset by all the expiration, all the death, in the temple. But we all must die. And all the expiration is inspiration. He says, "Behold I make all things new" (Rev. 21:5). That would certainly include sheep, goats, bulls and every lamb. They were offered up in fire, eternal fire that is the Judgment of God and doorway to the new creation. There, we must all lose our lives and find them. "Present your bodies a living sacrifice, holy and acceptable to God, which is your spiritual worship" (Rom. 12:1). Sometimes that can hurt, but it is always good. We expire death and inspire the Life, eternal life, tongues of fire.

Many years ago when one of my children was struggling with fear and shame, as we all struggle with fear and shame, she came to me after a worship service wherein we celebrated communion in the temple that is us. Rather excited and a little bit shocked, for she had seen a vision, she said:

> "Daddy, as I watched people go forward for communion, I saw
> these big cutter things (she called them cutter things–swords)
> that would swing out and cut people." She said, "Daddy, they
> cut off parts of their bodies, but they still came to commu-
> nion. They hobbled around communion and began to bump
> into each other, and when they'd bump into each other
> sometimes they'd fuse. Like...if someone didn't have an arm,
> they'd bump into someone that did and they'd join together,
> like fuse. And Daddy, I wasn't frightened. It was really cool,
> 'cause they made one huge body and nothing could hurt him."

She watched people "put on" Christ. When we come to the Table of the Lord, we come to the sacrifice and offering of Christ. We come to the Word of God and Judgment of God. That Judgment is a sword. It cuts away our arrogance. It breaks our closed earthen vessels. It opens wounds that have scabbed over and become hard. It causes us to expire, even as we are inspired. It joins us together as one. We forgive as we've been forgiven, such that all our weaknesses become strengths. They are the places where we are joined to others and the places we receive the strength that is Christ. The blood begins to flow, and we begin to live as Christ is revealed in this world through us—His body and His bride.

That's how we put on Christ. But how do we choose to put Him on?

I'm not sure we *do* choose, so much as *He* chooses us to choose. And how that happens is what will occupy most of the rest of our study of Genesis 1-3. But for now, I hope you see that there are two ways of thinking.

In Ephesians 4:17, Paul told us that unbelievers *"walk in the futility of their minds... alienated from the life of God... due to their hardness (porosis* – mineral-ization) *of heart."* That is, they're nuts because they refuse to bleed, to feel what others feel, to love. They're holding their breath—their life. They refuse to lose their life, that they might find it.

Psuche is Greek for "life." *Logos* is Greek for "Word" or "Reason."

They have Psycho-*Logos* and Psycho-Logic.
They think that their life is their own.

Theos is Greek for "God."
Theo-logic is *Theo-logos*, the Word of God, Jesus.
It's thinking that the Life is God's.
It's thinking with the mind of Christ, the Superman.

When I begin to think theologically, instead of psycho-logically . . .
I begin to expire and inspire.
I begin to love.

- I may hurt at times, but I no longer need to be afraid.
- I'm jealous of no one. I compete with no one. I'm grateful for everyone.
- I hate what separates everyone . . . and hides every someone.
- I hate evil and delight in its destruction.
- I'm not only Clark Kent, but I'm also Superman.
- I put on the Superman.
- I pay attention to every Clark Kent, because I realize each one is Superman . . . or at least hides the Superman.

Why would the Superman disguise himself as Clark Kent? Why did Superman hide himself from Lois Lane? Perhaps he wanted her to see his heart, before she fell in love with all that muscle? But now I am getting ahead of myself. We have yet to meet Eve or talk about the romance of God. We're still just on verse 7

> *And the LORD God formed man of the dust of the ground, and breathed into his nostrils the breath of life; and man became a living soul.*
>
> —Genesis 2:7 KJV

We'll move faster now. I apologize for taking so long with one little verse.

But Adam, that little verse says quite a lot.

Like Origen, and mindful of Paul (1 Corinthians and Romans), Gregory [of Nyssa] insists on the Adam-Christ parallel in his discourse on the foundations of apokatastasis [restoration]. If death entered the world due to the sin of one human, another human's obedience heals the consequences of that disobedience, and by means of his resurrection all humanity rises with him; thus, Christ annihilates the death that had been brought about by Adam's sin (Contr. c. Apoll. 21, GNO III,1, 160–161). Both Adam and Christ can recapitulate all humanity because humanity is a unity, a whole. This is a concept that Origen had already hammered home in his anti-Valentinian polemic. Throughout his In illud Gregory identifies the body of Christ with the whole of humanity, therefore also identifying the Church, which is the body of Christ, with all humanity at least in the perspective of the telos [the perfection, the end]. ...the salvific submission of Christ to the Father refers, not to Christ's own divinity, but to his "body," that is, all human beings. This constellation of concepts rests on a strong basic notion of the unity of human nature... .This unity is, not by accident, especially emphasized hy Gregory in connection with the unity of humanity at its first creation and the unity will be restored in the final apakatastasis... The totality of humanity was included in the first human being, and it is included in Christ as well. It is not simply the individual human being that is in the image of God, but also, and primarily, the full totality of humanity. The full realization of this being in the image of God will take place at the eventual apokatastasis, when the totality of human nature will be reconstituted into its perfect unity and will make up "the body of Christ." ... This super-body lives by it's union with its Head, who is Christ, whose life is shared by the body itself (De Perf. GNO VIII,1, 197-198). This is because the body shares the same substance and nature with its Head. And since the whole human nature, the body of Christ, "forms, so to say, one and the same animated being," the resurrection of one, i.e. Christ, "extends itself to the whole totality" (Or.cat. GNO III,4, 78)... Indeed, the world will come to an end when the number of human beings will be completed, and the body of Christ will be entirely built up. The perfection of this body will be reached in the telos, when every part of it has been made perfect. Then every single part will perfectly reflect all the characteristics of the head; thus, if the Head is Peace, Holiness, and Truth all the parts, too , will be peace holiness and truth (De perf. GNO VIII,1,197-200).
— *Ilaria L.E. Ramelli* <u>*The Christian Doctrine of Apokatastasis*</u>, *416-418*

...The church has a single intention: that God's kingdom may come, and that the salvation of the whole human race may come to pass. For every benefit, which the People of God during its earthly pilgrimage can offer to the human family, stems from the fact that the Church is "the universal sacrament of salvation", simultaneously manifesting and exercising the mystery of God's love. For God's Word, by whom all things were made, was Himself made flesh so that, as perfect man, He might save all men and sum up all things in Himself. The Lord is the goal of human history, the focal point of the longings of history and of civilization, the center of the human race, the joy of every heart and the answer to all its yearning. He is Whom the Father raised from the dead. Enlivened and united in His Spirit, we journey toward the consummation of human history, one which full accords with the counsel of God's love: "To reestablish (anakephalaio) all things in Christ, both those in the heavens and those on the earth" (Eph. 1:10).

—GAUDUM ET SPES PROMULGATED BY HIS HOLINESS. POPE PAUL VI ON DECEMBER 7, 1965, Vatican II

The Lord showed his own son and Adam as but one man. The strength and goodness, which we have, come from Jesus Christ; the weakness and the blindness which we have come from Adam... Jesus is all who shall be saved and all who shall be saved are Jesus.

—Julian of Norwich, Revelations of Divine Love

The Christian community is the provisional representation of the universal scope of the person and work of Jesus Christ.

—Karl Barth

On Metaphors

(You don't have to read this, but you might want to.)

Perhaps one of these questions, or one like them, has entered your mind as you've read this book:

   ✓ Was there *really* a Garden of Eden?

   ✓ Did God *literally* breathe spirit into dust?

   ✓ Is Adam a *metaphor*?

   ✓ Is Peter *serious*?

One morning during the first half of the 17th century, the great French scientist, mathematician and philosopher Rene Descartes entered a small coffee shop and sat down. The waitress asked, "Would you like cream with your coffee?" to which Descartes replied, "I think not." And ceased to exist.

OK . . . I'm not serious about that, but Descartes was. It was Rene Descartes that coined the famous axiom, *Cogito ergo sum*—"I think therefore I am," from which we can clearly infer that if "I think not, I am not."

This was the beginning of the En*light*enment, or the En*dark*enment, depending on how you look at it. Well, since that time, we've had a particularly difficult time with "metaphors," "literalism," "reality," and the Bible.

The Bible testifies to the idea that "I AM (is), therefore I think." Of course, in this axiom, it's understood that I AM is God, so if "I think not," I still exist—I just won't enjoy the coffee because I'm not thinking.

> "I think, therefore I am."
>   OR
> "I AM, therefore I think."

Now, I'm not just trying to be cute. There are profound implications to both axioms. According to the axiom, "I think therefore I am," my existence (and all existence—at least that which I could think about) is predicated upon *me* thinking. According to the second axiom, "I AM, therefore I think," my existence is predicated upon God thinking. God's thinking is His reasoning. In Greek: *Logos*. Existence is dependent on God speaking His Word.

An axiom is a philosophical statement that can't be "proven" or "disproven" by empirical means, but must be taken on faith. Think about it: If, like Rene Descartes, you did stop thinking and ceased to exist, you wouldn't be able to think about it. And, even if "I AM" subjected Himself to empirical analysis, you'd have to kill Him, to test the hypothesis that you would stop thinking. But then of course, you might stop thinking and therefore couldn't think about not thinking. And if you killed Him and did keep thinking, you'd be thinking with reason, and the axiom suggests that God's thoughts are Reason (*Logos*), which clearly would imply you didn't actually kill Him, or He rose from the dead, or you're insane.[1]

Don't think about that too much right now . . .

My point is that since the Enlightenment, as a society, we've learned to predicate all thinking upon ourselves. Before that time, thinking began with God and proceeded to man. After that time, thinking began with man and proceeded, possibly, to God.[2]

My point is that since the "Enlightenment," we've begun assuming that what is "literally" true is what is empirically true; we've assumed that the only things that are really true are things that are comprehensible to *me* and verified by *me*.[3]

My point is that "me" exists in three (and maybe a half) dimensions and can only experience things through my five senses. So, if all my thinking starts with

---

[1] Of course, this has been attempted. And for a time, the sky went black and the earth shook. We crucified the Logos of God, but according to Hebrews 7:16, He is an "indestructible life."

[2] We seized reason and assumed it (He) was our own. Of course, this is entirely unreasonable.

[3] Of course, "truth" is not comprehensible or verifiable to me, only recognizable by me—you can't prove that truth is true—you can only recognize it and assume it (or Him).

"me," I would tend to believe only what I could comprehend and verify with my five senses in three and a half dimensions. So, now, when "enlightened" modern people ask, "Is that *really* true?" they mean: "Can I verify that in three (and a half) dimensions with my five senses?"

Modern people say things like, "Is that *really literally* true . . . or just a *metaphor*?" For this reason, modern people have come to think of things like faith, hope, and love as simply "ideas" and not truly real. But according to Scripture, *"God is Love,"* and Jesus is His "Idea" (*Logos*), and it's impossible for anything to be more "real" than that . . . really!

✓   Was the garden *real*?

Do we know what we're asking . . . really? "Was the garden *literally* real?"

I just looked up the word "literalism" in the *Webster's New Collegiate Dictionary*, which my parents gave to me upon graduation from high school in 1979.[4] This is the first definition, "Adherence to the explicit substance of an idea..."[5] But, according to Scripture, "idea" (*Logos*) is the explicit substance of everything. *"In the beginning was the Idea (Logos), and the Idea was with God and the Idea was God... And the Idea became flesh and dwelt among us, and we have seen his glory, glory as of the only Son from the Father, full of grace and truth"* (John 1:1, 14).

See? We assume that the idea of a thing is less substantive than the thing. But Scripture teaches that all things depend on an idea. Saint Paul wrote: *"Therefore let no one pass judgment on you in questions of food and drink, or with regard to new moon or a Sabbath. These are a shadow of things to come, but the substance* ("reality" NIV, "body" KJV) *belongs to Christ."* Christ is the *Logos*, the Idea. Paul is arguing that the Logos is more substantive than the moon.

---

[4] *Webster's New Collegiate Dictionary* (Merriam: Springfield, MA, 1979)

[5] This is the second definition: "fidelity to the observable fact: REALISM." "Observable fact" is what "me" can observe in three-and-a-half dimensions with my five senses. I cannot "observe the fact" that "observable fact" is real or true—therefore, "truth" cannot be literally true . . . really.

A few years ago, Cornell physicist N. David Mermin summed up the implications of Quantum Theory with this statement: "We now know that the moon is demonstrably not there when nobody looks."[6] Physicists now observe—in three and a half dimensions with their five senses—that an "observer" (they still aren't sure what one of these is) with an idea in his or her head "collapses" the quantum state of subatomic particles.[7]

All matter is constructed with subatomic particles. And this clearly implies that *idea* is more substantive than *matter*. In other words, matter doesn't really matter but you do—whatever "you" are? And *if* you *are*, and you do matter or have matter, it implies that someone is observing you and you matter to *Him*. So, to even think implies that you are already being *thought* in the mind of an Observer—*I think, therefore I've been thought*. And if each of us is to not be utterly alone, but to think together in one universe, we must all be *thought* together in the mind of One Observer—One Spirit.

✓   Did God *literally* bend down and breathe spirit into dust?

Well, according to my *Webster's New Collegiate Dictionary* . . . *No* . . . because God and Spirit by definition can't be literal. "God is Spirit" (John 4:24), *"whom no one has seen or can see"* (1 Tim. 6:16). God is Spirit, who breathes spirit into us. Spirit by definition is not "observed" with the five senses in three and a half dimensions. Spirit cannot be observed. Spirit is the "thing" that does the observing. Spirit is the substance of who you are. So, according to my dictionary, if you take yourself *literally*, you are not;[8] you don't exist.

---

[6] Quoted in, George Herbert, Quantum Reality (Anchor: NY, 1985) 17.

[7] The observation of a "person" who "observes"—has an idea in his head—changes or actualizes a wave state into a particle state, a probability into and actuality.

[8] Yet most folks are convinced, they *really, literally* . . . are. According to Quantum Physicists this implies that someone is observing them—a Spirit with an Idea. It also implies that if you are to ever know another person and exist in the same reality as that other person, rather than simply your own reality, then an Observer must be observing you both. It's interesting that the first result of sin in the garden was that the man and woman desired to no longer be observed . . . yet, it's "not good that the *Adam* should be alone."

That's a lot to ponder, but for now I'm pointing out that by "literal," we usually mean "physical" and not "spiritual." As if the flesh (physical) gives life, and the spirit counts for nothing. But Jesus said, *"The Spirit gives life; the flesh counts for nothing. The words (ideas) I have spoken to you—they are full of the Spirit and life"* (John 6:63 NIV).

In Matthew 16, having just fed the four thousand with seven loaves and a few fish, and having previously fed the five thousand with five loaves and two fish, Jesus says to His twelve disciples, *"Beware of the leaven of the Pharisees and the Sadducees."* The Pharisees and the Sadducees sought the sign (the physical) and missed the substance (what the sign pointed to: Christ).[9] Jesus warns the disciples about this "leaven" as they cross the Sea of Galilee, having just fed the multitude, and the disciples begin to talk among themselves thinking that Jesus must be referring to the fact that they forgot to bring bread. Jesus responds,

> *"O you of little faith. Why are you discussing among yourselves the fact that you have no bread? ...How is it that you fail to understand that I did not speak about bread? Beware of the leaven of the Pharisees and Sadducees." Then they understood that he did not tell them to beware of the leaven of bread, but of the teaching of the Pharisees and Sadducees.*
>
> —Matthew 16:8,11–12

So . . . if you take your Bible literally, perhaps that means that you don't take it at all? And Jesus would say to you, "How is it that you fail to understand that I did not speak about _____ (whatever it is that you think He speaks about)?"

Well, I prefer to say that I take the Bible *literally*—actually I think that I take the Bible more literally than almost anyone I know—but I would not define *literal* the way modern people seem to define *literal*. I would not define it as *physical*. I would define it as *actual . . .* or, *according to the author's actual literary intent*.

When we speak, we all use literary devices, most notably, words. Some words and literary devices don't work well in the instruction manual for your car, but they might work very well in a love note to your wife. And visa versa. "Transaxel" may be found in one but not the other. Likewise, "Sugar lips" may be

---

[9] See Matthew 16:1–4

found in one but not the other. "Fuse" may be found in both, so it's important to ask, "How is this literary device being used and in what literary form, and what did he intend when he suggested a 'fusion of sugar lips?'" It's important to ask, "When the author used the Hebrew word, *yom*, often translated 'day,' what was his actual intent?" I've taught that the *literal* meaning is the author's actual meaning.

Well, that's how I've defined it, but I'm not the dictionary.

Maybe we should literally just not use the word *literal*, because we literally don't know what it means . . . I mean it.

I wrote this down long ago and now can't find the citation, but supposedly someone once asked Madeleine L'Engle if she believed that Genesis was "literally true?" She replied, "Literally true?! I believe it's more than literally true!"

I like that. If literal does mean "physical," Genesis is certainly far more than literally true . . . But that doesn't mean it's less than literally true. You may have drawn the conclusion that I'm saying it's "just a metaphor," but I'm not.

✓ Is Adam a *metaphor*?

We say things like, "It's literally true; it's not a metaphor." As if metaphors can't be literally true, as if metaphors can't be physical. But maybe everything physical is a metaphor of something spiritual. I mean Jesus acted as if *the leaven of physical bread* were a metaphor for t*he leaven of the Pharisee's teaching.* Jesus acted as if the "spiritual" leaven was more real than the "physical" leaven, but that doesn't mean that the physical leaven isn't real.

So, Adam may be a metaphor for all humanity or even Christ, but that doesn't mean that there wasn't a guy named Adam running around a garden thousands of years ago.

"Fine," you say. "Was Adam literally real?"

Yes. You are Adam.

"Is Adam a metaphor?"

Yes. Adam is you, and you are the image of Christ.

"But was there a particular guy, that a scientist could observe using his five senses, in an enclosed paradise garden several thousand years ago, as we normally measure time?"

> I'd like to think so, but to me, the question is becoming nonsensical because I've come to believe that I am Adam . . . and I am Eve . . . and Christ is the last Adam who transforms the ruined garden of my soul into the New Jerusalem that descends from Heaven.

Believe me: Nothing is impossible for God. I've seen astounding miracles. I've spoken to demons manifesting in human flesh—so to me, a talking snake is not far fetched. I've felt God heal my leg and, once upon a time, hold me to the ground. I know that an entire creation full of matter and physical laws is no obstacle to God. He actually speaks space and time into existence, BUT the substance does not belong to space and time. The substance belongs to Christ— the Word of God.

So, it seems to me that a person has entirely missed the point if they get worried about a physical garden somewhere in Palestine. Jesus is the point. And a person is horribly naive if they think God can't make a snake that talks. Nothing is impossible for God.

And in the final analysis, we don't judge the meaning of the story. The meaning of the story judges us. We don't make sense of it. It makes sense of us. Jesus is the meaning, and He is making sense of us all. We don't judge the Truth. The Truth is judging us.

We exist in three-and-a-half dimensions (if you count time as the fourth dimension), and God spoke His Word to create it all. The Word is True. And we? . . . Not so much.

In 1884 a pastor and schoolteacher named Edwin Abbott published a little book entitled *Flatland: A Romance of Many Dimensions. Flatland* is about two-dimensional creatures that live in a two-dimensional world called Flatland. Everything is comprehensible and verifiable until one of the characters has a revelation of the third dimension and then tries to explain the third dimension to the two dimensional citizens of Flatland. You'll remember that Saint Paul spoke of being "caught up into the third heaven" and hearing things he was "unable to speak."

Well, this Flatlander sees things that are not less than *literally* true, but more than *literally* true. He encounters realities that he cannot explain, not because they are untrue but because they are *more* true than what a two-dimensional mind can comprehend. To explain what he sees, he must use two-dimensional objects (like circles and squares) as metaphors for three-dimensional objects (like spheres and cubes).

However, the two-dimensional mind thinks the third dimension is just a myth. Flatlanders think third dimensional objects are just metaphors describing realities in their own two dimensional world. They can't take the third dimension "literally" and so consider it to be unreal. When the Flatlander with the revelation insists, "It's real!" he's thrown in prison, just like Paul . . . or sometimes crucified just like someone else.

If we lived in Flatland, our world would look like a two-dimensional piece of paper, and the only things that we could perceive with our senses would be two-dimensional objects like circles or squares.

If a three-dimensional object, like a sphere, intersected our world and stayed there, we'd see a circle. The man with the revelation might say, "That's a sphere," and we'd say, "You're an idiot. Its obviously a circle." The truth is that it is an infinite number of circles comprising a sphere. But Flatlanders could not comprehend a sphere, let alone verify the existence of one.

If a three-dimensional object like a sphere intersected Flatland and passed on through it, Flatlanders would see a point that would grow into an expanding circle, then shrink back to a point and disappear. They might call it a miracle. They might freak out. They might deny that it ever happened. But the man with the revelation would say, "That was a sphere," and they would say to him, "You're an idiot."

If a three-dimensional cylinder intersected Flatland at one particular angle, Flatlanders would see a circle, like the circle that forms when you set a cold can of beer on the dining room table and your wife yells at you for not using a coaster (hypothetically speaking of course). If the cylinder (beer can) intersects Flatland at another angle it can form a rectangle. The man with the revelation might say, "That's a cylinder." A Flatlander might say, "That's a rectangle."

The man with the revelation might see a cylinder intersecting Flatland at one angle and then moments later intersecting Flatland again at ninety degrees to that first angle. The first time the cylinder might form a rectangle in Flatland

and the second time a circle. Flatlanders would say, "Look a circle," and the man with the vision might say, "That's also a cylinder and the rectangle we saw a few moments ago." And the people of Flatland would say, "You're insane—a circle is not a rectangle, and there's no such thing as a cylinder. Two things cannot be one thing. Repent!"

Have you ever heard someone say, "God is three, yet one?" Can you comprehend that? Can you verify that? Is it true?

If I were to stand outside of Flatland, like I stand outside of a two dimensional piece of paper, and then jam three of my fingers through the paper speaking into Flatland saying, "The three is me," would I be lying?[10]

If the Word of God revealed through Scripture testifies: *the Lord God formed Adam of the dust of the ground and breathed into his nostrils the breath of life,*" who are you—O Flatlander—to say "Impossible!"

- Perhaps He took millions of years (as we measure years) and used countless genetic mutations to do it. Who are you to say that He could not?
- Perhaps He took an instant and transformed an animal into a sentient being with His Spirit. Who are you to say that He could not?
- If the Word testifies that Adam was a man in a garden, who are you to say it can't be?
- If the Word testifies that we are all Adam, who are you to say it can't be?
- If the Word testifies that we are all members of the *Eschatos* Adam, who are you to say it can't be?

---

[10] This little thought experiment becomes especially fascinating when you consider time to be one of the dimensions in Flatland. Imagine that Flatland is a poster board that you hold in front of you and that one dimension of that board is time—a time line. Then say, "I AM coming soon" and smash the board against your body. Your statement would have been true at every point on the timeline in Flatland. Jesus said, "Before Abraham was I am" and "I am coming soon." Jesus is the Truth and you are stuck in Flatland.

Imagine that Flatland is a two-dimensional plane inside your body. That would mean that in you, everyone in Flatland would "live and move and have their being," (Acts 17:28) literally, really, truly and it would not be "just a metaphor."

- If the Word testifies that two shall become one flesh, who are you, *little child*, to say it can't be?
- If the Word testifies that your heart is a garden that becomes a wilderness and then turns into a city which God calls His home, who are you—O Flatlander—to say it can't be?

The Enlightenment (or en*dark*enment) is over. Modern (post-modern) physicists now postulate up to twenty-six dimensions of space-time, just to attempt to begin to explain what they have observed in the lab. And what they observe is not what's most difficult to explain—that would be the observers: themselves. Actually, the most difficult "thing" to explain might be the observer that must observe all of us observers—if we exist at all, and are now, in this moment, relating to each other at all.

Well, that "thing" on the other side of the Big Bang, and that "thing" in my heart that can't be observed and verified by "me"—perhaps it's I AM.

I AM, therefore I think.

- ✓ Was there *really* a Garden of Eden? Yes.

- ✓ Did God *literally* breathe into dust? Yes.

- ✓ Is Adam a *metaphor*? Yes. But not only a metaphor.

   Actually, Peter (*me*) is a metaphor. Actually, all humanity, all *Adam*, and all creation is a metaphor, and the Word of God is not a metaphor. Yet all creation will be filled with the Word of God, and Peter and the rest of humanity will become His Body.

   Who are you—O Flatlander—to say it cannot be?

- ✓ Is Peter *serious*? Yes

He's trying to say that this story that we're reading is true; it could not be more true than it is. And it's making you true too.

I AM is thinking.

CHAPTER 5

Work Work Work... in
the Garden of Delight

Genesis 2:7–15

Genesis 1:26–28 *Then God said, "Let us make man in our im-age, after our likeness. And let them have dominion over the fish of the sea and over the birds of the heavens and over the livestock and over all the earth and over every creeping thing that creeps on the earth."*

So God created man in his own image,
in the image of God he created him;
male and female he created them.

And God blessed them. And God said to them, "Be fruitful and multiply and fill the earth and subdue it, and have dominion over the fish of the sea and over the birds of the heavens and over every living thing that moves on the earth."

That's what we read back in chapter one. This is what happens on the sixth day. By the end of the sixth day, everything is very good. This means Adam and Eve exercise loving dominion in a state of endless rest, in the image of God who loves in freedom. It is the eternal dance of Love that is Life.

But in chapter two verse seven, God makes man, and there is no woman. And God plants a garden (*gan*). That Hebrew word means "enclosure" or "walled garden," which makes you wonder what's on the other side of the wall around this garden. What we now read in chapter two is certainly not the Seventh Day of creation, for there is no woman; there is a wall around the garden; we're going to meet a nasty talking snake, and Adam just doesn't seem too bright—at least not yet.

Genesis 2:7–8, 15 *Then the Lord God formed the man of dust from the ground and breathed into his nostrils the breath of life, and the man became a living creature. And the Lord God* *planted a garden in Eden, in the east, and there he put the man whom he had formed... The Lord God took the man and put him in the garden of Eden to work it and keep it.*

This is "paradise." (That's the Greek term for "walled garden.")

And Eden means, "delight."

- Why is Adam put to work in the Garden of Delight? He's not serving cocktails to tourists from Cleveland. The Hebrew implies that he's tilling the ground.
- Does God need help? Does God need help in the garden? Does He need help beyond the wall? Didn't God just create almost everything simply by speaking? Why would He need Adam's help?
- Will we work in Heaven? I feel like I could use a rest!

On May 21, 1983, I left the scholastic world and entered the work world. I had a degree in geology from the University of Colorado. I did well because I loved geology. As a kid, geology was like my play, my recreation. I loved rocks. I was one of the "dirt people."

So, I graduated with great grades, but I couldn't get a job. 1983 was the year of the oil glut. On May 21, I graduated; on May 28, I got married.

At my wedding reception, all the little, old ladies on Susan's side of the family would wait for a lull in the conversation and then say, "So Peter, how are you going to support your beautiful, young bride?" It was the same question her father asked. All summer I desperately tried to find a job, and all summer I found nothing, until one day I saw this ad in the paper: "Demonstrate Hydraulic Equipment." I immediately pictured myself driving backhoes and front-end loaders at the Convention Center. When I arrived at the address in the ad, I couldn't seem to find the hydraulic equipment company. All I could find was a Kirby vacuum cleaner outlet. I walked by several times, and then it hit me: hydraulic . . . vacuum . . . *suck*tion.

I thought to myself, "I have to make a living!" I was desperate and terrified of failure. So, before I knew it, I was selling Kirby vacuum cleaners door to door in *fear*.

Kirby is a fine vacuum, and the world needs knowledgeable salesmen, but it turns out that I'm the worst Kirby vacuum cleaner salesman that ever lived. I sold one vacuum to a relative under cost, meaning the Kirby Company and I paid her to buy it. It felt *futile*. And let's be honest: Vacuuming—my household chore as a child—feels futile. You don't destroy the dirt. You just move the dirt around—dirt that will be replaced by more dirt the following week.

Well, every morning I had to go into the Kirby office before I hit the street. We were forced to take part in a morning ritual. I would stand in a circle with the other "Kirby professionals" smoking cigarettes and holding their hands as we sang together in unison:

> Oh when the Kirby pros go marchin' in,
> Oh when the Kirby pros go marchin' in,
> Oh yeah we count our sales by the number,
> For that money we adore.

We sang it to the tune of "When the Saints Go Marching In." I kind of mumbled the words. It felt a bit like idolatry. You may not sing the song, but most people do work for the money. And that is futility. Isn't it? We will all die, and the money will all burn.

My last sales call was to this poor, young, unwed mother renting an apartment without carpet. I knew I was there because she wanted the complimentary cutlery set. I also knew that the last thing she needed was the $800 Cadillac of vacuum cleaners. I had to call in before I left her residence to report on the demonstration.

I explained her situation to my boss. But he kept giving me lines to feed her. I finally said, "She has no carpet, no money, and no food for her kids." Not satisfied, he proceeded to coach me in how to make the sale: "Show her how skin gets caught in her mattress and how, unless she vacuums it out with our patented cleaning system, that dirty skin could lead to disease, decay, and possible death!"

> But I couldn't do it. I felt like a mercenary . . . or worse.
> Trying to make a life, I felt like I was taking life.

Karl Marx taught that this was the problem with our industrialized, capitalistic civilization: Capitalism leads to *alienation*. We use people to love things (like money) rather than use things (like money or vacuums) to love people. And so, we become alienated from people, using people and competing with people for things—alienated from people and from our work, for we just work for capital—for money. That is, in an industrialized society, there's nothing of Peter Hiett in the vacuum he sells. It's just the same as every other vacuum on the assembly line. So, Peter Hiett doesn't give his life, he just uses his work to consume others' lives—no communion of life.

I read about a guy who kept hearing rattling in the door of his brand new car. Finally, in frustration, he took the door apart and found a bolt hanging on a string with a note taped to it that said, "Placed here by Rob." See, Rob was desperate to put something of himself into his work. And I was, too. The proletariat is too . . . it's just that Marx didn't know how to make that happen.

Well, I just couldn't get myself to sell that poor woman an $800 vacuum. My job *sucked*. (And of course, I'm referring to *suck*tion.) Work *sucked*—FEAR, FUTILITY and ALIENATION.

I quit vacuum cleaner sales that very day. The next year I went to seminary, and now I work in a church. But I'm still anxious. I worry about providing for my family. I'm *afraid* that I don't know how to make church *work*. Yet this is how I make a "living."

And now, instead of one boss with a clearly defined goal, to sell the Cadillac of vacuum cleaners, I have hundreds of bosses, each with a different and poorly defined agenda, and there's no way I can please them all—that's *futile*!

And it's *alienating*. We've got budgets, programs, capital expenditures . . . people become tithing units or ways to boost my ego. For most pastors, it's really not about money but power, prestige, and influence. So, if we're honest, we pastors sing:

Oh when the saints go marchin' in
Oh when the saints go marchin' in (to my building),
Oh yeah we count our parishioners by the number,
For the power, prestige, and influence we adore.

You see, as a part of the competitive, capitalistic, Christian religion industry, I turn people into things and use them as food for my ego—alienated from people and alienated from my product. I used to sell vacuums to make money, and now I sell Jesus to make parishioners. And the Jesus that sells best is an assembly line, market-researched, upper-middle class, American Jesus sold to people who want to use Him to get into Heaven, keep their tails out of Hell, and get out of church in time for brunch!

We pastors sell Jesus *to* people who want to use Him, and we sell Jesus *for* people that want to use Him—including us.

What does that make us?
And what does that make Jesus?
And what does that make you?

And now, you may say, "Right, I got your point! Don't work for money. Don't work for people. Work for God!" Right?! . . . We're all supposed to be working for God: "*Go and make disciples...*" etc. etc. But does that make it better?

1. Have you ever read the Sermon on the Mount? "*You therefore must be perfect, as your heavenly father is perfect*" (Matt. 5:48). That's terrifying. I can't make myself perfect in the image of God. Talk about *FEAR*!

2. "*Unless the Lord builds the house, those who build it labor in vain*" (Psalm 127:1). Exactly! So, why do we labor? Isn't it *FUTILITY*?

3. And *ALIENATION*—does God need us to "*go and make disciples of all nations?*" Does God need you to convince people to put their faith in His perfect unconditional Love—in Christ Jesus—so He won't have to torment them endlessly in unspeakable wrath? Does God need you to save people from Himself? If you think so, isn't that kind of alienating . . . from God and from people? Does God *need* you to work for Him?

Does God need you to take some knowledge from some tree or something and get to work making yourself and everyone else in God's image ? Make money? Make churches? Make people in the image of God?

I used to be in the vacuum industry, and now I'm in the religion industry. And work sucks!

Well, I hope you know that I'm joking . . . kind of . . . and not at all. I mean, I have a wonderful job, and work often feels like a gift, but I think you can all relate on some level. Can't you? I suspect that most of us don't picture our jobs as paradise.

We think, "Paradise would not be my job, and certainly not work . . . because work feels like it's cursed."

> **Genesis 2:7** *Then the Lord God formed the man [Adam] of dust from the ground and breathed into his nostrils the breath of life, and the man became a living creature. And the Lord God planted a garden in Eden, in the east, and there he put the man whom he had formed.*

Notice that the garden is in Eden on the east side. We'll see that Eden appears to be a large region roughly the size of Old Israel. The garden is on the east side, like Jerusalem is on the east side of Old Israel. In fact, Orthodox Jews believe the Temple Mount is the original location of the creation of Adam. In Ezekiel 28, God seems to locate the Garden of Eden on the "holy mountain of God," Mount Moriah, Mount Calvary, the Temple Mount—they're all basically in the same place.

You see, this is the beginning of the greatest story ever told—the story of Wisdom and Life Himself, hung on a tree, on a hill, and a river that flows from a throne in an eternal city of precious jewels that is a temple and the Garden of Delight.

> **Genesis 2:8–10** *And the LORD God planted a garden in Eden, in the east, and there he put the man whom he had formed. And out of the ground the LORD God made to spring up every tree*

*that is pleasant to the sight and good for food. The tree of life was
in the midst of the garden, and the tree of the knowledge of good
and evil.*

My third book will be all about the two trees in the middle of the garden. For
now, just notice that they are there, in one spot, on that mountain with Adam.

Genesis 2:11–14 *A river flowed out of Eden to water the garden, and there it divided and became four rivers. The name
of the first is the Pishon. It is the one that flowed around the
whole land of Havilah, where there is gold. And the gold of that
land is good; bdellium and onyx stone are there. The name of
the second river is the Gihon. It is the one that flowed around
the whole land of Cush. And the name of the third river is the
Tigris, which flows east of Assyria. And the fourth river is the
Euphrates.*

No one is certain of the location of the Pishon. The Gihon most likely refers
to the Nile, since Cush refers to Ethiopia, Sudan, and Egypt. Of course, we all
know the Tigris and Euphrates. The Nile to the south, the Tigris and Euphrates
to the North and East, surround the land of Israel.[1] How it could be said that
they all come from one river I don't know . . . but there's much I don't know.

---

[1] The writer of Genesis has identified the "land" prepared in Genesis 1 with the Garden of Eden described in Genesis 2. The Garden of Eden anticipates the tabernacle
where God desired to dwell with His chosen people . . . .The Garden of Eden extended
from the "river that flows through all the land of Cush" to the "River Euphrates." Since
in Genesis the land of Cush is linked to Egypt (Genesis 10:6), the second river, the
Gihon (Genesis 2:13), was apparently understood by the author as "the river of Egypt."
. . . When we move to Genesis 15, we find that the land promised to Abraham—the
Promised Land—is marked off by these same two rivers, the Euphrates and the River
of Egypt (Genesis 15:18). Note that the area marked off by these two rivers in Genesis
15 is essentially the same region covered by the Garden of Eden in Genesis 2. When
the general boundaries are compared, it becomes clear that the writer of the Pentateuch
intends us to identify the two locations with each other. God's promise of the land to
the patriarchs is thus textually linked to His original "blessing" of all humanity in the
Garden of Eden. We find the same linkage in the prophetic literature and the New

Genesis 2:15 *The LORD God took the man and put him in the garden of Eden to work [abad – "work" or "till"] it and keep [shamar – "keep" or "observe"] it.*

The Lord God took the Adam and put him in the Garden of Delight *to work . . .* in Paradise! And soon, he'll be joined by a very beautiful and very naked lady, with whom God commands him to: *"be fruitful and multiply."* Work, work, work! Plow the field. Plant the seed. Do some gardening. That doesn't sound so bad.

You know, gardening is strange work, for when you garden, it becomes obvious that you really don't make stuff—life; God makes it, and He lets you help. You can't make one zucchini squash . . . but when you're at peace with that, it's really fun to help—to work and keep a garden.

Do you have a garden? Have you ever had a garden? If so, I bet you know that you can get pretty good zucchini down at Safeway or Whole Foods . . . maybe even better zucchini and cheaper zucchini. Right? But you still garden. You *"till it and keep it"* because you want to.

1. You're not *ANXIOUS* because you know you can always buy zucchinis if need be.

2. It's not *FUTILE* because you're really not growing zucchinis. You're growing fun, relaxation, and wonder. It's wonder-full how a seed turns dirt into a zucchini. Just observing it makes you feel like a new person. Your work is really a form of rest. You could call it play.

3. And it's not *ALIENATING.* You feel connected to your zucchini because you grew it. And when you give it to your neighbor, you're not just giving some fruit, you're giving your self.

You garden because it's fun!

Testament. God's promise of blessing through the seed of Abraham is linked to his blessing of the nations and all humanity.
—Dr. John Sailhamer, *Genesis Unbound* (Multnomah, Sisters OR 1996) pp. 68,72

It's fun because you don't have to do it for a living. You don't need to do it for a living because people like my grandpa garden for a living. They're called farmers. But for them, gardening is not always fun because they do it for a living.

I think my grandpa must have been made in God's image because they both were into cursing the ground: "This G*# damned Nebraska soil!" Grandpa loved the farm, but I think, for grandpa, work often sucked—like it was cursed somehow—but not for Adam in Genesis 2, in Paradise. What was work like for Adam in Paradise?

In physics, I learned that work is force applied over distance. And that's interesting because that means

- Skiing bumps on Mary Jane Mountain—my second favorite form of recreation—is work. It is exhausting, tiring work. But it doesn't seem like work. We call it play!
- Dancing is work, but it's also rest. It's re-creation.
- Play, dancing, and recreation are work.

So, perhaps no one works as hard as children. One day it hit me watching the kids: Everything they did was what Susan and I did, except they were having fun! They played house. They had toy hammers, saws, and an Easy Bake Oven. They even had a vacuum cleaner that didn't suck, and they'd vacuum with it for hours—but not just vacuum, *dance* vacuum—work was play and play was a dance. They even played church, and they played hard—wrote sermons, preached sermons, sang songs, took up an offering . . .

But they did not make a living at it. They did not believe that life depended on their work. They didn't work at love, and they didn't work to live. Jesus said that in order to enter the Kingdom (to get back to the garden), we must become like children (Matt. 18:3).

And one other thing: They loved to help. Elizabeth used to write sermons for me because she knew that I considered it to be hard work. When I was a little boy and my dad worked in the garden, I always wanted to help, and I knew I needed my dad's help. He helped me till the soil and plant the seed. I'm sure it was more work for him, but he wanted me to share his joy.

When my girls were about four and five, I built a beautiful stone staircase on the side of our house out of huge rocks that I collected from the side of the road driving home from our church on Lookout Mountain just to the west of

Denver. Some of those stones had to weigh a few hundred pounds. And the girls would always say, "Can I help?" And I'd usually say, "Sure."

I'd lift a hundred pound boulder and let one of them put their hand on the side as I struggled and strained. It was much more challenging work with their help, but I wanted to let them help because I wanted them to share my joy—and besides, I was shaping them in my image. They'd say, "Mommy, Mommy, look at the stairs that me and Daddy built. Look at the stairs that *WE* built." Susan would say something like, "Becky, Elizabeth, *YOU* built those stairs?" And I'd say, "Yep, *WE* built those stairs!" They loved to help, and I loved to let them help. I didn't need their help. I wanted them to help. But if anything I was *their* helper. God the Father has just created the Universe. Does He need Adam's help to till the garden? Or does He want Adam's help because He longs to share His joy and make Adam in His own image because He is Adam's Helper? God is Love, and Love works because Love wants to work. The work is Life. God wants to give Adam His Life. Adam is to work in the Garden of Delight, and it's a blessing—He's not asked to "make a living." It *is* living.

What happened to work?

How come it feels like a curse?

Well, as we'll see, Adam and Eve tried to make a living from their work. The snake convinced them that their lives depended on their work, so they worked to live, and then they worked to love, rather than living and loving their work . . . work, that is to be Life and Love.

Remember, they were the gardeners; they tended the garden and the trees; that was their work. And their work was life—the trees were *"pleasant to the sight and good for food"* (Gen. 2:9). Their work was Love and Life. They didn't work to make a life or a living.

Work was living, *and* living was work until the snake suggested that the produce of one tree could make a life in the image of God. It was the one tree that they were warned not to work—the tree of the knowledge of good and evil. God told them it would make death. We'll discuss it in much more detail when we move into book three. But for now, I just hope you'll notice that they "worked" this tree to make a life in the image of God. They worked to live . . . and everything died.

And as you know, God showed up cursing. He cursed the snake, and He cursed the ground. We'll see that the curse was actually a gift to Adam and his bride. It would teach them:

- You yourself cannot make your life with your work.
- You cannot create yourself with the knowledge of good and evil (the law).
- You are created and saved by *"grace...through faith, and this* [faith] *is not of your own doing, so that no one may boast. For we are his workmanship, created in Christ Jesus for good works, which God prepared beforehand that we should walk in them* [or perhaps dance and play in them?]*"* (Eph. 2:8-10).
- And faith in that truth is Good. God gives you the Good.
- Lack of faith in that truth: "God is Salvation," is evil.

So, as the Apostle Paul writes, God subjected creation *"to futility ...in hope"* (Rom. 8:20). Work has been cursed so you could receive the blessing that is Grace—His name is Jesus. It literally means, "God is Salvation." And He delivers you from the curse. He bears your curse, and *He* makes your living. He is your life, for He gives you His Life—Himself.

For it is written,

> *"Cursed be everyone who does not abide by all things written in the Book of the Law, and do them." ...Christ redeemed us from the curse of the law by becoming a curse for us—for it is written, 'Cursed is everyone who is hanged on a tree.'"*
> —Galatians 3:10, 13

So, here's a fascinating question that we will continue to ponder: What was hanging on that tree in the garden? What knowledge did Adam (that first Adam) and Eve take, and what knowledge and what Life has God given?

Well, for now, just observe: Jesus redeems us from the curse, and Jesus gives us His life. Our living does not depend on our work. It is the gift of God in Jesus, The Life. When we believe that in faith, we no longer work to live. We live to work. As Paul writes, *"To live is Christ, and...if I am to live in the flesh that means fruitful labor for me"* (Phil. 1:21-22).

We live to work, and that work is a blessing—like play, like dance, like worship, like gardening. It's recreation that is my re-creation when I work by grace in the faith of Jesus.

Blessed work is the faith of Jesus in His Father in me; it's the dance of the Trinity in me. Jesus said, *"My food is to do the will of him who sent me and to accomplish his work."* (John 4:34) How weird is that? He was nourished BY work—not so that he *could* work.

You know, when my kids would dance and play church, they were usually looking at me, and my joy was their strength. And my joy was derived from their joy . . . in my joy . . . of their joy, in my joy, (*perichoresis*), and it manifested as dance and play—sometimes exhausting and painful, yet nourishing to the soul. It was Life.

See? Jesus worked, danced, and played for His Father. So, He seems to have known something about His Father that we have forgotten or perhaps never have known. Perhaps He knows that God is Love; He knows Love—but not only *about* love; He *knows* Love: I-contact.

> *And whatever you do, in word or deed, do everything in the name of the Lord Jesus, giving thanks to God the Father through him.*
>
> —Colossians 3:17

"Whatever you do..." Do you realize that a Christian cannot have a secular job? Because whatever job you have is your calling. Even if God calls you to quit, you are to quit to His glory. No Christian has a secular job, and no Christian is unemployed. You are all employed by God. He may use General Motors to pay your salary, but *He's* your employer. Even if you're unemployed, He has employed you in His service wherever you go—even the unemployment line!

Now, if you say, "Okay . . . what does He want me to do?" Well, I don't know. I'm not a dentist or a carpenter or a mom . . . *you* are. Ask Him. If you're a dentist, I would guess He'd want you to fix teeth and not overcharge people. If you're a carpenter, He might want you to love people by making good tables and chairs. If you're a mom, I suppose He'd want you to love your children as He loves you. In Colossians 3, after saying, *"Do everything in the name of the Lord*

Jesus, giving thanks to God the Father through him," Paul gives advice to wives, husbands, children and slaves:

> *Slaves (doulos), obey in everything those who are your earthly masters, not by way of eye-service, as people-pleasers, but with sincerity of heart, fearing the Lord. Whatever you do, work heartily, as for the Lord and not for men, knowing that from the Lord you will receive the inheritance as your reward. You are serving the Lord Christ.*
>
> —Colossians 3:22–24

Critics say Christ didn't abolish slavery. But maybe He did. You are not a slave if you're willing to serve, and even less if you love the one you serve. "Slaves," says Scripture, "you work for Jesus." And "Masters, you do as well." Christ abolishes slavery from the inside out by turning every master into a willing slave of those they once enslaved. You serve Jesus, and Jesus serves His Father who works all things together for good . . . even Jesus and yourself.

> *Have this mind among yourselves, which is yours in Christ Jesus, who, though he was in the form of God, did not count equality with God a thing to be grasped, but emptied himself, by taking the form of a doulos* [That means "slave!"] *being born in the likeness of men. And being found in human form, he humbled himself by becoming obedient to the point of death, even death on a cross.*
>
> —Philippians 2:5–8

Scripture says that He did this for *"the joy that was set before him"* (Heb. 12:2). What was the joy set before him? Wouldn't it have been the delight of His Father and communion with us—His Bride? Wouldn't it have been I-contact—the Joy of Love, which is Life? Life is expiring and inspiring; it's respiration: I-contact.

You see, selling vacuums door to door felt like slavery. But it didn't have to be slavery, not if, in my heart, I was working for my Father with the faith of my Lord. Jesus wasn't a slave, for He chose to do His work out of Love. He took the form of a slave with the heart of God, and God is Love. He trusted His

Father and so delighted in serving His Father. He didn't work for money, or the approval of man, but for the delight of His Father.

Dorothy Sayers points out that, from the outside in, the work at a prison and the work at a monastery look like the same work, under the same law: poverty, obedience, and chastity. Yet, from the inside out, the difference between the prison and monastery is the difference between cursing and blessing, between death and life, and between bondage and the freedom of Love.

You see, I think Paul is saying, "If you don't like your job, get a new boss and become a new man." In other words, whatever you're doing, don't do it for money or merely for people; do it for your Father in Heaven, and do it in the Spirit of Jesus. In doing this, you will have entered into the Life of the Trinity—or the Life of the Trinity will have entered into you. Love will have entered into you. And Love works. *"Love bears all things, believes all things, hopes all things, endures all things. Love never ends"* (I Cor. 13:7-8).

And now, maybe that's the catch . . .

We can't just decide to love, can we?

We can't just decide to trust like Jesus, can we?

We can't just decide to have the mind of Christ, can we?

We can't just save ourselves, by ourselves, with our work, can we?

We can't just make ourselves in God's image, can we?

We need a helper . . .

Work in a cursed world shows me that.

"God is Love" (I John 4:8,16). And Jesus is *"the Life"* (John 14:6).

The evil one tempted that first Adam and Eve to take from the "tree of the knowledge of good and evil" in order to make a life in the image of God.

"Knowledge of good and evil" sounds like the law, doesn't it?

The law describes Love. And God is Love. And the Word of Love is Life.

So, the evil one tempts us to make a life by making love (and I don't mean sex—Genesis 1:27—I think God commands them to have sex).

READ SLOWLY:

> The evil one tempts us to make a life, by making—manufacturing—love.
> But God is Love, and Jesus is the Life.

> Doesn't Adam realize that he can't make love or a life?
> Love just made him and breathed into him, His Life!

> Doesn't humankind realize that we can't create our own life in the image
> of Love?

> But Love creates us and gives us Life!

No, I don't think we realize that. And it's a rather stunning observation once you begin to see it. We all seem to assume that we have created ourselves, and continue to create ourselves in God's image with this thing we call a "free will." We call our will "free" because we assume that no one determines our will but ourselves—as if we were *uncreated creators*. No wonder we aren't grateful for our lives. And no wonder we're terrified of losing "our lives;" we think we make our lives, and so we work ourselves to death . . . not life.

We don't realize that we are created by Love who gives us Life.

- Another way to say that: *We don't have faith in God and His Word; we don't have faith in Grace.*
- And please note: *We're not saved until we do!*
- Another way to say that: *We're not fully created in the image of God until we trust our Creator, which means resting in the truth that we are created.*

We don't realize . . . but we *will* realize.

That's what the rest of our study of Genesis 1-3 is about; that's what the rest of the Bible is about; that's what the rest of your life in this God-cursed world is about. It's still the *sixth* day of creation in this world. Fear, futility and alienation reveal that. But God is giving you a new heart, a new will, His own heart—Jesus, the Life.

[God] is the source of your life in Christ Jesus, whom God made our wisdom, our righteousness and sanctification and redemption

—1 Cor. 1:30 RSV

Imagine if you had that heart. And if you can imagine it, maybe you already have it—at least a little. You see, Faith comes to us as a seed—a little seed. It's planted in the broken soil and decay of our earthen vessels—our stony hearts. It looks dead, but it's actually the Life. We can't make the Life. At best, we can observe it planted and buried in the dirt that is us—old us. You know, a seed that becomes a tree and bears fruit doesn't just suck up the dirt and hide it in a bag; the tree actually changes the dirt into fruit. The tree transforms the dirt, including it in the great dance of Life.

And, by the way, that's what's so fun about gardening. When I was a kid, I loved to *"work it and keep it;"* I loved to *"till it and observe it.,"* filled with wonder over the miracle of a seed that dies and comes to life and bears much fruit, transforming dirt into life.

When I believe that I am created by Love, who gives me life, work isn't fear, futility, and alienation; work is Life.

1. I stop working in FEAR.

> I can't make money; I can't build a church; and I can't save a soul.
>
> But *God* can, and God does—through me.
>
> It's been hard, but I'm learning that God is my provider.
>
> Jesus said, *"You are Peter, and on this rock* [on this *petros*], *I will build my church"* (Matt. 16:18). "Peter, I will build it—not you—but *on* you."
>
> And, of course, I can't save a soul, and I sure don't need to save one from God, when *"God* is salvation."
>
> When Jesus was crucified He cried, *"It is finished"* (John 19:30). When He commissioned His disciples, He said, *"All*

authority in heaven and on earth has been given to me" (Matt. 28:18). That is, "I'm in charge. Go, therefore, and use your Easy Bake Ovens. Get out your Junior Carpenter Tool Chest, and go to town! Peter, preach and stop stressing! I will save my lost sheep; I will build my church, and I am your living."

2. Work stops feeling FUTILE and becomes fruitful.

God planted a garden, and I am the garden; I am God's field.

Faith and mercy is the harvest of this earth—not numbers on charts, money in bank accounts, or bodies in seats. It will all burn. But faith, hope, and love abide (1 Cor. 13:13). "*The fruit of the Spirit is love, joy, peace, patience, kindness, goodness, gentleness, faithfulness, and self-control*" (Gal. 5:22).

So, the way God measures success is very different from the way this world measures success. You could be an absolute failure in this world: broken, abandoned, beaten, naked, scorned, and nailed to a tree—a failure in this world—but the very *glory* of God and harvest of this earth!

When I remember what God is growing, I'm already fruitful. Faith grows in fear. Hope grows in futility. Love grows in the soil of alienation. I can't make a seed, and I can't grow a piece of fruit, but God grows fruit in me. And it "abides." It's not futile.

3. I'm not ALIENATED from my work. My work is communion.
   I am the work, the work of Love.
   I become the dance, the dance of Life.
   I am the body of Christ, who is the image of God.
   That's the body of the Life that is the manifestation of Love.

So, I sold vacuums trying to make a life and do what love required, and it was fear, futility, and alienation. It was a curse. But maybe instead of a curse, it could've been a blessing.

> **Genesis 2:15** *"The LORD God took the Adam and put him in the garden of Eden to work it and keep it."*

Is that a curse or a blessing?

As we have noted, Love is Life. The great dance of Love is Life. And all our work is to be Love. Jesus said,

> *"You shall love the Lord your God with all your heart and with all your soul and with all your mind." This is the great and first commandment. And a second is like it: "You shall love your neighbor as yourself." On these two commandments depend all the Law and the Prophets.*
>
> —Matt. 22:37–40

Is that a curse or a blessing?

It is interesting that in Genesis 1, God just speaks a Word and it happens—creation happens—until we get to this Word: *"Be fruitful and multiply and fill the earth and subdue it..."* (Gen. 1:28). That is, "Adam, work it."

Is that a curse or a blessing?
And will it happen? And how will it happen?

It is also fascinating that when Jesus, who is the Word through whom all things are created, states the great and first command—the command which encompasses all of God's commands, which is also the "job description" of humanity—He doesn't say "should," but "will." He says, *"You will love."* . . . I should you not![2]

---

[2] "I Should You Not" is the title a Downside Up short film that "should" be released around the same time as this book. Once released, it can be found at http://www.downsideup.com/

Most English translations translate the verb as "shall," but the tense is a simple future active indicative. "Shall" is an antiquated and confusing English tense, but the future active indicative is a very simple tense. It means, "will." So, Jesus who is the Truth and the Word says, "You *will*." Do you believe Him? Maybe "you will."

God is Love, so the Word of Love says, "*You will love the LORD your God with all your heart, mind, soul, and strength and your neighbor as yourself.*" You will "*work it and keep it.*" You will love, and Love is Life.

Is that a curse or a blessing?

If I think it depends on me . . .
If I think that I must make myself love in order to live, it's a curse.
    I work to live, and work sucks!

If I think it depends on God . . .
If I think that Love makes me and causes me to live, it's a blessing.
    I live to work, and work is Life!

Susan and I discovered that our families used to routinely go out to dinner at the same restaurant when we were about seven. Imagine if God spoke to me at the Denver Drumstick and said, "You better love that tow-headed girl in yonder booth, serve her, work for her and gladly give all your money to her for the rest of your life . . . OR DIE!" That would've sucked. It would've been a curse, and I probably would've gone insane and died.

Ironically, I did love that "tow-headed girl in yonder booth," serve her, work for her, and gladly give all of my money to her for the rest of my life . . . THAT IS MY LIFE!

You know, if God had whispered in my ear, "Hey Peter, see that tow-headed girl over there? You will love her with all your heart. She will be your wife." Well, that word wouldn't have been a curse, but a blessing . . . maybe even a seed that would one day bear fruit. That word of love might have worked for me, even as it worked me.

So, I sold vacuums trying to make a life, and it felt like a curse . . . But it wouldn't have been that way, if I hadn't believed that *I* had to make my life.

Actually, a life had already been making me. A life had already been working me, and I had already begun to truly love this life. Of course, I didn't think of it as work, but more like play or joining a dance—but it was work. In high school, I spent all my money on her. In college, I'd drive for days just to see her a few hours. I would diet, exercise, wash the car and endure countless hours of walking through gift shops "just looking" because that's what she liked. And I would go to work—that is, I would go to my job.

- When I thought I had to make a life, the work was a curse.
- When I remembered that she was my life, work could actually be a blessing. For then, I didn't work in fear, but gratitude.

- At least sometimes, we all work to make money, to purchase "a life"—pay for food, buy a home, feel secure, and earn respect. We work for life.
- But sometimes, we work to spend money in gratitude for "a life"—but we usually don't call it work, but re-creation or just LIFE! Work is life.

- Sometimes, we work at love and it feels like death.
- But sometimes, Love works us, and then we live.

In 1981, Love was working me, and I felt totally alive.

I remember the day I first went shopping for her ring. I drove from Boulder to Harry's Jewelers in downtown Denver. REO Speed wagon was blasting on my stereo: "Roll with the changes...Don't let her go!"

When I got to the jewelry store, Harry, who was a family friend, kept showing me stones. You know, they all look pretty much alike, and Harry kept explaining their relative worth, but I didn't really care. I knew how much I had to spend. The money represented all I had; it was my summer jobs, my savings, my work and your work—my government student loan money. (Thank you.)

I'm just saying the money was a lot of work, and here's the weird thing: I wanted to work. I mean, I really didn't care about the stone. I only cared about spending all my money on the stone. At one point, I remember wanting to jump the counter, grab Harry by the collar and scream:

Harry, I want to pay more!

Harry, I want to spend everything I have!

Harry, I want all my blood, sweat and tears to buy this stone!

Harry, it's for my bride!

I know she'll say yes, 'cause she's already asked me to ask her.

She's chosen me to choose her.

Harry, I could never pay for her, but I want to give everything to her.

Harry, charge me more! I need to bleed for it. I want to hurt for her.

Harry, it's crazy, I know. But it's love, and love has become my life.

See what I mean? Love was working me, and it was Life.

Actually, Love was working us, and Love would "make a life," actually four lives—four fruits: Jonathan, Elizabeth, Becky, and Coleman.

Work, work, work in the Garden of Delight.

Now, you may say, "Gosh, that's nice for you Peter, but I don't have a husband, or I don't have a wife." Well, when God put Adam in the garden to *"till it and keep it"* he had no wife, and he couldn't find his Helper. But Love will find him and give him a Life. God is Love, and His Word is Life, and He is still making Adam in His image.

Old Testament scholars point out that the garden is a picture of the tabernacle and later the temple, which was built on the traditional site of the Garden of Eden. The Hebrew words translated *"work it and keep it"* can also be translated *"worship and obey."* To work the garden is to worship and obey. To worship is to commune with God in His temple. The Body of Christ is a temple. We comprise His temple. When you love God in others, Love is finding you and giving you His Life. You are His temple.

To the side of the Temple Mount, there is a garden. Jesus was hung on a tree in that garden. His tomb was in the same garden. When He rose from the dead, Mary thought He was the gardener. He is. And He is her Helper. And she is His temple. He said, *"Apart from me you can do nothing"* (John 15:5b).

When we love, God is making us His Life. God the Son is serving God the Father through us, and God the Father is glorifying God the Son in us, and we are being animated by the Spirit of God. Love works us, and it is Life: *Perichoresis*.

"So, what do I do?"
Nothing maybe?
...Maybe the Word is doing you.
...Maybe Love is working you.
...Maybe He's working in His Garden of Delight.

Just worship Him, look at Him, ponder Him . . . and you will obey Him.

You don't make Love. Love is making you and giving you His Life.

*   *   *

Picture your boss at the end of a conference table. You're about to get a review. If you're in school, picture the teacher or principal. Maybe your boss is a group, so picture the group. Maybe your boss is yourself. In my experience, that is the hardest boss to work for.

Bless your boss. They're a gift to you. Sometimes the Lord speaks through your boss. Bless them. But now say, "I love you, but the Lord is my boss. I work for Him."

Picture Jesus. He walks in and kisses your old boss. They trade seats. Look at Him: a crown of thorns in His skull, fresh wounds in His hands and feet, and His eyes are a flame of fire—burning with love and desire for you. He said, *"Whoever has seen me, has seen the Father"* (John 14:9).

He pays your salary. He makes the sun rise. He grows the zucchinis. He gives you your next breath. You work for Him.

Now look down at your hands. There are nail prints. There is a gash in your side. You work for Him, and He's working in you as you glorify your Father. The Father looks like Jesus, and you look like Jesus. His work is your work. Love is working you and giving you His Life.

When I believe, my work becomes His work, and that work doesn't suck. It's the edge of Paradise. Have you ever looked someone in the eye and said, "In the name of Jesus, you're forgiven"? It's Paradise. It's gardening in Paradise. At times it may hurt, but it's the edge of Paradise. And it's your job.

To work is to pray. —*Augustine*

It is impossible for a Christian to have a secular job. —*Rob Bell, Velvet Elvis*

In hardness of condition and lack of liberty there is little to choose between Dartmoor [prison] and a Trappist monastery, and the looker-on might readily suppose that in both "the problem of work" had been "solved" in the same way. "Poverty, obedience, chastity" is the rule of life in both; and the convict might appear to have the advantage, since he is far likelier than the monk to return to the world some day and in the meantime enjoys a good deal more freedom of speech. Yet between the employed and the employed, between the secure and the secure, between the bound and the bound there is a difference too great to be seen in the schedules of employment.
—*Dorothy Sayers, The Mind of the Maker*

The works of monks and priests in God's sight are in no way whatever superior to the works of a farmer laboring in a field, or of a woman looking after her home.
—*Martin Luther*

Work is not primarily a thing one does to live, but the thing one lives to do... Incompetence and untruth always result when the secular vocation is treated as a thing alien to religion. When you find a man who is a Christian praising God by the excellence of his work—do not distract him and take him away from his proper vocation to address religious meetings and open church bazaars. Let him serve God in the way to which God has called him.
—*Dorothy Sayers, Creed or Chaos*

CHAPTER 6

The Helper

Genesis 2:15–25

Genesis 1:27–28 *So God created man in his own image, in the image of God he created him; male and female he created them. And God blessed them. And God said to them, "Be fruitful and multiply..."*

When my family lived in Northern California many years ago, we were in a small group with our good friends, the Harrises. They had a son named Conner, who was about five. One night at small group, Micki Ann told us about their family's recent trip to the ballet in San Francisco. Of course, it was a high society affair and a bit of a stretch for Conner.

Conner sat next to his grandpa, who was hard of hearing. The music was playing when a male ballet dancer came dancing onto the stage wearing the customary tights that male dancers wear when dancing ballet.

Conner watched a while and then leaned over to his grandpa and whispered, "Where's his penis?" His grandpa said, "What?" So, Conner said it louder: "Where's his penis?" His grandpa said, "What?" "Where's his penis?" Conner said even louder because the music was getting louder; actually it was reaching a crescendo. Finally, his grandpa said again, "What?" And Conner yelled. But just as Conner yelled, the music stopped. So, everyone at the San Francisco Ballet heard five-year-old Conner scream, "Where's his penis?"

Well, I just want to say that I feel like five-year-old Conner at the ballet. You see the Bible is just packed with sexuality, yet mentioning sexuality to church folks makes me feel like Conner at the ballet. And I know I'm not the only one who feels this way. Many of you tightened up at the end of the last chapter and are fairly nervous right now.

Some of us grew up in an age of sexual repression; some of us grew up in an age of sexual indulgence or idolatry. Actually, repression and indulgence may both be the same idolatry—the idolatry of our own will. Well, in the early '60s, we were taught that sex is a dirty, filthy thing, so you should save it for the person you marry. But in the late '60s things had changed, and people talked about sex like they talked about scratching an itch. Now, people seem to think they should indulge their every desire. Yet at the same time, we sue others for indulging their desire.

It seems that repression and denial lead to indulgence and broken hearts, which lead to more repression and denial. People usually think repression and denial are the job of the church: "Don't think about that thing that Conner mentioned at the ballet!"

When I talk about sexuality in sermons, I get letters. And often those letters come from people whose strategy is repression, but their lifestyle is indulgence. For them, church is a means of repressing desires. So, when the preacher gets up and says *that word* (that Conner Harris mentioned at the ballet) it's a problem. And the word fills them with fear, pain, and shame.

For some, there has been so much fear, pain, and shame they can no longer even hope for pleasure.

And now here's our problem: Already in Genesis 1, in the very first commandment to humanity, God said, *"Be fruitful and multiply."* You see, that is extremely difficult to do without the thing Conner Harris mentioned at the ballet. And that thing only works when fueled by some desire, but maybe God isn't into repressing desire as much as redeeming desire—perhaps even increasing desire—for the Good.

Now in Genesis 2, God is going to get into the details, not because sex is *bad* but because sex is *good*. In chapter 1, He made it and called it good. If I gave my son a new BMW and then said, "Jon, don't take the Beemer four-wheeling, and never put Cheez Whiz in the crankcase," I wouldn't be saying that because the BMW is *bad* but because the BMW is *good*—really good.

So, God says, "Conner, ballet dancers wear very tight underwear. And Conner, the thing you mentioned at the ballet is *good*—very good; I made it. And so I'll help you know what to do with it. Trust me. You're only five." Well, we are all like five-year-old Conner Harris. Whether we're ninety-five or five; we're all sexual beings, and we're only beginning to learn what to do with that fact.

I'm asking you to grow up a bit, trust the Word of God a bit, and allow your Father in Heaven to teach you. I'm tired of the church abdicating sexuality to MTV. Our strategy is not repression or mere indulgence. Our strategy is surrender, sanctification, and redemption.

The evil one has lied to all of us, so this topic may be one of great pain, shame, sorrow, and longing for you. You may even find your heart shutting down. You may be a prostitute, a nun vowed to celibacy, a hermaphrodite, or a eunuch incapable of having sex. Nonetheless, you are a sexual being made for communion. On the other side of the pain is a new creation literally constructed out of the things you suffered here—things now transformed from sin into grace, sorrow into joy, and shame into the most ecstatic communion. So, don't hide your heart. Don't shut it down. Surrender it to the One who made it.

> **Genesis 2:15–18** *The Lord God took the man and put him in the garden of Eden to work it and keep it. And the Lord God commanded the man, saying, "You may surely eat of every tree of the garden, but of the tree of the knowledge of good and evil you shall not eat, for in the day that you eat of it you shall surely die."*

Trust me: we're going to talk a whole lot more about this tree of knowledge, but for now I would just point out that, in this story, there are two ways of knowing:

1. Adam and Eve will know some stuff through this tree and die.
2. Adam and Eve will know each other in another way, and give birth to life.

1. One is seizing control—taking.
2. One is surrendering control—giving and receiving.

1. One feels like a final exam.
2. One feels like a honeymoon.

> **Genesis 2:18** *Then the Lord God said, "It is not good that the man should be alone..."*

The first thing in all of Scripture that God declares "not good" is loneliness. And if it's not good, Adam is definitely not finished in God's image. God is good, and God is a Trinity of loving persons, so if Adam is alone he's certainly not finished in the image of God.

And please notice: "Not good" is the condition of Adam before the fall. So, "not good" wasn't simply a result of the fall. Adam is "alone" before the fall. And in the Bible, the concept "alone" is a pretty good description of what we loosely call Hell. Hell = Adam alone. *Hades, Sheol*, death, and "Outer Darkness" = Adam alone. Adam is alone in paradise, and it's not good. Have you ever been alone in paradise?

Several years ago, I went on a mission trip to Brazil with my life-long friend Andrew Trawick. At the end of the trip our missionary host, Ken Flurry, took us to the beach—the most beautiful beach I had ever seen. The jungle came down to the sand. Couples frolicked in the warm waves. I lay there in the sunlight on the warm golden sand.

I remember thinking: "This is paradise." Then I looked to my right and saw my friend Andrew stretched out like a pasty white pale fish in swim trunks. I looked to my left and stared at the big old hairy belly of my missionary friend, Ken Flurry. Then I remembered my bride, whom I had not seen in two weeks, and I thought: "This isn't paradise . . . this is hell!"

Alone in paradise . . .

I've been to the Caribbean about four times on romantic vacations with my wife Susan. It's the closest thing I can think of to paradise. Yet without Susan, the Caribbean would just be a sandbox.

If I had traveled to the Caribbean when I was Conner's age, I would have liked it because I liked sandboxes when I was five (whether I was in Colorado or in the Caribbean). If Susan would have come with me, at age five, we might have even played together in the sand. But we would have had no concept of paradise.

We would have been in paradise but not at all *in* paradise or truly experiencing paradise. But that wouldn't be because we'd sinned; it would be because we were immature—not finished. We would have not yet had a capacity for paradise.

Adam is alone in paradise. Alone. Or is he?
Actually, Adam is in the very presence of God, who is love.
Adam is alone in the presence of Love.

I guess Adam can't conceive of Love, receive Love and commune in Love. Maybe he doesn't truly know Love, so he can't trust Love!

And that is NOT GOOD, for "God is Love."

Quoting a Greek Poet, Saint Paul wrote: *"In [God] we live, and move, and have our being"* (Acts 17:28). We literally swim in God, who is Love. So, are any of us truly alone? Be honest: do you ever feel lonely? I do.

So, if Scripture is right and I swim in God, who is Love, I must have something like a thick, fleshy skin surrounding my heart. So, although I swim in Love I don't feel Love, as if I'm surrounded by heaven and yet trapped by hell—trapped in an earthen vessel, incapable of I-contact.

Old Adam is surrounded by heaven, yet he is alone.
Jesus the New Adam said, *"The kingdom of heaven is at hand."* (Matt. 4:17)
So, why do I feel alone?

Lots of people want to go to Heaven. Moslem fundamentalists picture Heaven as a harem full of virgins; Christians tend to picture it as mansions and all-you-can-eat buffets.

My friend Andrew is an evangelist. After preaching the message he used to ask the crowd, "How many of you want to go to Heaven?" Recently he shared with me that he changed his invitation because of something my father asked him long ago. My father said, "Andrew, why would people want to go to Heaven?" What is Heaven: mansions, buffets, and virgins . . . or God? Now Andrew asks, "How many of you would like to know God and have a relationship with God?" Don't worry. I'm sure that Heaven is at least mansions, buffets, and very attractive women, but that's the sandbox. Paradise is communion with God: I-contact.

But I worry about us rich, American, consumer Christians. Do we even *want* God? Do we even want the good? For God is the good. And that brings up a fascinating question: How can Adam choose the good if he doesn't *know* the good or even *about* the good? And how is Adam to know the Good?

Genesis 2:18 *"Then the Lord God said, "It is not good that the man should be alone; I will make him a helper fit for him."*

"...A helper fit for him."

1. It's interesting to note that in Hebrew the word "helper " is a masculine noun.

2. It's also interesting to note that Adam is still a he/she . . . for where is she? She's hidden in he. And I'm "hidden in Christ." And maybe the "sexist language" of Scripture is more than we know.

   Whatever the case, women, do you see that this story has been about you all along? Eve is in Adam. And men, fasten your seat belts, for by the end of the Scriptures, we'll discover that we are all the Bride of the *Eschatos* Adam.

3. It's also interesting to note that this word "helper" (*ayzer*) almost always refers to God in Scripture. It occurs twenty-five times in the Psalms, and each time we're reminded, "God is our Helper" (Not Egypt, chariots, or horses—*God* is our helper.) Now God will help Adam find his helper.

   > **Genesis 2:18–19** *Then the Lord God said, "It is not good that the man should be alone; I will make him a helper fit for him." Now out of the ground the Lord God had formed every beast of the field and every bird of the heavens and brought them to the man to see what he would call them.*

I've gotta admit: I didn't see that one coming. Just when I expected a dating service, God conducts a biology lesson. He'll do something like this with Noah in chapter six and bring to him male and female, two by two. Well, what he asks of Adam seems a bit strange, but we have a name for it: taxonomy. Basically it's science. We could spend a good bit of time on this, but I hope you see that science is no threat to God; it's a commandment from God: "Name the animals. Study my creation." *"The heavens declare the glory of God, and the sky above proclaims his handiwork"* (Ps. 19:1).

People turn science into idolatry, worshipping and serving the "creature [or creation] rather than the creator" (Rom. 8:25), but that's nothing new. We shouldn't worship the creation, but we're commanded to read the creation. And, all the while, God is asking us this question: "Adam, who's your helper? Have you found a helper fit for you Adam?"

Now, if you are like me, you want to yell, "Come on God, just tell Adam! Tell me! Tell us all where to find help! Tell us who our helper is!" I mean, why doesn't God just write it in the sky? Why doesn't He just write it on a golden tablet that materializes on your bedroom floor? Why doesn't He just tell you?

Well, there are different ways of knowing and different things to be known. Hold that thought . . .

For now, let's continue with our text. But before we read it, I'd like to suggest a theory—I can't claim that this is verified in any detail by any ancient rabbinic sources—I conjecture that while God paraded the animals in front of Adam, He had a Cole Porter sound track playing in the background. It goes like this:

> And that's why birds do it, bees do it
> Even educated fleas do it
> Let's do it, let's fall in love...
>
> Penguins in flocks on the rocks do it.
> Cuckoos in the privacy of clocks do it.
> Let's do it, let's fall in love.
> —Cole Porter, "Let's Do it (Let's Fall in Love)"

Genesis 2:18–22 *Then the LORD God said, "It is not good that the man should be alone; I will make him a helper fit for him." Now out of the ground the LORD God had formed every beast of the field and every bird of the heavens and brought them to the man to see what he would call them. And whatever the man called every living creature, that was its name. The man gave names to all livestock and to the birds of the heavens and to every beast of the field.*

> *But for Adam there was not found a helper fit for him. So the*
> *Lord God caused a deep sleep to fall upon the man, and while he*
> *slept took one of his ribs and closed up its place with flesh. And*
> *the rib that the Lord God had taken from the man he made into*
> *a woman and brought her to the man.*

Now I must confess, none of the ancient rabbis knew anything about Cole Porter or had any of his soundtracks. However, they did write commentaries on Genesis. They wrote Midrash. In their exposition of Genesis 2 (*Bereshit Rabbah*)[1] the animals are pictured walking by Adam in pairs, and Adam comments: "Everything has its partner, and I have no partner." Meanwhile, God keeps asking: "Adam where's your partner? Who is your helper?"

Have you ever wondered why God made sex?

It didn't have to be this way. God could have arranged things so that you simply split in half like an amoeba or, maybe, grew a bud on your back. You sneeze. It pops off: "*Hey! It's Junior.*" He could have made it so you went to a class, filled out a form, and a baby would appear under a burning bush or something.

If you're into biology and worried about new genetic material from a combination of parents, He could have made it so we reproduced like fish. The gal leaves an egg; if the guy so desires, he drops of some seed—no mess, no hurt feelings or confusing attachments, just civic responsibility. A new generation raised, if need be, by an autonomous collective. He could've done that, but He didn't. He made sex.

Why such a messy, vulnerable, passionate, and painful procedure? Apart from fish, perhaps, He made a very sexy creation. He must have had a reason.

Years ago, my associate was preaching in our old building—with large plate glass windows right behind the pulpit that looked out on a field and the mountainside. He was preaching on Valentine's Day. It was a great word on intimacy, relationships, sex, and marriage. Aram didn't know it at the time, but right be-

---

[1] H. Freedman and I. Epstein trans., *Bereshit Rabbah* (London: Soncino Press, 1939) 135–146 "Then he paraded them again before him in pairs, [male and female]. Said he, 'Every one has a partner, yet I have none': thus, BUT FOR ADAM THERE WAS NOT FOUND A HELP MEET FOR HIM!"

hind him, through the window, as Aram was saying it, two deer were doing it! And everyone saw! It was such a lofty word made flesh for all to see. What does it mean? Haven't you ever wondered, "God, this is so bizarre: the pleasure, the passion, the shame, and this is where life is born? What does it mean?"

God brings the animals to Adam and asks a question. Do you hear the question?

> *Adam*, they're each male or female, each has a helper in their likeness through whom life is created—life through naked, intimate, vulnerable communion.
> *Adam* . . . who is your helper? In whose likeness are you?
> *Adam*, who longs to fill you and create through you?
> *Adam*, to whom will you cleave?
> *Adam*—humankind, who is your helper?
> *Adam*, can you see me, hear me, would you know *me*?
> Would you allow yourself to be known and loved by *me*?
> *Adam* could not find, he did not see or perceive, "*a helper fit for him.*"

So, God begins the great lesson. He puts Adam to sleep and takes a rib (or, in Hebrew, a "side"). He takes the side and fashions it into Eve. Adam had been one body, and now Adam is two—male and female. God brings the woman to the man.

> **Genesis 2:23-25** *Then the man said, "This at last is bone of my bones and flesh of my flesh; she shall be called Woman, because she was taken out of Man." Therefore a man shall leave his father and his mother and hold fast to his wife, and they shall become one flesh. And the man and his wife were both naked and were not ashamed.*

So, at last Adam has found his helper . . . or not.

> **Genesis 3:1** *Now the serpent was more crafty than any other beast of the field that the LORD God had made. He said to the*

> *woman, "Did God actually say, 'You shall not eat of any tree in*
> *the garden'?" –*

You know, she didn't turn out to be that great of a helper. So, did Adam find his helper? How could Eve be his helper? She's part of the one that needed help. Adam even said, "...*bone of my bones and flesh of my flesh*," that is, "she is me and me is she." So, God had asked both of them, "Man—male and female, who is your helper?"

The helper Adam got was more of himself; the helper Eve got was more of herself. "*Eve took the fruit from the tree and ate, and she gave some to her husband who was with her, and he ate*" (Gen. 3:6). Adam was there! And he didn't stop her. That's a lousy helper.

But now, let me remind you, Paul has been teaching us about an Old Adam and a New Adam. In Romans 5:14 he revealed that Adam (that Old Adam) was a *tupos*—a type, an imprint, a form of the one who was to come: the *Eschatos* Adam.

The Old Adam is like an empty place, like a womb. He's like a clay form or mold into which a sculptor pours molten bronze producing an eternal master-piece, while the earthen vessel is cut away and discarded. Old Adam is the place in which the *Eschatos* Adam will be revealed.

> So, Old Adam didn't stop Eve; he took the fruit just like Eve.
> He took Eve's sin at the tree because he was a bad helper.

But maybe there's another Adam that takes Eve's sin at the tree . . .
> Because He will "not leave her nor forsake her,"
> Because He wants to sacrifice His life for her,
> Because He wants to expire for her . . . and in-spire her,
> Because He wants to show her that He is her Helper.

Perhaps the Old Adam creates a longing in the Bride so that when she hears the New Adam cry, "*It is finished*," and she sees Him deliver up His Spirit, she drops at the base of the tree in the garden where He is crucified crying, "My Lord and my God . . . my Helper."

Well, that may be a new thought for you, and we'll have to explore it further, but for now, it's still day six. God is still asking: "Humankind, who's your helper?" Adams are looking for Eves, and Eves are looking for Adams, and we're all trying to find helpers. They are great blessings. . . like appetizers before a meal or signs on a highway. They're great blessings, but if by God's grace we find an adam or eve, they still fail, and sin, and grow old, and die, and don't fully fill the emptiness that gnaws at our insides.

It turns out that Adam is a lousy helper for Eve, and Eve is a lousy helper for Adam. Adam is Eve, and Eve is Adam, and we're just not good at helping ourselves or saving ourselves. And God is still asking the question: "Who's your helper?"

But now, He not only uses birds, bees, and penguins in flocks to ask the question. He uses our very bodies to ask the question and point to an answer. He doesn't write it in the sky—at least not with letters—or drop it in our bedrooms on tablets of gold. He writes it in our flesh.

He must really want us to *know*, in the most intimate of ways. He's saying: "Humankind—Adam, look at yourself. Contemplate every urge, every desire!" He's asking, "Don't you hate being alone? Are you ready to know and be known by Me—your Helper? I am *the* Good."

Throughout the Old Testament, God tells Israel, *"I am your helper,"*[2] *"For your maker is your husband. The LORD of hosts is his name"* (Isa. 54:5). And they have the hardest time hearing. It's like there's a skin over their ears . . . or hearts.

In the New Testament, we meet Jesus. The name Jesus means, "God is salvation" or *"Yahweh* is help." Jesus is the Word of God in human flesh—even I AM in a temple of flesh. God said, *"I will make a helper fit for him* (humankind)" (Gen. 2:18b). He did. We wrapped Him in swaddling clothes and laid Him in a manger.

- Jesus is the Helper (1 John 2:1), the *parakletos* in Greek.
- Do you know what *parakletos* means? "Called along side."
- Do you remember where we are made? At a tree in a garden. We are made from His wounded side—His body broken and blood shed.

---

[2] Psalm 32:30, 70:15, 115:9–11, 121:1–2, 146:5, Hosea 13:9 See also Ezekiel 16 and all of Hosea

- Do you remember what He told His disciples? *"Whoever has seen me has seen the Father… And I will ask the Father, and he will give you another Helper, to be with you forever"* (John 14:9,16). Father, Son and Holy Spirit, are all our Helper: eternal I-contact
- Jesus, the *Eschatos* Adam, is our husband, and we are His Bride.

> *"Therefore a man shall leave his father and mother and hold fast to his wife, and the two shall become one flesh." This mystery is profound, and I am saying that it refers to Christ and the church*
> —Ephesians 5:31–32

Remember all the Dan Brown, *Da Vinci Code* controversy about Jesus and Mary Magdalene? Well, they weren't totally off the mark. It turns out that Jesus is, and will be, married to a bride that was once a harlot and that Bride is us. But now, here in the sixth day, God is still asking Adam, He's asking you, "Who's your helper?"

So, why sexuality? Why not a-sexual reproduction, like amoebas and foraminifera? Why gender, and why marriage? Why the covenant of marriage and why failed marriages? Why the longing, frustrations, pain and shame? Why sexuality and broken sexuality? Why the glimpses of ecstasy that make you yearn for deeper and lasting ecstasy?

Paul tells us: It all *"refers to Christ and His Church"*—the Bride. In all these things, creation and desecration, good and evil, God is still asking, "Who's your helper?" "Who's your savior?" And He doesn't want you to answer with just some words. He wants you to answer with your whole being!

Thirty-five years ago, my wife Susan and I were both in high school and hadn't been dating for long. I brought her to youth group because she was smokin' hot, and I knew that I wasn't supposed to date non-Christians, so I wanted to make sure she was one. I wanted to go parking with her, so I needed to get her saved! (What an evangelist.)

She had learned about Jesus as a little girl, but she wasn't sure she wanted to know Jesus or be known *by* Jesus *now*. Late one night, during that first year that we were dating, she awoke from a sound sleep to see evil spirits surrounding her bed. A figure, darker than the night, appeared at the foot of the bed. It reached out its arms and said, "You're mine." It was all she could do to say the name

"Jesus." (She had learned about that at youth group.) Well, when she said the name, she heard a horrid scream and watched as all the evil shrank into a hole and disappeared. She rolled over and grabbed her Bible, opened it, and her eyes fell on this verse: Hebrews 13:5-6, *"He has said, 'I will never leave you nor forsake you.' So we can confidently say, 'The Lord is my helper.'"*

She read that verse and, immediately, prayed this prayer: "OK Jesus, you can come in." The prayer was more than just words. It was an answer to the ancient question. She answered, and is still answering, with her whole being.

To the extent that I'm a good helper, I teach my bride about Jesus.
To the extent that I'm a bad helper, I teach her to long for Jesus.

> *"This mystery is profound, and I am saying that it refers to Christ and the church"*
> —Ephesians 5:32

Have you seen those ads for "ChristianMingle.com," the Christian dating service? Their motto is "Find God's match for you." Well, God is God's match for you. And sexuality, male and female, was created to help you find Him, for He's always looking for you. No matter who you are, no matter what you've done or where you've been or what may be your fantasies, the Point is Him . . . and you.

I want to make that clear as we dig deeper into Genesis, sex, marriage and family. So, please note:

- We are all sexual beings: Whether you're eighteen and can't contain yourself or ninety and trying to remember, straight as an arrow or all your desires seem out of balance, never even been on a date or been married thirty years, we're all sexual beings, and our sexuality is the creation of God to help us know our Helper.
- We are all frustrated sexual beings: Why? Because we're still waiting for our Helper. Human sexuality is the sign but not the substance. We're frustrated by design . . . to nurture a longing for our Helper. If you think your husband or your wife is your *Helper*, you'll destroy him or her because you're expecting God, and they can't be God. But if you know they're not God, maybe you can worship God at the temple that is your spouse.

- We are all uncomfortable, frustrated, sexual beings: We're uncomfortable because we've all looked in the wrong places for our Helper. So, now we hide from the question; we cover our need in shame. We've looked in the wrong places or maybe looked in the wrong way.

As I mentioned, there are two ways of knowing:

1. We can *seize* control, like you seize fruit on a tree. But everything you know in that way is dead or will die. OR
2. We can *surrender* control, like a bride surrenders to her groom, like the Church surrenders to her Lord. To truly know Love, you must surrender to Love. If you seize love, control love, you crucify love and don't know love as Love. You only know a description of Love, like the law.

At the end of Genesis 2, the man and woman are naked and unashamed. By the end of Genesis 3, they're sowing fig-leaf underwear and hiding in the trees. The snake has tempted them to "help" themselves, tempted them to complete themselves by taking the knowledge of good and evil. He's tempted them to help themselves—not by knowing the Good, but by taking knowledge of the Good. Now they hide their need, for they've chosen control; their need feels like shame. So, they hide their need and hide from the question, "Who's my helper?"

Our old Adam loves control. Our flesh loves control (or *is* control): It is dirt trying to create itself in the image of God with more dirt and maybe some fig leaves. It's like a thick skin grown over our ears and around our hearts that makes us insensitive, that keeps us from being known and knowing in return; it keeps our spirit locked inside our earthen vessel; it keeps us from I-contact.

Now if you think I'm exaggerating the biblical implications of our sexuality, I'd remind you of Genesis 17 and the sign of the covenant. In Genesis 17, God promises to bless a man named Abraham and his seed. Then God says to Abraham,

> *This is my covenant, which you shall keep, between me and you and your offspring after you: Every male among you shall be circumcised. You shall be circumcised in the flesh of your foreskins,*

[you shall cut the skin off of the tip of that thing that Conner Harris mentioned at the ballet] *and it shall be a sign of the covenant between me and you.*

—Genesis 17:10–11

We don't know exactly what Abraham thought at that point, but I bet it was something like this:

Um . . . couldn't we just wear T-shirts? Couldn't we just memorize a list and take an oath? Couldn't we just build you some buildings and start some program? Maybe we could start a school and get some knowledge of good and evil, make some lists and learn some principles or something. Anything but that! That's sensitive! That's private! That's uncomfortable! That's personal . . .

For four thousand years, we've been saying the same thing: "God, I'd like to know *about* you, but I'm terrified to *know* you or let you know me—let you touch me . . . there."

Moses told the Israelites to circumcise the "*foreskin of* [their] *hearts, and be no longer be stubborn*" (Deut. 10:16). Jeremiah prophesied saying: "*Circumcise yourselves to the Lord; remove the foreskin of your hearts*" (Jer. 4:4). . . . How do you do that?

"*And the Lord your God will circumcise your heart and the heart of your off-spring, so that you will love the Lord your God with all your heart and with all your soul, that you may live*" (Deut. 30:6). Life is I-contact, *perichoresis*, the Great Dance. So God will circumcise your heart. . . . How does He do that?

Saint Paul writes:

You were circumcised with a circumcision made without hands, by putting off the body of the flesh, by the circumcision of Christ, having been buried with him in baptism, in which you were also raised with him through faith in the powerful working of God, who raised him from the dead. And you, who were dead in your trespasses and the uncircumcision of your flesh, God made alive together with him, having forgiven us all our trespasses, by canceling the record of debt that stood against us with its legal demands.

—Colossians 2:13–14

Bride of Christ, have you been to the cross and seen the *Eschatos* Adam hanging on the tree? It does something to you, doesn't it?

- It cuts away your arrogance and pride. It breaks your earthen vessel.
- It reveals the heart of God: Jesus *"from the bosom of the father."*[3]
- He surrenders His Spirit. You inspire then expire yours.
- It feels like death, but it's the beginning of Life: I-contact.
- You don't just know about God. You know God.
- Adam–humanity: who is your helper?

. . . Just look at that wound in His side.

But when they came to Jesus and saw that he was already dead, they did not break his legs. But one of the soldiers pierced his side with a spear, and at once there came out blood and water. . . . When he had said this, he showed them his hands and his side. Then the disciples were glad when they saw the Lord. Jesus said to them again, "Peace be with you. As the Father has sent me, even so I am sending you." And when he had said this, he breathed on them and said to them, "Receive the Holy Spirit."

—*John 19:33–34, 20:20–22*

This spiritual intercourse with God is the ecstasy hinted at in all earthly intercourse, physical or spiritual. It is the ultimate reason why sexual passion is so strong, so different from other passions, so heavy with suggestions of profound meanings that just elude our grasp.

—*Peter Kreeft, Everything You Wanted to Know About Heaven*

---

[3] John 1:18 RSV

CHAPTER 7

Warm Bodies in a Cold War

Genesis 2:18–25

I grew up during the Cold War. It was the Cold War abroad, and it was the "Cold War" at South Elementary School in Littleton, Colorado. Along with Field Day, the very worst day for me was Valentine's Day. Talk about stress! It was worse than the Cuban Missile Crisis. For an entire week before that dreaded day, we would each work frantically preparing our valentine receptacles: shoe boxes with rubber cement, construction paper, glitter, and bright plumage attached to the outside of each receptacle to attract valentines.

We set them on the windowsill next to the playground, and for ten agonizing minutes, we distributed our valentines. I'm sure some teacher reminded us it was about giving, but we all knew that was just a line. It was all about *getting* valentines. It was survival of the fittest—"the will to power" (Nietzsche).

So, if you gave a valentine to some girl, for instance, and she didn't give one to you, it was a crisis. Why? Because you just exposed a weakness for her that was not reciprocated by an equal and opposite weakness. All at once, she was in a position of power in a Cold War situation. You might as well just fall at her feet crying: "I'm not worthy! Please don't flaunt your full valentine receptacle over mine—so light, so empty, so void of cards and candy hearts, save for one cowboy valentine from Mrs. Black saying, 'Howdy, Partner'!"

There should be a law: "Every child will receive the exact same number of valentines, and every valentine will be exactly the same—*no differences.*" Otherwise, folks get crucified. That's the danger of love in this fallen world. That's the danger of acknowledged differences in a Cold War situation. That's the danger of revealed weaknesses. They destroy the balance of power and folks get crucified.

The Cold War was all about a balance of power. Our government is constructed to maintain a balance of power. Democracy is a balance of power. The U. S. Declaration of Independence states: "We hold these truths to be self-evident, that all men are created equal." Yet, if anything is *not* self-evident I would think it would be that. I mean, some men are created short and some tall. Some men have low IQ's; some men have high IQ's. Some have low EQ's; some have high EQ's. It appears that God created them that way—unequal. So, it's really not self-evident that all are created equal or even that all should be allowed to vote. Indeed, the founders wouldn't let minorities, slaves, and women vote. Maybe minorities, slaves, and women should be the only ones allowed to vote.

Now, some of you are a bit stressed because I'm messing with the balance of power in a Cold War situation. So, let me say this: I'm very grateful for the system of government in the United States of America. It may be the very best system of secular governance in a fallen world where power needs to be balanced between sinners for the good of the whole. However, it is not "self-evident that all men are created equal," especially if by equal we mean the same.

The Bible *does* teach that each person has equal value, for each person is the breath of God. Each person is equally loved by God, that is, loved with all He has and is. However, the Bible is pretty clear that we're each different. The same breath fills unique and different earthen vessels taking the form of each of those vessels. Scripture teaches that we're equally loved but each unique and very different. And although it feels like a curse in this place, it will be revealed as a blessing in another place. But now we're in this place . . . So, in fear we legislate equality.

Even so, there is one fundamental difference that's pretty tough to completely legislate away.

> **Genesis 1:27–28a** *So God created man in his own image, in the image of God he created him; male and female he created them. And God blessed them.*

People come in two very distinct models, and God blessed the difference. Yet, so often it feels like a curse. I mean, it's difficult to think of anything that has produced more pain than the difference between men and women. Men have objectified, abused, and raped women for ages. But women have also raped men. Their weapon may not be physical strength, but there are other types of strength that may be far subtler and even more painful.

Whatever the case, pain is like a "sexually-transmitted reality"—an STR. So, it only makes sense that we would do all that we could to eliminate the differences and balance the power.

In modern society, we've done a pretty "bang up" job. Nowadays, males probably have the most reason to feel inferior. Women can do just about everything men can do . . . but men can't have babies. About the only thing men can do that women can't is go potty standing up.

When my daughter Elizabeth was a toddler, she used to stand in front of the toilet throwing tantrums and making a terrible mess because she couldn't get her plumbing to work like her older brother, Jon. Yet, her plumbing is designed to make babies. She couldn't see it at the time, but making babies is an even more amazing ability than writing your name in the snow (The great benefit to going potty standing up, here in Colorado).

About a year ago, my twenty-four-year-old daughter, Elizabeth, was watching home videos with her boyfriend in our TV room when I heard all this laughter. Elizabeth came running up to my office and said, "Dad, you've got to see this! This explains everything."

They were watching a video that I took one afternoon in our backyard in Danville, California back in 1992. The kids were just playing on the grass in the backyard when my son, Jonathan, who is just a year older than Elizabeth, said, "Daddy, I have to go pee pee." Well, being the lazy guy that I am; and being rather proud of my masculine abilities; and having just trained Jonathan in those abilities; and realizing that what I was about to say frustrated my wife, I said, "Go pee pee in the grass." He did, and I congratulated him for a job well done.

At that, Elizabeth said, "I have to go pee." The camera panned to my daughter, still in diapers, trying to get things to work like they did for her brother. You could hear my wife, Susan, obviously perturbed, talking through the window, "You can come inside and go pee pee." Elizabeth was distraught . . .

Meanwhile, you could hear me apologizing: "Elizabeth...honey...I'm sorry, it won't work that way. But Sweetie, you have special parts that can do special things, too."

The video ends with Elizabeth looking up at the camera with a look on her face that said, "Daddy, where is it, and how do I get one?" Now, please understand: I'm not just trying to be crass. I mean it when I say, "*That* is a profound and fascinating question!"

"How do I get one?"

Well, I suppose a person could just *take* one, Lorena Bobbitt style. If you don't remember the story, she used a knife. "*Take* one"—but once taken, it wouldn't work well. But that is one strategy: just yank the fruit from the tree.

Sigmund Freud argued that all little boys suffer from castration anxiety, and all little girls must deal with penis envy. Maybe Freud was on to something, but it doesn't only work in one direction.

It must have been some time around the sixth grade: I remember thinking, "Wow! Breasts are good. I wish I had breasts. If I had breasts, I'd just stare at them all day." But then I thought, "Maybe not because if I had them I might not enjoy them, at least not in the same way."

So, how could I "know" breasts? Remember, there are different ways of knowing. How could I know them? I could just *take* them. Men do that. They just take fruit from the tree; we call it rape. They want to "know the good" but they end up "knowing evil." They take life, but know death. And we have to enact all sorts of legislation to protect people's "privates" and balance the power.

Now, modern science has even learned how to reroute plumbing such that women can get an operation and write their name in the snow. Men can grow breasts, and they're working on the men having babies dilemma. You see, we've told ourselves that sexual differences are only plumbing-deep. So, all the valentines are really just the same.

And when that doesn't work, we tell ourselves, "If you don't like what you've got, you can just *take* that of another. That's how you get what you don't have. You don't need a helper; you just help yourself." Now please hear me, I'm not trying to shame anyone, I'd just like everyone to ponder this question: Are the differences between us a curse or a blessing?

It's clear that the safest possible world would be an entire world without gender—without any diversity at all for that matter. We've done it in church with gender-neutral Bibles, non-gender specific theology, and the elimination of gender roles in ecclesiastical structures. It makes some sense, but it's still confusing.

I think my worst day in seminary was one particular day in 1985—Cecil M. Robeck's class on pastoral theology. We were talking about the roles of men and women in the family and church. I just raised my hand and asked a question, something like: "I don't think I hate women; I just don't understand how you reconcile what you're saying with 1 Timothy 2:11-13." I'm still a bit confused about that, but what happened next was like World War III. It was apocalyptic.

Professor Robeck didn't answer my question. He just invited comment. A plethora of young female seminarians stood up and just ripped into me for about a half-hour. It was clear that there had been a great deal of abuse and pain—clear that I was questioning the balance of power in a Cold War situation. Then this guy—whom I'm convinced just wanted a date—got up and apologized to all the women on my behalf. Then Professor Roebeck ended the discussion.

But nobody addressed the question: "What do we do with 1 Timothy 2:11-13?"

> *Let a woman learn quietly with all submissiveness. I do not permit a woman to teach or to exercise authority over a man; rather, she is to remain quiet* (literally: "to be in tranquility"). *For Adam was formed first, then Eve; and Adam was not deceived, but the woman was deceived and became a transgressor. Yet she* (singular) *will be saved through childbearing—if they* (plural) *continue in faith and love and holiness, with self-control.*
>
> —1 Timothy 2:11–13

I don't care who you are, that just seems like a really bizarre thing to say. Clearly there is a cultural element to this. But Paul mentions Adam and Eve, who basically had no culture. And wasn't Adam deceived? I'm pretty sure that just about every adam I've ever met has been deceived. And does Paul really mean to say that unless females give birth they aren't saved? That flies in the face of everything else he wrote!

152 | God and His Sexy Body

Paul wrote stuff like this as well:

> *...In Christ Jesus you are all sons of God, through faith. For as*
> *many of you as were baptized into Christ have put on Christ.*
> *There is neither Jew nor Greek, there is neither slave nor free,*
> *there is no male and female, for you are all one in Christ Jesus.*
>
> —Galatians 3:26–28

That's a bit troubling, too: If you get baptized, do you lose your genitals . . . or gain some? When Jesus rose from the dead, was He still a dude? Does everyone in Heaven get neutered upon entry?

And what is the difference between male and female? Is it simply an issue of plumbing? The Bible never really spells that out. In 1 Timothy and 1 Corinthians, Paul seems to say that women shouldn't ask questions in church. Yet in other places, sometimes the same places (1 Cor. 14:26, 34), he seems to tell them to speak. Some argue that someone else has been tampering with the Bible. Some argue that the translations are poor. Some argue that Paul was a butthead. It's clear there are cultural issues. Paul even commands us to judge for ourselves (1Cor. 11:13). So . . . what do you think it all means?

In some places in Scripture, women certainly instruct men (Acts 18:26), start churches (Acts 16:14,40), and even prophesy, judge and lead a nation under God's command (Judges 4 and 5). In the Gospels, women not only fund Jesus and the church (Luke 8:3), but it's like they *are* the Church—and not the messed up church, the perfected Church—that does the "*beautiful thing*" (Matt. 26:10, Mark 14:6), that comes first to the *Eschatos* Adam, risen form the dead, in the garden, (John 20:11-18, Matt. 28:9, Mark 16:9, Luke 24:10). It really is remarkable that, in the Gospels, women in the vicinity of Jesus can seem to do no wrong.

So, what's the difference? It's not very clear. I have two associate pastors, and they're both women and extremely gifted and extremely female. But what's the difference? In Ephesians, in reference to marriage and our text from Genesis, Paul writes, "*The husband is the head of the wife*" (Eph. 5:23). The Greek philosopher, Maria Portokalos in the popular movie, *My Big Fat Greek Wedding*, explains this verse to her daughter saying, "Let me tell you something, Toula. The man is the head, but the woman is the neck. And *she* can turn the head any way she wants." So, what is "headship?" You'll be hard pressed to find a legal definition in Scripture or some detailed list. The Bible never seems to spell it out. Maybe we can't define it—but we can "know it," for there are different ways of "knowing."

But now, before we go any further, let me clarify: I didn't write the Bible. And I'm still confused by many of these questions. But God seems to be okay with all these questions. In fact, it appears as if He's responsible for the war. I mean: He made us male and female. And the differences are not shallow but deep. And the differences are not simple but subtle. And the different roles referred to in Scripture for men and women, husbands and wives, are not clear but highly debatable. It's like God set us up. Now we're in a war. And the war is so cold that, at times, we can barely even talk about it.

But this is the strangest thing about our cold war. Henry Kissinger said it best (the great statesman with so much experience negotiating disputes during the Cold War): "I am convinced that no one will win the war between the sexes, for there is far too much fraternizing with the enemy."[1]

That's so true! My greatest wars have been with a female named Susan. And we'll fight over things that are invariably related to our gender. At times, I'll become deeply offended at her female perspective and conclusions—sometimes even jealous of how she's able to arrive at those conclusions. And then we will go to war, and often the war will grow cold. We won't talk. We won't connect.

Yet, along about the third day, I won't be able to maintain my resolve, for I'll find myself overwhelmed with this intense desire to go fraternize with the enemy. And then, not only do our gender differences appear to be less of a problem, but those differences actually become the attraction. The very thing that offended me becomes the very thing that utterly captivates me.

C. S. Lewis wrote:

> Have as much equality as you please–the more the better–in our marriage laws: but at some level consent to inequality, nay, delight in inequality, it is an erotic necessity.[2]

---

[1]   Michael Hodgin *1001 Humorous Illustrations for Public Speaking*, (Grand Rapids, MI: Zondervan, 1994) 328.

[2]   C.S. Lewis *The Quotable Lewis*, editors Wayne Martindale and Jerry Root (Wheaton, IL: Tyndale, 1989) 184.

Pain is sexually transmitted, but *ecstasy* is also sexually transmitted. *Life* is sexually transmitted. *You* have been sexually transmitted—an STR. Isn't that strange?

Different valentines—blatant inequality—fraternizing with the enemy, warm bodies and hot sex in the midst of a cold war, which produces life: Who would have thought of such a thing? It's almost as if it were a sign from another world or *for* another world.

If no one wins the war between the sexes . . .

If no one wins . . . that means all surrender.

Maybe it's an erotic, ecstatic necessity.

Well, Elizabeth pointed at the TV and said, "This explains everything," as she sat on the couch fraternizing with the enemy. You know, I kind of hope this boyfriend is the one, and if he is . . . well, there won't be anything left for Elizabeth to envy.

> **Genesis 2:18–22** *Then the LORD God said, "It is not good that the [adam] should be alone; I will make him a helper fit for him." Now out of the ground the Lord God had formed every beast of the field and every bird of the heavens and brought them to the man to see what he would call them. And whatever the man called every living creature, that was its name. The man gave names to all livestock and to the birds of the heavens and to every beast of the field. But for Adam there was not found a helper fit for him. So the Lord God caused a deep sleep to fall upon the [adam], and while he slept took one of his ribs and closed up its place with flesh. And the rib that the Lord God had taken from the man he made into a woman and brought her to the man [the Adam].*

Remember that Jesus is the *Eschatos* Adam, and we are His Bride, who will be presented to Him in splendor (Eph. 5:27). We are created at His wounded side with body broken and blood shed and His own Spirit delivered up in expiration.

God "brought her to the Adam."

Genesis 2:23–24 *Then the man said, "This at last is bone of my bones and flesh of my flesh; she shall be called Woman, because she was taken out of Man." Therefore a man shall leave his father and his mother and hold fast to his wife, and they shall become one flesh.*

Adam (humankind) had been incomplete without his helper. God has divided Adam into two parts that become one. He's still incomplete, but he's learning how two can become one.

When the two parts become one body, they join together in a very specific place with very specific organs designed to connect the depths of their being. That's I-contact. The organs (especially on him) look like internal organs on the outside of the body.

Picture Adam: so muscular, sleek, and well-proportioned—his body makes sense . . . but what's *that* doing there? It looks like it should be on the inside, not on the outside. And think of Eve! She has a place on the inside for what's on Adam's outside. He has a part she does not have, and she has a part he does not have. It is their inequality and their difference. In that one place, his fullness fits her emptiness. And the two become one flesh.

My wife is my own body. And it's just as Adam said, "...*bone of my bone and flesh of my flesh.*" *She* is *me*, and *me* is *she*. He wanted *she* because *she* was *he*—his own body. In seventh grade, I realized that breasts are good, and I wanted some. And, of course I did; they are my own body.

On May 28, 1983, they became mine.

Now, I let Susan wear them, but they're my own body. And now, not only are Susan's breasts my own body, but so are Susan's feet, her hands, her eyes, her heart, and her gifts.[3] And you know, sometimes when she aches, I think I kind of start to ache. When she feels good, I feel better.

I wanted my own body. Does Jesus have a body?

According to our text, the two that become one started out as one—one body. So, of course two-year-old Elizabeth was frustrated and confused. According to both Paul and the book of Genesis, she just realized that she was missing part of her own body. How is she going to get it back? If she marries her boyfriend, she will get it back, and *"the two shall become one flesh."*[4] And if she ever divorces her husband, it's not just severing that part—it's severing her heart. No wonder God hates divorce.

"...and they shall become one flesh."

In many places, Paul talks as if our "flesh" is a bad thing, but maybe that's not because it's a physical thing, but because it's a separated thing. My flesh only feels its own pleasure and its own pain. I eat a cheeseburger, and you do not taste it. You eat a cheeseburger, and I do not taste it. Maybe the problem with my flesh is that it is cut off from all other flesh, incapable of *perichoresis*, unable to commune, unable to join the dance that is Love. It needs to be circumcised; a portion needs to be cut off and, in that place, joined to another. My flesh only feels for itself.

But when two become one flesh, when I cleave to my wife in intimate communion, there is a moment when her pleasure is literally my pleasure . . . like she eats a cheeseburger, and I taste it. Maybe the problem with flesh is not that it feels a little pleasure, but that it only feels its own pleasure—that it only helps it-

---

[3] Once I complained to God about how He had gifted my wife with certain spiritual gifts that I've always wanted. He gifted her in a way He hadn't gifted me. And this thought entered my head: "Hey Peter she has breasts and you don't . . . yet you do . . . and you seem to like that arrangement. Maybe she's strong where you're weak so you'll both be strong and know My joy." I enjoy our body.

[4] We'll discuss just what it is that constitutes marriage in chapters to come. It's not a piece of paper that you can get from the county judge.

self. But in the moment when bride and groom cleave to each other in intimate communion, they help each other and feel ecstasy.

Adam and Eve help each other, and the two become one flesh. "*...as it is written,*" writes Paul, " '*The two will become one flesh.*' But he who is joined to the Lord becomes one spirit with him" (1 Cor. 6:16-17). Adam and Eve help each other, but that help is a sign and not the substance. The substance belongs to Christ, for God is our Helper.

> *In the same way husbands should love their wives as their own bodies. He who loves his wife loves himself. For no man ever hated his own flesh, but nourishes and cherishes it, just as Christ does the church, because we are members of his body. 'Therefore a man shall leave his father and mother and hold fast to his wife, and the two shall become one flesh.' This mystery is profound, and I am saying that it refers to Christ and the church.*
> —Ephesians 5: 30–31

Jesus is our Helper.

Back to Genesis:

> **Genesis 2:25** *"And the man and his wife were both naked and were not ashamed."*

This is a very sexy creation. "Not ashamed"—that's sexy.

But now, what would they be ashamed of?

Well, where is it that we feel shame? And what do we cover?

- We cover that point where our difference is exposed.
- We cover that point that reveals our need and incompleteness.
- We cover that place where we are unequal and thus vulnerable to pain and the abuse of power.
- We cover that place that is connected to our heart.
- We cover that place that manifests the deep sexuality that is encoded within every cell in our body.
- We cover that place where bride and groom make I-contact.

- We cover that place of communion.
- We cover that point where diversity becomes unity in the image of God.
- We cover that point where two become one and produce life.
- We cover that point where Adam enters the bride—his temple—his body—and gives her his seed, and she bears fruit that is life: love, joy, peace, patience, kindness, goodness, gentleness, faithfulness, self-control.

We cover *that*. We cover the difference.

The theologian Emil Bruner wrote, "The physical differences between the man and the woman are a parable of the physical and spiritual differences of a more ultimate nature."[5] One fills, and the other is filled. One refers to Christ, and the other refers to His Bride. We cover *that*.

But Adam and Eve were both *"naked and unashamed."* In fact, they were rejoicing in their differences,—not threatened or offended by the difference, but rejoicing in the difference. Indeed, they were rejoicing in their individual need for the other's individual difference. Unashamed and needy: that's an incredibly sexy creation!

Bride of Christ, realize that you need your Groom, and you shouldn't be ashamed of that fact. Sin is not needing God, your Helper; sin is denying that you need God, your Helper. Sin is knowing that you need yet denying that you need. Sin is hiding your nakedness from Him and being offended at His love for you.

Well, God made a very sexy creation, and Satan plotted to produce a very sex*less* desecration. He hates diversity. He especially hates diversity in unity; he hates *perichoresis*; he hates love.

So, he tempts Eve to help herself: "Take from the tree of the knowledge of good and evil. Make yourself in the image of God. Complete yourself with knowledge of the Good, knowledge you take, knowledge you control, knowledge of the good to make yourself good."

---

[5]   Emil Bruner, *Das Gebel und die Ordungen* (Tuebingeni J.C.B. Mohr, 1933), 358. *cited in* Larry Crabb *Men and Women, Enjoying the Difference* (Grand Rapids, MI: Zondervan, 1991), 151.

Jesus said, *"No one is good except God alone"* (Mark 10:18), and *"I and the Father are one...whoever has seen me has seen the Father"* (John 10:30, 14:9). Jesus was "the Good" in flesh.

- In the garden, Eve saw the Good hanging on a tree, and she was tempted to take the Good to make herself Good, in the image of God.
- In a garden in Jerusalem, the leaders of Israel saw the Good and hung Him on a tree. They were trying to take the Good to make themselves Good—to make themselves God. They had "Jesus envy" (Mark 15:10).
- I see the Good and try to take the Good to make myself Good, but I kill the Good and make myself bad. I see Love and try to take Love to make myself Love, but I crucify Love, incapable of Love; I see Love and turn Him into law, and everything dies.
- I see Jesus . . .

There are different ways of knowing and being known.[6]

Well, as I was saying, the devil tempted Eve, and she ate. And Adam, who was with her, also ate. Then they covered their differences with leaves from the tree—I presume it was the tree of law, the tree of the knowledge of good and evil. They covered their need and hid themselves . . . in the trees.

They cover *that* part, and they *should* cover that part, because for the first time they feel fear, shame, self-consciousness, and envy—they've become takers rather than receivers and givers. They will abuse revealed weakness in a Cold War situation. Valentine's Day will be all about consuming valentines and not exchanging valentines. It will be about *lust* rather than love. They hide *that* part, and they *should* hide that part. It needs to be protected with leather, skin, and law.

It must have been the greatest sorrow for God as He slaughtered an animal (I bet it was a lamb). He slaughtered an animal and used its skin to make clothes

---

[6]   If I think that I can *take* Jesus, according to the law in the power of my own flesh; if I think that I can create me, using Him; if I subordinate Him to me . . . I crucify Him and create a lie about me: the old man. I know *about* him, but I don't *know* Him.
But if I *receive* Jesus by faith through Grace—which is surrender . . . I become His Bride, His body, His temple. His life is my life. His will is my will. I'm finished in the image of God: the new man. I know Him. (We'll discuss this much more in book 3).

to cover their nakedness, which had now become shame; the blessing now felt like a curse—a point of weakness in a Cold War situation.

Now we cover *those* parts, and we *should* cover those parts . . . except in one situation: the covenant of marriage. It's almost like marriage is to be a walled garden in a fallen and cold world—a sanctuary bound by a covenant where two people can experience communion and, if for only a moment, taste the ecstatic relationship of another world and long for another world, even *yearn* for the Helper. For no human being is *the* Helper. They are only helpers to help you taste, but they will fail; they are helpers to help you look for, and recognize, *the* Helper.

Do you see?

God knew what would happen before He made Adam male and female. He knew that Adam (that's us) would fall before we fell because He's omniscient, and because Adam was "alone" in the presence of Love—he didn't know his Helper.

We know God knew because male and female is the story of Christ and His Bride: *"For this reason a man shall leave his father and mother and cleave to his wife. This mystery is a profound one, and I am saying it refers to Christ and the Church."* Christ was crucified *by* the Church—it was our sin that put Him there—and crucified *for* the Church. For us, He willingly died. Male and female is the story of Christ and His Church.

In 1 Timothy, Paul writes, *"Adam was not deceived."* Well, he couldn't have meant any of us adams, for Paul taught that all adams had sinned. He could only mean the *Eschatos* Adam, Jesus. The moment we sin, Jesus decides to bear our sin. He takes the fruit from the woman (Gen. 3:6), for *"He will not leave us nor forsake us"* (Heb. 13:5). He *"takes away the sin of the world"* (John 1:29). He bears *"the sins of the whole world"* (1 John 2:2) because He wants to. He is our Helper.

Male and female is the story of Christ and His Bride; it's the Gospel written in our flesh, from the dawn of time and from the day you were born. God knew what would happen, and God predestined that it would happen. Jesus Christ and Him crucified is no accident; it's God's very precedent—His judgment from the foundation of the world.

God knew about the "cold war" and even arranged for it, that we might see how He ends the war and fall in love with His Judgment. God arranged for it, that we might fall in love with His judgment, not threatened by His Judgment, but romanced by His Judgment.

He set it all up, that we might willingly receive His Valentine in the receptacle that is our heart, that we might recognize our Helper.

> *Now is the judgment of this world; now will the ruler of this world be cast out. And I, when I am lifted up from the earth, will draw all people to myself." He said this to show by what kind of death he was going to die.*
>
> —John 12:31–33

Chad Thompson was like me, so Valentine's Day was usually hard for Chad. His mother, Ruth Ann, was a friend of mine in California, and she told me the story. One year, Chad came to Ruth Ann and said, "This year, Mommy, I want to give a valentine to every kid in my class." That really troubled Ruth Ann because Chad wasn't popular, and she knew the gift wouldn't be reciprocated, but she helped him anyway. Together, they worked hard on each one, so a bit of Chad went into each one.

On Valentine's Day, she waited for him with a knot in her stomach. She had prepared a plate of cookies anticipating a little boy with a broken heart. When the bus arrived, she watched intently as children got off the bus, laughing and playing. Then . . . her heart sank. As always, Chad was in the back by himself. His hands were empty (not a note, not a scrap). Tears came to her eyes as she ran out to meet him. Chad saw her and exclaimed: "Not a one mom, not a one." He smiled and said, "Mommy, I didn't miss a one."

When Jesus, our Lord, ascended from the garden in which we had crucified Him on the tree, I picture the Father waiting like Ruth Ann waited at the bus stop for Chad. He sees Jesus—fresh wounds from nails driven through His feet and hands, a tremendous gash in His side. The Father runs to embrace Him. Jesus exclaims, "Not a one Father, not a one. I didn't miss a one. I died for them all—the sins of the whole world. I breathed our breath into them, and I gave each my gift of flesh and blood, fashioned to fit each and every wound."

> Do you see the difference? He has made Himself last of all and slave of all, subordinate to all . . . in Love.

Do you see the difference? He's like you, yet different than you.

He is steadfast Love that *never* ceases and Mercy that *never* comes to an end. He is the Faithful One.

And you are not. That's why He scares you. That's why you fear Him. Not because His Love may end, but because it does not end, not at the border of Israel, not at the doors of the church, not at the end of time.

That's why He scares you, and that's why He scared them two thousand years ago.

That's why we took His Life in a garden on a tree.
And that's why He gave His Life in the same garden on the same tree.

He is Faithful Love, and we are not.
And yet, we will be.
He is our Helper.

In 1 Timothy, Paul wrote: "...*Adam was not deceived, but the woman was deceived and became a transgressor. Yet she will be saved through childbearing...*" We are all saved through childbearing: It's the seed of the woman that crushes the head of the snake (Gen. 3:15). We, the Church, give birth to Christ in this world (Matt. 12:46, Rev. 12:5). Paul writes to the Galatians, "*I am again in the anguish of childbirth until Christ is formed in you!*" (Gal. 3:19). Get that? We're all giving birth to fruit—fruit of His Spirit—faithful Love, and God is Love. Of course, the woman (singular), that is us (plural), will be saved through childbearing. We give birth to Christ in this world.

Christ is the Ultimate Adam, and we are His Bride and even His mother. Men play one role in that drama, and women play another. If you're a woman, you might say: "That's a bad deal; men are Jesus?" NO! Men are supposed to be *like* Jesus.

Sometimes I preach, and I think: "Wow, it must be such a privilege to be a woman. Something in her is made to receive Jesus, the Groom, and experience ecstatic communion with Him." Sometimes I preach and think, "It's an honor to be a woman." And sometimes I think, "It's an honor to be a man—to imitate Jesus and share in the fellowship of His sufferings."

It's a privilege to be feminine and a privilege to be masculine. Yet, on a deeper level, we're all feminine, for we are all His Bride, and maybe we're all masculine, for we're all His Body at work in this world.

And we will all be His Body in consummated ecstasy. Susan and I are one body, neither male nor female, but both. I'm sorry if I'm freaking you out, but we will all be one body. We will have "*put on Christ*" (Gal. 3:28), and we will all be "*one in Christ Jesus*" (Gal. 3:29).

And if you're still wondering what headship is, Paul makes it clear in Ephesians that it's not simply some principles we could follow or some laws we could obey. It's more like a person we could know or be known by:

> *In him we have redemption through his blood, the forgiveness of our trespasses, according to the riches of his grace...as a plan for the fullness of time, to unite (anakepahlaiomai – bring together under one wounded head) all things in him, things in heaven and things on earth... And he put all things under his feet and gave him as head over all things to the church, which is his body, the fullness of him who fills all in all.*
> —Ephesians 1:7, 10, 22–23

Jesus said, "*If anyone would be first, he must be last of all and servant of all*" (Mark 9:35). Jesus is the first at choosing to be last. The Head leads by subordinating Himself to the beloved in sacrificial love. That's biblical headship. That's the beginning of the Great Dance; that's the revelation of Love.

Without Christ, this whole world is hiding their differences in shame. This whole world is trapped in a cold war. No one truly gives valentines, so no one truly receives valentines. There is no expiration and inspiration, no respiration, no life.

But Jesus was bound and determined to fraternize with His enemies. He is the warm body, broken for you and bleeding for you in this cold war. He is Holy. That means "very different." But don't be afraid to invite Him in. We are afraid of Love, but if we submit to Love, we will be filled with Love, give birth to Love, and perfect Love will cast out fear.

The cold war will turn into a raging party—actually a wedding banquet.

*   *   *

Imagine this:

You're there. You're in the crowd. He's about thirty feet in front of you. They have Him hanging only a few feet above the ground so people can spit on Him and mock Him. He's been a threat, and now the establishment is balancing the power. He is exposed in weakness. His weakness is love.

The hatred for Him is utterly intense. You feel it, too. Confess it. In other words, confess your sin. Maybe it's someone you haven't forgiven. Maybe it's envy, resentment, anxiety, or fear. Maybe it's lust, adultery, or refusal to feel. Whatever it is . . . think of it. Confess it. Now hold out your hand.

A thick, black nail materializes in your hand. It's your sin. No sooner than it does, someone grabs the nail. It's a Roman soldier. He walks to the cross and drives it through Jesus' flesh into the wood as he yells, "Go to hell, king of the Jews!"

Now, please understand that this is not something that may happen. This is something that has already happened.

The sky grows black; the earth shakes.

Any balance of power is an illusion. It's all His.

But there He is, covered in spit, blood, and open wounds.

He lifts His head, and His eyes lock on yours. Don't look away.

His eyes burn like fire, but don't look away.

You watch His lips as they form these words: "I love you."

That's the difference.

Are you offended? When we first see the Truth, it feels like a pit in the stomach. It's shame. You can hide there, and then I believe it's called hell. You can hide your shame, or you can surrender your shame so that He might fill you—the emptiness that is you. He longs to fill you. And when He does, what appeared to be an offense will become an ecstatic blessing. It begins here and even now.

Pray, "Jesus, I confess myself, and I call upon you, my Helper."

He is the Helper fit for you.
See? God has made "a Helper fit for you"—Himself!

Unlikeness makes one feel strange or endangered—"different" to the point of alienation. At the least, unlikeness draws pity or snorts of scorn or blank, uncomprehending looks. Therefore, the partners strive to seem the same. They dress themselves in "like" opinions, in "like" habits, in "like" tastes and goals—but at bottom this sort of sameness is a truce and not the truth. They have become ashamed of their nakedness.

Then, truly, "in the day that you eat of it you shall die." These spouses spend a great deal of energy denying much of the truth of themselves, of their own natures, repressing it so that they may live life with as little pain as possible. So close to another human being, yet so isolated. So lonely.

—*Walter Wangerin, Jr., As For Me and My House*

"Ah, equality!" said the Director. "We must talk of that some other time. Yes, we must all be guarded by equal rights from one another's greed, because we are fallen. Just as we must all wear clothes for the same reason. But the naked body should be there underneath the clothes ripening for the day when we shall need them no longer. Equality is not the deepest thing, you know."

"I always thought that was just what it was. I thought it was in their souls that people were equal."

"You were mistaken," said he gravely. "That is the last place where they are equal. Equality before the law, equality of incomes—that is very well. Equality guards life; it doesn't make it. It is medicine, not food. You might as well try to warm yourself with a blue-book."

"But surely in marriage . . .?"

"Worse and worse," said the Director. "Courtship knows nothing of it; nor does fruition. What has free companionship to do with that? Those who are enjoying something, or suffering something together, are companions. Those who enjoy or suffer one another, are not. Do you not know how bashful friendship is? Friends—comrades—do not look at each other. Friendship would be ashamed. . . ."

"I thought," said Jane and stopped.

"I see," said the Director. "It is not your fault. They never warned you. No one has ever told you that obedience—humility—-is an erotic necessity." . . .

She had been conceiving this world as "spiritual" in the negative sense—as some neutral, or democratic vacuum where differences disappeared, where sex and sense were not transcended but simply taken away. Now the suspicion dawned upon her that there might be differences and contrasts all the way up, richer, sharper, ever fiercer, at every rung of the ascent. How if this invasion of her own being in marriage from which she had recoiled, often in the very teeth of instinct, were not, as she had supposed, merely a relic of animal life or patriarchal barbarism, but rather the lowest, the first, and the easiest form of some shocking contact with reality which would have to be repeated—but in ever larger and more disturbing modes—on the highest levels of all?

"Yes," said the director. "There is no escape. If it were a virginal rejection of the male, He would allow it. Such souls can bypass the male and go on to meet something far more masculine, higher up, to which they must make a yet deeper surrender. But your trouble has been what old poets called Daungler. We call it Pride. You are offended by the masculine itself: the loud, irruptive, possessive thing—the gold lion, the bearded bull—which breaks through hedges and scatters the little kingdom of your primness as the dwarfs scattered the carefully made bed. The male you could have escaped, for it exists only on the biological level. But the masculine none of us can escape. What is above and beyond all things is so masculine that we are all feminine in relation to it. You had better agree with your adversary quickly."

"You mean I shall have to become a Christian?" said Jane.

—*C. S. Lewis, That Hideous Strength*

I was a wall, and my breasts were like towers; then I was in his eyes as one who finds peace.

—*Song of Solomon 8:10*

Nothing is more repugnant to capable, reasonable people than grace.

—*Charles Wesley*

CHAPTER 8

God's Sneaky Way to get a Person Crucified

Genesis 2:24

Genesis 2:24 *"Therefore a man shall leave his father and his mother and hold fast to his wife, and they shall become one flesh."*

> He took a hundred pounds of clay
> And then He said, "Hey, listen"
> "I'm gonna fix this-a world today"
> "Because I know what's missin'"
> Then He rolled his big sleeves up
> And a brand-new world began
> He created a woman
> And-a lots of lovin' for a man
> Whoa-oh-oh, yes he did.

> —Gene McDaniels, "A Hundred Pounds of Clay,"
> (#3 on the Billboard Chart, 1961—the year I was born)

In 1978 at the age of sixteen, I suffered from some chest pains. The doctors took some X-rays and were surprised to find that my heart was actually a trophy room. I mean the kind that big game hunters have, and I was sitting in the middle of this trophy room in a big stuffed leather chair, smoking a pipe and humming the 007 "James Bond Theme" song.

Over the mantle was the stuffed head of Carron McKinley.[1] In the ninth grade she held my hand one day when we went for a walk. Lisa Jenkins was a cheerleader, and it was announced that we were "going together," even though we never went any place. (She made a very attractive end table . . . with that little cheerleader skirt.) Betty stood in the corner like a stuffed bear, ready to kiss me.

---

[1] Names have been changed to protect the innocent.

(We had kissed for thirty minutes straight! I know that because I was watching the bank clock across the street so I could tell my friends.)

Carron, Lisa, Betty, and a few others were my trophies. I mean, I had won their affections and conquered their hearts. Now, I called myself a "Christian," so I don't mean that I had sex with them but that they fell for me.[2] But this is the weird thing: as soon as they'd fallen for me, they seemed less attractive to me, perhaps because they had fallen for me. It's as if they were fruit, and I would see the fruit on the tree; I would see that they *were good and delightful to the eyes, and to be desired to make one wise,*" good, and complete but . . .

> As soon as I picked the fruit, it died.
> As soon as the big game hunter bags his trophy, it dies.

As soon as he takes a life, it's no longer life . . . but death, soon to be stuffed, mounted, and placed in the corner of his room. So, I'd pursue a girl until I thought I had a girl, and then I'd lose interest in the girl and call it off. Sometimes, she'd call it off, and I'd say it was a "mutual calling off." But at that point, I absolutely did not want to call it off because she had called it off . . . but I still kept her as a trophy in my trophy room because she fell for me (at least a bit) and after all, I did *kind of* call it off; they were my trophies.

Now, understand, I knew *about* these girls, but I didn't really *know* any of these girls. You can't know a trophy; a trophy is dead. I thought I captured love, but I didn't *know* love. Carron, Lisa, Betty, Ann, Sally...Jesus. Like I said, I called myself a "Christian," so I had Jesus too—hanging on the wall in my trophy room—next to Carron's head.

I didn't *know* them, and I was terrified to let them *know* me. I projected an image that I hoped was me—easy-going, confident, athlete, on the swim team—but of course, it wasn't me. I was an actor impersonating my image of myself, trying to impress other actors impersonating their images of themselves. And no self could ever afford to truly be naked in front of another self—in any serious emotional and spiritual sort of way.

I had recently started dating a new girl. I remember praying that she'd never come to a swim meet because she'd see me lose—naked of all glory, covered only in a speedo and pasty white flabby flesh. I tried not to think about that;

---

[2] I should clarify: each one fell for me enough to give me a kiss.

I'd hide from myself in my trophy room—pretending to gain life by consuming life. I was a consumer, terrified of being consumed. I was a taker, acting like a giver. I was something of a monster . . . and often still am.

But this girl I was dating . . . just wow! She was one hot, "hundred pounds of clay." "Chantilly lace and a pretty face and a pony tail hanging down. A wiggle in the walk and a giggle in the talk [made my] world go round."[3] She was absolutely gorgeous until, of course, I thought I had captured her heart, and then the song would just stop. I'd say, "Let's take it slow," and she'd say, "OK." Then the song would start again, and I'd start hunting again. I'd ask her out again.

No wonder people play hard to get. We all want to get, but no one can afford to be gotten. We all want love, but when we think we have love we crucify love, and then can't know love or be known by love. (There are different ways of knowing.)

Well, one spring night in 1978, I said, "Let's call it off," and Susan Coleman said, "OK, I really think we should call it off."

> I really hurt her, and I terrified myself.

> I remember thinking: "Maybe I can't love and can never be married because if I ever bagged a wife I couldn't love that wife. Once I took the good, it would no longer be the good. Once I captured love, I could no longer love.

My trophy room had felt safe—and it was starting to feel safe as Hell. It was all about me and that me was false. "I" was trapped in that room called "me." I was alone. And that would explain the heartache: Surrounded by love, I was unable to love, unable to make I-contact. I was alone.

Alone is the first thing that God declares "*not good.*" It was the one thing "not good" before the fall and also before the Seventh Day, when everything is good. It's "not good," and Adam doesn't know it's "not good," for he doesn't know the Good. He hasn't taken from the tree of the knowledge of good and evil. Adam was alone in the presence of God who is Love, who is Good: "*God alone is good*" (Mark 10:18).

---

[3] Jerry Foster, Bill Rice, and Jiles Perry Chantilly Lace, 1958

On the sixth day of creation, in Genesis 1:26, God says, *"Let us make man (Adam) in our own image, after our likeness."* Theologians argue over exactly what the "image of God" entails, but it appears to be at least three things:

- ✓ First: God says *"our* image." God is a Trinity. He is "not alone." He is three persons and one substance, and that one substance is love. God is love. So, Adam (which means "humanity") is to be made in the image of love—a communion of persons. That communion creates life. When God says, *"Let us make man in our image,"* He has been doing nothing but creating.

- ✓ Second: Adam (humanity) is to be *a* creator in the image of *the* Creator. The image is to be a creator—not a consumer—a giver, not a taker.

- ✓ Third: Scripture is very clear that the image of God is not perfected on earth until 3pm on a Friday, the sixth day of the week, just before Easter, along about 33AD as Jesus the ultimate Adam, hanging naked on a tree in a garden lifts His head and cries out before God and His Bride, *"It is finished."* Scripture says He is: *"the perfect image of the invisible God, the first born of all Creation"* (Col. 1:15). So, the image of God is a creative communion that looks like Jesus . . . or is Jesus. He is the *Eschatos* Adam.

On the sixth day: *"God created Adam (humanity) in His own image, in the image of God he created him, male and female he created them"* (Gen. 1:27). As the sixth day ends, God sees *"everything that He has made. And behold, it's very good"* (Gen. 1:31). But Peter Hiett, the trophy hunter is not very good. Thank God that He's still creating us in His image! Thank God that the Seventh Day is yet to come!

Adam is alone in the presence of Love. Adam is "not good" in the presence of "the Good." Adam is like a closed earthen vessel containing darkness, surrounded by eternal light. Adam is alone.

So, Adam can't find a helper.

And God says, *"I will make a helper fit for Adam"* (Gen. 2:18).

So, God divides Adam into male and female.

He takes one hundred pounds of clay, in Hebrew *adamah*. But He doesn't take this clay from the ground. He takes this *adamah* from Adam. *Dam* is Hebrew for "blood." He takes *dam* and *adamah* from Adam; Eve is made from Adam's bleeding side—his body broken and blood shed. Like we are made from Christ's bleeding side—His body broken and blood shed—on a tree in a garden.

Well, Adam was not yet fully made in "the image of God," just as I was not yet fully made in "the image of God," sitting alone in the dark trophy room of my heart.

Adam did not yet have faith in Love. He did not know love or even about love, so he couldn't trust Love[4]. How is he going to get faith in Love? How is God going to create humanity in His image? Well, God puts Adam to sleep and divides him in two. God brings Eve to Adam, and Adam exclaims: *"'Bone of my bones, and flesh of my flesh'*—Chantilly lace and a pretty face ... "

> **Genesis 2:22–24** *And the rib that the Lord God had taken from the man he made into a woman and brought her to the man. Then the man said, "This at last is bone of my bones and flesh of my flesh; she shall be called Woman, because she was taken out of Man."*
>
> *Therefore a man shall leave his father and his mother and hold fast to his wife, and they shall become one flesh. And the man and his wife were both naked and were not ashamed.*

Two persons, one substance: communion, creating life—not exactly the same thing as God, but a sign pointing to God—hopefully full of God. God invented marriage, and He seems to be something of a wedding fanatic.

---

[4] In Genesis 3:22, after Adam and Eve have eaten from the tree, God says, "Behold, the Adam has become like one of us, knowing good and evil..." The text clearly indicates that Adam did not originally have knowledge of the good. He didn't know that God was good or that Love was good. Indeed, he didn't truly know who or what Love is. "In this is love, not that we have loved God but that he loved us and sent his Son to be the propitiation for our sins" (1 John 4:10). We are just beginning to know this. But as we realized in the last book, it's still the sixth day.

- It appears that the first ceremony must've happened in the garden, and God walked Eve down the isle . . . in a rather suggestive outfit.

- The first commandment that we read in Scripture is the honeymoon commandment, my favorite: *"Be fruitful and multiply"* (Gen.1:28).

- Jesus' inaugural miracle in the Gospel of John was to turn water to wine to keep a wedding banquet going and . . . fun.

- And now if you think a chapter on marriage doesn't apply to you, think again. Paul makes it clear that every believer is at least engaged. He quotes our verse from Genesis and claims that it's all about your relationship with Jesus:

Therefore a man shall leave his father and mother and hold fast to his wife, and the two shall become one flesh." This mystery is profound, and I am saying that it refers to Christ and the church.
—Ephesians 5:31–32

- In the end, according to the Revelation, we're all going to a wedding banquet—*"The Marriage of the Lamb,"* where our relationship with Jesus is ultimately consummated in ecstasy. Heaven is the ultimate marriage—the fulfillment of all our deepest dreams and desires.

In this life, we have to wait for the fulfillment of all our deepest dreams and desires. We live in a world under a curse. Yet marriage is a relationship established before the curse. It's like a unique and tangible opportunity to sample the ultimate relationships that constitute the Kingdom of Heaven while still walking in this fallen, sixth-day world—communion in a sanctuary bound by a covenant.

Scripture refers to marriage as a covenant.[5] When people form covenants they take vows. Marriage vows are a promise to love. So, whenever I perform wedding ceremonies I ask the question: "What is love?" Most people seem to think that love is some sort of feeling or possibly a hormone—like something we describe in Hollywood musicals:

---

[5] Malachi. 2:14, Proverbs. 2:17, Ezekiel 16:8

> Some enchanted evening
> you will meet a stranger;
> you will meet a stranger across a crowded room
> and suddenly you'll know..." [6]

What will you know? You'll know that your hormones are working. That's great! But is that love? Hormones are rather unreliable, so people form covenants bound with a vow. Nat King Cole sang:

> Love is a many splendored thing;
> It's the April rose that only grows in the early spring.
>
> [That's too bad, for April roses only last about as long as your standard honeymoon.]
>
> Once on a high and windy hill,
> two lovers kissed in the morning mist,
> and the world stood still. [7]

I hope you see the problem here. You can't vow that—you can't vow to always smell roses whenever your bride enters the room. You can't promise that the world will stand still whenever you are "kissed in the morning mist" by your groom. And isn't it for this very reason we take vows, because our passion is unreliable? So maybe love is more than a hormone, passion, or feeling. Maybe love is a decision, and that's why we take vows and make covenants.

Is Love a feeling? Is Love a promise?

In the Old Testament, there is a special word that is often translated *steadfast love*, *love*, *mercy* or *lovingkindness*. That word is *hesed*. My seminary professor used to say, "It means covenant love." When people formed covenants in ancient times, it appears that they would slaughter an animal and lay the pieces on

---

[6] Oscar Hammerstein II, vocal performance of "Some Enchanted Evening," by Richard Rogers, published in 1949, *South Pacific*

[7] Nat King Cole, *Love is a Many Splendored Thing*. Lyrics: Francis Paul Webster

the ground; then they would walk between the pieces reciting the terms of the covenant saying something like, "May it be done unto me as it was done unto this animal if I break the terms of this covenant." [8]

Marriage is a covenant. Divorce is breaking a covenant. If you've been divorced you know: It's less like annulling some legal document registered with the county clerk and more like taking a living body, one body, and tearing it in two.

In Matthew 19, when Jesus quotes Genesis and explains marriage and divorce, the disciples say, "Well, it's better not to get married!" And maybe they're right? Ask any businessman about unconditional covenants with no escape clause. They'll tell you that you'd have to be crazy to enter into one. Marriage is crazy. It's a covenant with no escape clause—except death. Someone must die.

I know a fellow named Josh. For three years he was absolutely consumed with a woman. He rescued her from an impoverished and abusive family. She married Josh for his power, money, and good looks. And yet she was so intimidated by him; she never gave him her heart. Actually, she gave her heart to anyone that would pay.

She became a prostitute. Josh would walk the streets at night, find her and buy her back from pimps. She gave herself to vile men, but was frigid with Josh. She grew ugly. The counselor said that she was "hiding her shame." Still, Josh thought of her, dreamed of her, followed her everywhere. When she wept, he wept. When she laughed, he laughed. He wouldn't forsake her. He once shared that if he had it to do over again, he would—in a heartbeat. Eventually, one Friday (with the help of some corrupt politicians) this woman tried to kill Josh. And she did . . . People argue about whether or not it's "OK" to get a divorce. If anyone ever had a valid grounds for divorce . . . His name is Josh. Joshua is His Hebrew name. "Ye-shua" was how they said it in Aramaic. "Ye-sus" is how you say it in Greek. "Jesus" is how we pronounce it in English. Every week we remember the covenant He fulfills and the covenant He makes as we break the bread saying, "His body which is for you."

---

[8] For a fascinating example on this practice, see Genesis 15. Notice that only one passes between the pieces.

Divorce is breaking covenant.

It feels less like annulling some legal document and more like breaking a living body in two.

God made a covenant with His people, and the law—which is a description of love—describes the terms of that covenant. And we broke it.[9] Jesus paid the price of that broken covenant of law, and Jesus established the covenant of Grace that cannot be broken—for it is eternal.

Never forget that the picture of love, and the revelation of Love, in our faith is not an "April rose," an "enchanted evening," or "Chantilly lace and a pretty face." Our picture of Love is God in flesh—the *Eschatos* Adam—the Great Bridegroom, Joshua/Jesus hanging naked, drenched in His own blood, impaled on a tree in a garden because of His covenant love for *each* one of us, His Harlot Bride.[10]

His blood is shed to atone for all the ways that we have broken covenant with Him.

His body is broken to form the new and eternal covenant for each of us.

You see, when you vow yourself to fallen people, you can get crucified. When you let them, it's called forgiveness.

Love isn't just a feeling. Love is a vow.

Some time ago, driving down the freeway listening to the radio, I heard Rush Limbaugh announce that the legislature in West Virginia was considering

[9] The great and wonderful Good News is that God not only made a covenant of law with the people of Israel (Deut. 4:23–24), but long before that He made a covenant of Grace with their fathers (Deut. 4:30–31). When God made a covenant with Abraham in Genesis 15, He took all the vows and He walked between the pieces. He keeps covenant on both sides. Apart from Him we can do nothing (John 15:5).

[10] Ezekiel 16 describes this romance. The whole book of Hosea is a prophetic representation of this drama. The Revelation reveals the consummation and transformation of the harlot bride—us.

warning labels on the back of marriage licenses. I think he was mocking the idea. I think it's a pretty good idea.[11] In fact, I stole the idea and made a warning label of my own. Whenever I marry a couple, before they take the vows, I tape this warning to the groom's chest:

> WARNING: Marriage is a covenant ratified by God. The surgeon general has determined that there are certain hormones in the bloodstream at the time of your wedding, which may cause dizziness and poor perception. These hormones can mostly subside on your honeymoon. Use extreme caution. The person you are about to marry is a reprobate.

At this point in the ceremony, wide-eyed enchanted couples will look at me as if to say, "What about the one hundred pounds of clay? What about male and female in the image of God? What about, 'God is a wedding fanatic?' and 'marriage is an opportunity to taste heaven on earth?' What about love: 'Chantilly lace and a pretty face?' Isn't marriage God's plan?"

So, I tell them:

> Yes! Marriage is God's plan. Just like Jesus Christ and Him crucified is God's plan.

Is God crazy?

> Yes, He is crazy with love for you! And yes, He does have a plan for you! But it's far more than a house in the suburbs and 2.5 kids. God's plan for you is to kill the prideful, self-centered, lonely old you and transform you into His own image.

And who is He?

> He is the crazy Bridegroom, hanging on a cross because He vowed Himself unconditionally to us: His unfaithful Harlot Bride.

---

[11] Actually, I don't believe that civil government has anything to do with deciding who's actually married or not married. But a warning would be highly appropriate.

Jesus is the perfect image of the invisible God, and God said it right there in Genesis chapter one: *"Let us make Adam in our own image"* (Gen. 1:26).

God's agenda is to make us look like Him, so God makes us male and female. He fashions one hundred pounds of clay: "Chantilly lace and a pretty face," estrogen, testosterone, and all these burning desires.

And why does He do it? To suck folks in, to set an ambush—"Chantilly lace and a pretty face"—to lure them into an unconditional covenant with one other sinner and no escape clause but death . . .

So, I tell them:

> God is sucking you into an unconditional covenant with one other sinner and no escape clause but death!
>
> - So that you'd be forced to love . . . even when it hurts.
> - So that you'd expire your self and be inspired by Love.
> - So that you'd learn to forgive as you've been forgiven.
> - So that you'd begin to look like Jesus.

Marriage is God's sneaky way to get a person crucified.

Like *U2* sings, "I can't live, with or without you."[12] I can't live "with you"—for you shatter my idolatrous image of you. And I can't live "without you"—because *"it's not good for the Adam to be alone."* . . . "I'm so lonely I could die," sang Elvis Presley.[13]

"I can't live with or without you."

And a voice from Heaven booms "Exactly! That's the point. You can't live." You—sitting in your stuffed chair, smoking a pipe, humming the 007 "James Bond Theme" song, and staring at the trophies of your own selfishness. You— lonely, arrogant, old Adam, trapped alone in a hell of your own making, dead,

---

[12] U2 "With or Without You."

[13] Elvis Presley "Heartbreak Hotel."

but unable to die to yourself—You must be crucified. You must expire to be inspired.

You know, people get divorced based on the grounds of "incompatibility."

Who's compatible with a cross?[14]

If your bride publicly humiliates you, strips you naked, whips you and nails you to a tree, it doesn't mean that your marriage isn't working, maybe it means it is—for now, you look a lot like Jesus!

Marriage is God's sneaky way to get a person crucified!

Perhaps you're not married. And so, you've felt left out. Well, Jesus wasn't married—yet He was and is married to you. He died for you, and He invites you to die for Him too. And He invites you to die for His Bride; you are His body. Believe me, she is a spouse capable of nailing you to a tree. She's already done it to Jesus.

This is my point: Jesus is in you, and His Bride is all around you, and He still suffers for His Bride through you, even as He fashions you in His own image. You are married to Jesus, and Jesus in you is married (or at least, betrothed[15]) to those around you—even if they, or we, haven't yet experiencd the consumation of our covenant.

When you give yourself to others, as Christ gives Himself to you, you will get crucified. Church can get you crucified. And Church is to be "the Kingdom

---

[14] If you've been divorced based on the grounds of "incompatibility," I don't mean to shame you—apparently, at one point God gave Israel a "certificate of divorce" (Isa. 50:1)—but, I do mean to point out that what God means by *marriage* may be rather different than what we mean by *marriage*. And if God did in fact "divorce" Israel, in Christ, He died for her to win her back. That may not be an option for you. But no matter what, you must believe, "His mercies are new every morning" and He will take all our failures—including divorce—and turn them into beautiful demonstrations of His Grace.

[15] In Jesus' day, betrothal was like marriage that awaited its consummation by means of sexual communion.

of Heaven" on earth. Sometimes people wonder how Church can promise so much and yet, at times, be so painful. Well, it's a marriage.

Marriage between a man and a woman is just the reference. Christ in you loving others (including your husband or wife) is the reality. Love is the reality. Love can get you crucified and heaven is Love!

What is Love?

When I perform wedding ceremonies, I tell the couple:

- Love is not simply a feeling that you can conjure up.
- Love is not a vow that you can make.[16]
- Love is your Creator, and He makes you with His Covenant Vow, His Covenant Word—Jesus. And Jesus is happy. He came that His joy might be in you.
- Your hope is not your passion or your ability to keep promises. Your hope is God's ability to keep promises in you—He is the promise keeper. Your hope is Christ's passion in you—the passion of the Christ. Your hope is to confess your sins one to another and call on Jesus to live out His life in you.

Marriage is God's sneaky way to get a person crucified.

And crucifixion is God's sneaky way to give us new life—His Life.

I broke up with Susan that spring evening in 1978 (around Easter). But as soon as she said, "OK, we'll date other people," the song started once again: "Chantilly lace and a pretty face, a pony tail hanging down..."

The following morning I drove to her house. I wanted to capture the good. I wanted to possess her beauty once again. She wasn't home. Her mother told

---

[16] James 5:12 "But above all, my brothers, do not swear, either by heaven or by earth or by any other oath, but let your 'yes' be yes and your 'no' be no, so that you may not fall under condemnation."

Proverbs 2:16 teaches that the adulterous woman "forsakes the companion of her youth and forgets the covenant of her God." It's as if God takes the vows, and God cuts this covenant. In marriage we participate in His covenant.

me that she'd gone to the park to feed the ducks. It was a grey day, damp with a steady drizzle.

As I drove down Gallup Street, I saw her in the distance. The park looked like a garden; I watched her walking in the garden, weeping. She didn't see me, but I watched her. She was walking alone in the grey rain, holding a bag of crumbs. . . weeping. I just sat in the car and watched her.

Her heart was naked and exposed. If she had a throne room, the walls had been breached and broken. And it was out of that place that she was bleeding. As I stared at her, I was captivated by something that I must've missed before. Not "Chantilly lace and a pretty face," but love—bleeding for me: a heart that had allowed itself to be crucified by me and for me. I was captivated by the image of God in her. It was like I had bagged a trophy and placed it in the trophy room, but it had come to life and was attempting to bag me. The hunter became the hunt*ed*. The thing I sought to possess began to possess me!

Like a beast or a monster, I had tried to capture love, and Love captured me. But Love is not content to just capture me; Love seeks to transform me; Love seeks to even impregnate me and become incarnate in me; Love seeks to live its life in me—transforming me into its own image—from a monster that consumes love, into a lover that is the presence of Love. Love makes me its very own Body—sometimes broken and sometimes bleeding.

I have never bled as much for anyone, or felt as broken for anyone, as I have for Susan. I have never experienced as much passion for anyone, as that which I have experienced for her. I love her.

I tried to posses love, and Love possessed me all the way to the altar. An altar is a place set aside for sacrificing things. The minister boomed,

> Do you now give yourself to this woman in all love and honor,
> in all faith and tenderness, to live with her and cherish her,
> according to the ordinance of God in the Holy bond of Mar-
> riage...til death do ye part? [17]

And with a tremendous smile plastered across my face, I said: "I do!"

---

[17] I don't know if these were the exact words, but they're close.

It was the best decision that I ever made—but maybe I didn't make the decision; the decision made me. It's still making me.

Jesus is God's decision, and He's making all of us.

Jesus said, "*No one is good except God alone*" (Mark 10:18).

As we noted in the last chapter, Jesus is *the* Good in flesh.
As we also noted: God's people in the Old Testament, and the New Testament, play the harlot, but are the Bride—the Church.

- The harlot bride sees "the Good" and wants to possess "knowledge of the Good," to make herself good. But instead, she makes herself bad.
- She tries to take "knowledge of the Good" on a tree in a garden and comes to know: God is Good, and she is bad.
- She sees "the Life" and tries to take "the Life" on that tree in that garden in 33AD.
- She knows about "the Good," but can no longer know "the Good," for she just crucified the Good—the last Adam, Jesus.

But what we took, God gave—He *for*gave. That's His decision.
We take Love, and He gives Love, making us in the image of Love.
We consume, and He creates. He creates creators out of consumers.

- At the cross we took "*knowledge of the good*," and God revealed *the* Good. God is good, and Jesus has made Him known.
- At the cross we took "Life" and God gave Life—Jesus is "the Life" — Body broken and blood shed is the fruit of that tree.
- We consume that fruit, which is Christ's death, but He is "the Life" and He rises in us.
- *The* Good knows us, such that He literally impregnates us with Life—His Life, Eternal Life, The Life of the *Eschatos* Adam. We are His Body and Bride.

The cross is a tree,[18] and the tree is a trap. It's the monster trap.[19]
It kills monsters (like me in my trophy room) and turns them into lovers.
It traps sinners and turns them into saints, the image of the living God.
It's there that we begin to expire, so we can inspire. Life is respiration!
It's there that Adam, humankind, begins to have faith in Love.

That's what Adam (including Eve) was lacking in the garden on the sixth day, before the fall: Adam lacked faith in Love. That's why Adam was alone, even in the presence of Love.

Well, for now I'm just saying that marriage is a reference to the story of Christ and the Church, the creation of faith in Love. And I'm also saying: You're married . . . even if it hasn't yet been consummated quite yet. Hopefully you know that the communion table is not only a picture of our sin and God's Grace in Christ Jesus two thousand years ago, but it's also a reminder of a great wedding banquet still to come and even a taste of that banquet right now.

> *And when the hour came, he reclined at table, and the apostles with him. And he said to them, "I have earnestly desired* (literally: *"In lust I have lusted"*) *to eat this Passover with you before I suffer. For I tell you I will not eat it until it is fulfilled in the kingdom of God."*
>
> —Luke 22:14–16

That's the wedding supper of the Lamb. You're married. God is Love, and Love was crucified for you. Every time you sin, Love bears the pain of that sin on a tree in a garden at the boundary of time and eternity. That's not meant to make you hide in shame but surrender your shame and see that Love chooses to bleed

---

[18] I hope this sparks your interest, for there is an amazing story to tell about the trees in the garden of Eden, the "tree" in the garden on Calvary, and the tree in the New Jerusalem. We'll tell it in the next book.

[19] Dead in our sin, we crave the broken body of the living, like zombies. And we crave the shed blood of the living, like vampires. We're monsters even as Jesus says, "Eat me and drink me." He traps monsters and turns them into lovers at His cross.

for you—in the hope that you would choose to bleed for Love. He says, "Take and drink the covenant in my blood." It's life!

That bleeding is Life!

- When one person bleeds, it looks like a man hanging on a cross.
- When two people bleed it looks like a good marriage.
- When everyone bleeds—one part into the other—it looks like a living body dancing in a garden of delight.

Life is bleeding. Life is respiration. But we don't simply come to life the moment we see "Jesus Christ and Him Crucified," just as I didn't simply become a good husband the moment that I saw Susan feeding the ducks in the rain. No. She bled. Then I bled. Then we kissed. Then I offended her, and she offended me. She still bleeds, and I still bleed. You see, the monster was exposed that day in the garden in the rain, but it takes at least a life-time for Love to create faith in Love and to create you in the image *of* Love.

Love creates life, and He usually takes His time. Love is a covenant promise ("I will never leave you nor forsake you."), and Love is a passion ("See my hands and feet. Place your fingers in my side"). And Love reveals Himself in promises and passion over time. Love creates faith in Love, with a story of love. And that story is written over time. Love makes us real in time.

At weddings I usually read the following. It's not just true for married people. It's also true for anyone that surrenders to the life of Love. It comes from the great theological treatise, *The Velveteen Rabbit*:

> *"What is* REAL?" asked the Rabbit one day, as they were lying side by side near the nursery fender, just before Nana came in to tidy up the room. *"Does it mean having things that buzz inside you and a stick-out handle?"*
>
> *"Real isn't how you are made,"* said the Skin Horse. *"It's a thing that happens to you. When a child loves you for a long, long time, not just to play with, but* REALLY *loves you, then you become* REAL."
>
> *"Does it hurt?"* asked the Rabbit.

"*Sometimes,*" said the Skin Horse, for he was always truthful.

"*When you are Real, you don't mind being hurt.*"

"*Does it happen all at once, like being wound up,*" he asked, "*or bit by bit?*"

"*It doesn't happen all at once,*" said the Skin Horse. "*You become. It takes a long time. That's why it doesn't often happen to people who break easily, or have sharp edges, or who have to be carefully kept. Generally, by the time you are Real, most of your hair has been loved off, and your eyes drop out and you get loose in the joints and very shabby. But these things don't matter at all, because once you are Real, you can't be ugly except to people who don't understand.*"[20]

I had a seminary professor who used to say, "Some things are loved because they're valuable, but the best things are valuable because they've been loved."

You're one of God's best things. Can you think of anything else, or anyone else, in all His creation, before whom or with whom He went to greater lengths? He has born all things to reveal Himself to you. He is your Helper.

God is loving eternal value into you. God is making you real. You can't be ugly except to people who don't understand. And when all people do understand—when you arrive, "finished," in that Seventh Day—you will radiate the glory of God (Rev. 21:11). There is no greater beauty. It's the Good.

Robertson McQuilkin was the president of Columbia Bible College. A Bible college or seminary is a wonderful place, but it can also be a place where people go to take "*the knowledge of the good*" and make themselves good . . . and that's *not* good.

Well, Robertson was the president. Being in his position would have been a dream come true for me, and it was a dream come true for Robertson. His office must've looked like a trophy room. But then tragedy struck; his wife, Muriel, was diagnosed with Alzheimer's disease. "Chantilly lace and a pretty face, a po-

[20] Margory Williams *The Velveteen Rabbit* Illustrated by William Nicholson (New York: Doubleday, 1922)

nytail hanging down" must've been what attracted Robertson to Muriel forty years earlier. But now Muriel couldn't even remember who Robertson was or who *she* was. But Robertson knew.

His friends advised him not to neglect his calling, but Robertson believed the covenant was his calling, so he resigned from his position as president to care for Muriel, feed Muriel, and bathe Muriel. Muriel didn't know who she was, but Robertson knew who she was and told her who she was: she was the Bride. He recorded his experience in one of my favorite little books titled: *A Promise Kept.*

One day a former student asked him: "Do you miss being president?" Mc-Quilken writes:

> I'd never thought about it...But that night I reflected on his question. Finally I turned to the Lord: "Father, it's OK. I like this assignment and I have no regrets. But something has oc-curred to me. If the coach puts a man on the bench, he must not want him in the game. You needn't tell me, of course, but if you'd like to let me in on the secret, I'd like to know: Why don't you need me in the game?[21]

Roberston didn't sleep well. He woke contemplating the puzzle. On their morning walk around the block, Robertson held Muriel's hand in order to steady her as she shuffled along. A familiar form came walking up behind them; he was the local drunk. He staggered around Muriel and Robertson, out into the street and then back onto the sidewalk, where he stopped and stood directly in front of them. He looked them up and down and then said, "'Tha's good. I likes 'at. Tha's real good. I likes it.' Then he headed off down the street mumbling to himself over and over: 'Tha's good. I like it.'"[22] Robertson chuckled, and they headed home. He writes that it was when they reached the garden and sat down that the words came back to him, and he realized that God had answered his prayer: "I like it, it's good." It's the Good!

---

[21] Robertson McQuilkin *A Promise Kept*, (Wheaton, IL: Tyndale, 1998) 58–59.

[22] Ibid. 60

Robertson tried to capture the Good.

And the Good captured Robertson and shaped Robertson in His own image.

One day, Robertson and Muriel were stuck in an airport lounge due to a flight delay. They sat across from an attractive, female, executive type working on her computer. Of course, Muriel made a constant commotion and this young executive said something without looking up from her computer. Robertson assumed she had mumbled a protest: "Pardon?" he asked. "Oh," she said, "I was just asking myself, 'Will I ever find a man to love me like that?'"

Maybe you're asking a question like that.

Maybe we're all asking a question like that.

Will I ever find my Helper?

The whole world was looking for a helper and couldn't recognize *THE* HELPER when He took the bread and broke it saying, "*Take, eat; this is my body,*" and likewise the cup saying, "*Drink of it all of you. This is my blood of the covenant, which is poured out for many for the forgiveness of sins*" (Matt. 22: 26-28).

The Covenant:

- He knew what He was doing when He cut the woman from the man and brought her to the man.
- He knew what He was doing when He "cut that covenant" (Gen. 9:9) with old Noah and every living creature on Mt. Ararat.
- He knew what He was doing when He called Abraham into the darkness on the side of Mt. Zion, when He had him cut the animals in two and made him watch as the Fire passed between the pieces, and He confirmed the covenant . . . both sides (Gen. 15:7-21).
- He knew what He was doing when He called Moses up onto Mt. Sinai, when He instituted the sacrificial system and gave Moses the terms of the covenant—the law (Exodus, Leviticus, Numbers, Deuteronomy).
- He knew what He was doing when He broke the bread and poured the wine . . . and, at the end of the day, He cried, "It is finished" as He fulfilled the covenant of law and ratified the eternal covenant of Grace, hanging on a tree in the garden.

Marriage is God's sneaky way to get *Himself* crucified.

> He wanted Adam to capture Him so He could capture Adam's heart and create Adam in His own image!

> He wanted His harlot Bride to nail Him to the tree so He could reveal His love to her and create faith—faith in Love within her!

> The Covenant of God creates the Passion of the Christ, and the Passion of the Christ creates Faith in you—the eternal, imperishable Seed in you—the life of Christ in you: His Bride!

Marriage is God's sneaky way to get Himself crucified.

And crucifixion is God's sneaky way to give all of us His Life.

> *...he poured out his soul to death*
> *and was numbered with the transgressors;*
> *yet he bore the sin of many,*
> *and makes intercession for the transgressors.*

> *"Sing, O barren one, who did not bear;*
> *break forth into singing and cry aloud,*
> *you who have not been in labor!*

> *For the children of the desolate one will be more*
> *than the children of her who is married," says the LORD.*

> *...For your Maker is your husband,*
> *the LORD of hosts is his name;*

> *and the Holy One of Israel is your Redeemer,*
> *the God of the whole earth he is called.*
> —Isaiah 53:12–54:1,5

Christian writers (notably Milton) have sometimes spoken of the husband's head-ship with a complacency to make the blood run cold. We must go back to our Bibles. The husband is the head of the wife just in so far as he is to her what Christ is to the Church. He is to love her as Christ loved the Church—read on—and give his life for her (Eph.V, 25). This headship, then, is most fully embodied not in the husband we should all wish to be but in him whose marriage is most like a crucifixion; whose wife receives most and gives least, is most unworthy of him, is—in her own mere nature—least lovable.

—*C.S. Lewis, The Four Loves*

Then our good Lord Jesus Christ asked me: "Are you well satisfied that I suffered for you?" I said: "Yes, good Lord, and I thank you very much. Yes, good Lord, may you be blessed." Then Jesus our good Lord said: "If you are satisfied, I am satisfied. To have ever suffered the Passion for you is for me a great joy, a bliss, an endless delight; and if I could suffer more I would do so."

—*Julian of Norwich, Journeys into Joy*

CHAPTER 9

The Sacrament of the Covenant

Genesis 2:24–25

Genesis 2:24–25 *Therefore a man shall leave his father and his mother and hold fast to his wife, and they shall become one flesh. And the man and his wife were both naked and were not ashamed.*

> Lord Almighty, I feel my temperature rising.
> Higher n higher, it's burning through to my soul.
> Girl, girl, girl, girl, you gonna set me on fire.
> My brain is flaming. I don't know which way to go.
> Your kisses lift me higher. Like the sweet song of a choir
> You light my morning sky, with burning love...
> Burning, burning, burning and nothing can cool me.
> I just might turn to smoke, but I feel fine.[1]
> I'm just a hunk, a hunk of burning love.
> Just a hunk, a hunk of burning love.
>
> —Elvis Presley, *Burning Love* (#2 on the Billboard Chart, 1972)

A few years ago, the worship team at my church played "Burning Love" for the offertory, before the Word was preached, and we communed with the Body Broken and Blood Shed in the sanctuary of the Covenant of Grace. It was a "problem" for some. And I think I understand why.

Three thousand years ago, a high priest walked onto a raised platform in the center of a village. At the priest's side was a young woman dressed in a robe. She was beautiful—a virgin. It was a spring high holy day, and hundreds of peasant farmers gathered round as the priest announced, "Whoever produces the year's best barley, oats, and wheat will have her, take her, to the glory of god."

---

[1] Pop Quiz: How many things can you think of in Scripture that "burn" with fire but are not consumed?

As he lifted his arms, she dropped her robe and danced luridly to the sound of drums. Hunger grew within the men of that crowd. They wanted her—to possess her. When the dance was done, she was clothed and whisked from sight. Sacred prostitutes came to the front: male and female. The high priests assigned them partners from the crowd. Men left their wives to perform their duty to the glory of their god—Baal.

Of course, that's not an exact account, but it is based upon historical evidence. Baal was the Mesopotamian god of fertility. In Hebrew, the word means "possessor." Cultic prostitution was part of the worship of Baal. Throughout history, religion has been closely associated with sexuality. That was certainly true in biblical times. Allegedly, Andrew Greeley once wrote, "The most fundamental insight that primitive man had about sexuality is one that we frequently overlook or forget: that it is a raw, primal, basic power, over which we have only very limited control. Primitive man invariably viewed sexuality as sacred."[2]

Well, I don't think it's just primitive man. In modern society, sex itself has become a religion, complete with high priests and priestesses such as Dr. Kinsey, Dr. Freud, Dr. Ruth and even Reverend Hefner.

Human religion is largely the way we comprehend and manage mysteries. Religious leaders market the mystery, explain the mystery and dissect the mystery, which often kills the Mystery. That, in itself, is rather mysterious. We've spent two thousand years trying to comprehend and manage the sacrament of communion, but Jesus never told us to manage it or comprehend it. He told us to do it. You can know all about communion and never commune. Similarly you can know all about sex and never truly have it. There are different ways of "knowing."

---

[2] I wrote "allegedly," for long ago I catalogued this quote and now can't remember where I read it. Whatever the case, it's abundantly clear that the religions of the world have always been pre-occupied with sex—either in the form of repression or indulgence. And I don't need a sociologist to tell me why. As a young man working as a landscaper, riding a lawnmower all day in the hot sun, it seemed that my mind would only ruminate on one of two topics: sex or God. Only God was a mystery deep enough and lovely enough to get me to think about something other than sex. No wonder people worship sex.

For much of history the church has viewed sex as a rival religion, and we don't know what to do with this profound and powerful mystery . . . but then again, we don't know quite what to do with communion either. Should we define it, wage war over it, regulate it and restrict it . . . or just take it?

According to historian John Boswell, the church put so many restrictions on sexual activity in the Middle Ages that, for all but forty-four days a year, sexual relations between married couples were forbidden.[3] It's no wonder that the Middle Ages were filled with roaming bands of stressed out barbarian thugs looking for a fight.

For much of history, confused and threatened by sexuality, the institutional church has portrayed sex as something unclean—not something that could become unclean, but something inherently unclean. In light of that fact, it's not surprising that many in the Church have come to believe that the knowledge of good and evil is equivalent to sexual knowledge. The obvious reading of Genesis one and two reveals that this assertion is absurd.[4] Nonetheless many have taught that, the first and original sin was sexual intercourse. Because church leadership often viewed sex as inherently bad, the institution propagated a strategy of repression and denial.

But mere repression often leads to indulgence:
Don't think about SEX! Don't think about SEX!...
Don't think about it!!!!! Don't you dare think about SEX!
...Now, what are you thinking about?

Repression often leads to indulgence . . . and denial . . . and more repression and indulgence. We cover it with shame and live out of the shame—such that our life is a lie, which we hide from the truth. And Jesus, the Great Bridegroom, the *Eschatos* Adam, is the Truth, the Way and the Life. Hide from Jesus and you're dead, lost, and alone.

A few years ago, a woman at my last church wrote me a letter informing me that she was leaving due to "sexual references in sermons." She said they made her "uncomfortable and grieved her spirit." Ironically, I learned that she really

[3] Philip Yancey, Finding God in Unexpected Places, pp. 13–14.

[4] It's extremely difficult to argue that the first and original sin was sexual intercourse, when the first and original command of God was, "be fruitful and multiply."

struggled with promiscuity. Her strategy for dealing with her promiscuous desire was repression. I think it lead to indulgence and more repression and left her rather dead, lost, and alone.

You know, it was no sin that Adam (humankind) needed God, his Helper, to fill him and complete him and make him fruitful. It was no sin that Eve needed Adam to fill her and complete her and make her fruitful. It was no sin for Adam to want to fill her, complete her and make her fruitful according to the very first command of God; remember he is the rest of her body! It's no sin to need God, and it's no sin to desire your husband or wife. However, sin *is* hiding your need from God and trying to fill that need with something other than God.

There was a man who always told me dirty jokes in the parking lot at church, but then he would get visibly upset when I'd mention sexuality in a sermon in the sanctuary. I think he felt it necessary to hide his felt needs and desperate desires from God—to deny them before God—but they still were expressed in the parking lot and sometimes expressed in rather disturbing ways.

I remember one person saying something like, "Well, I certainly wouldn't want my daughter learning about sex . . . in the sanctuary . . . before communion!" She must've thought sex was the opposite of communion in a sanctuary, in the sight of God.

At youth group, I got the idea that sex was unimportant, and even dirty, and that's why we should save it for the person we marry. Now, we *should* save it for the one we marry, but is that why? . . . Because it's dirty? Is dirt bad—unimportant, or is it good? Dirt is fairly important to farmers . . . and to seed (*sperma* in Biblical Greek). Well, seed turns dirt into new life that mixes more dirt with light, producing fruit, which multiplies the life: "*Be fruitful and multiply*" (Gen. 1:28).

So, what is sex? Is it Good? Bad? Unimportant? And should we sing "Hunk, a hunk of burning love" in the sanctuary . . . before communion?[5]

Recently, I was reading a popular Christian author bemoaning how, for so many modern people, sex was like a religion "reminiscent of ancient fertility cults...Sex is the sacrament in the new age." He obviously has a point, but he may be missing a bigger point.

---

[5] I want you to chew on these questions for the rest of the book.

He then quoted another popular Christian author. It's obvious that both are evangelical Protestants and sons of "enlightened" modernity, having inherited a host of policies for regulating communion, and having developed a rather "scientific" explanations of communion. This second author notes how strange it is when people in some churches take communion, "lovingly holding and distributing tiny bits of bread and drops of wine." He then writes, "In religion, simple things become infused with a greater meaning. They gain a fascination and an emotional importance far beyond their practical function. So, it is with sex in our time: it has become a sacrament."[6]

I think he's saying that just as some people make such a big deal of "pieces of bread and drops of wine," so in the same way we've made too much of sex, for sex is "just body and blood" like communion is "just bread and wine." I think he's saying that sex is "just biology," and sadly, "It's gained a fascination and emotional importance far beyond its practical function." He's saying our problem is that folks have "infused" a "simple thing" with "greater meaning;" that we make "too much of sex." We turn it into a sacrament.

> Well, it seems that Jesus made a pretty big deal of "pieces of bread and drops of wine."
>
> And it seems that God made a pretty big deal of "sex:"
>
> **Genesis 1:27–28** *So God created man in his own image —in the image of God he created him. Male and female he created them. And God blessed them. And God said to them, "Be fruitful and multiply.*

Biologists will tell you that this, the first of all the commandments, seems to indicate some sort of intimate sexual communion. God doesn't tell them to comprehend it or even manage it, but to do it.

---

[6] Tim Stafford *The Sexual Christian*, 39 cited by Doug Webster *The Easy Yoke* (Colorado Springs: NavPress, 1995) 124.

Please hear me: I truly admire both of these authors and highly recommend their work. So, they are not "straw men," but their casual analysis of sexuality and communion betrays a fundamental evangelical Christian perspective on the body and blood that I find to be rather unbiblical.

Genesis 2:8 *"The Lord God planted a garden in Eden."*

"Eden" means "delight." "Garden" implies seed, dirt, life, trees and fruit. "Garden" in Hebrew, (*gan*), means "walled garden." In the words of G.K. Chesterton, this walled garden created space for "good things to run wild"[7]—a sanctuary.

Genesis 2:18 *"It is not good that the man (Adam) should be alone. I will make a helper fit for him."*

Adam was alone in the presence of Love. He was unable to experience communion in the sanctuary of delight. He didn't know and so could not trust Love. He did not know: *"the Lord [Yahweh]; he is our help"* (Ps. 33:20) and that we are His Bride.

Genesis 2:21-24 *So the Lord God caused a deep sleep to fall upon the man, and while he slept took one of his ribs and closed up its place with flesh. And the rib that the Lord God had taken from the man he made into a woman and brought her to the man. Then the man said, "This at last is bone of my bones and flesh of my flesh; she shall be called Woman, because she was taken out of Man." Therefore a man shall leave his father and his mother and hold fast to his wife, and they shall become one flesh.*

Scripture tells us that this refers to Christ and the Church. Christ Jesus gave His Church "pieces of bread and drops of wine," saying, "This is my body given to you. Take and eat."

The name Jesus means, *"Yahweh is Salvation/Help."*

So, like a walled garden contains delight . . .
Like the stone temple contained the Eternal Fire . . .
Like our bodies of flesh contain Spirit . . .
So, a covenant contains a sacrament: a communion of delight.

---

[7] G. K. Chesterton, Orthodoxy: The Romance of Faith (New York: Bantam, 1990), 95.

Genesis 2:25 *And the man and his wife were both naked, and were not ashamed.*

Well, I was just pointing out that Jesus makes a big deal of communion, and God makes a big deal of sex. So, perhaps we haven't made too much of sex (or communion, for that matter), but rather, far too little. And sex is far from bad. It's more like a remnant of the Good. I hope you realize that this all happened before the fall. (Even Christ and the Church is referenced in Genesis 2—before the fall.) All this talk of "communion" and preparation for communion happened before the fall. So, the fall is not the result of sex . . . yet perhaps, the fall was necessary if we were to ever know communion, if we were to ever know "Body broken and Blood shed."

Don't get stuck on that thought. We'll come back to it in Genesis 3. For now, I just hope that you grasp this: Sex did not cause the fall, and sex is not the result of the fall. Sex is more like a vestige of life from before the fall. Sex is a vestige of Eden bound by a covenant, much like the garden was protected by a wall. Sex is a vestige of communion in a sanctuary, a vestige of *perichoresis*—the Great Dance, Love and Life.

Or maybe it isn't a vestige, but more like a promise.[8]

Maybe sex, in a covenant sanctuary of delight, isn't a vestige of life, but more like the promise of life—eternal life. And in a fallen world, perhaps it must be managed . . . to the inside of that covenant sanctuary—not because it's bad, but because it's profoundly good. But there, in that sanctuary, it must run wild, for it's a taste of the uninhibited life that constitutes the Kingdom of God.

Maybe it's more than a vestige and more than just a promise. It's like a promise incarnate—a covenant wrapped in flesh. Sex must never be God. Yet, can it

---

[8] After all, we don't know that Adam and Eve actually had sex, or desired sex, or even thought it was "good," until after they took "knowledge of the Good." They didn't have faith in Love. Love is good. So, maybe taking "knowledge of the Good," did lead to sex, but that doesn't mean that sex is bad, anymore than the Good is bad. But, how we take the Good can be very bad. In the beginning God commanded intimate communion, but Adam and Eve did not "know" truly intimate communion. Intimate communion is Love. God is Love. We didn't "know," but we are coming to "know," we are learning to love, through the death and resurrection of the *Eschatos* Adam.

reference God? Indeed, it may be such an effective reference to God that if we forget God we'll naturally worship the reference and turn it into an idol. But if we say that the reference doesn't matter, then it no longer refers to God, and it no longer has much meaning. "It's just body and blood," we say, "And we wonder: "Why does God or Jesus (God incarnate) matter? Why does a relationship with God matter to us . . . or to God?"

What is "cleaving?"
What is "holding fast (*dabaq*)" to your wife?
What is sex?

In biblical times, a couple would go through a wedding ceremony, then proceed to the wedding chamber where the "friend of the bridegroom" stood outside the door. When the couple had consummated their marriage, the groom would call to the "friend," who would then call to all the waiting and expectant guests, "He's done it. It is finished." Then a party would begin that would last for a week, for the covenant had been consummated.[9]

When John the Baptist was told of Jesus baptizing His followers, John said, *"The friend of the bridegroom, who stands and hears him, rejoices at the bridegroom's voice"* (John 3:29).

So, what is sex in the covenant of marriage?

- It's a communion that consummates the covenant.
- It's a sign and a seal of that covenant.
- It's an outward expression of inward realities, like a promise incarnate.
- It's a means of grace through which life is transmitted and fruit is born.

---

[9] I've searched the Scripture and I haven't found any reference to brides and grooms taking vows to form covenants. It seems that something else formed the covenant—the moment the groom gave his body and blood to the bride and the two became one. It appears that this is why there is no specific instruction regarding "pre-marital sex," (at least not as we think of it) in Scripture. Sex basically meant that you were married: Exodus 22:16–17, the boy who seduced the virgin would pay the bride price and the two would be married. Even if the father absolutely refused to give his daughter away, the boy still had to pay the bride price. In Scripture, the punishment for sex before marriage is marriage.

- It's word made flesh; It's love made flesh; It's a mystery—*mysterium* in Greek; *sacramentum* in Latin.

You see, what I just described is the theological definition of a "sacrament."

When you come to the communion table, you partake in the "sacrament of the covenant."

- It's a communion that consummates the Covenant.
- It's a sign and a seal of that Covenant.
- It's the outward expression of inward realities, like a Promise incarnate, like the Promise of God wrapped in Body and Blood.
- It's a means of Grace through which Life is transmitted and fruit is born.
- It's Word made flesh; It's Love made flesh; It's the mystery of Grace.
- It's the Body and Blood of your Groom, which you receive into the most empty, restless and yearning parts of your soul—parts which you once considered dirty and covered in shame, but in which you now receive eternal Seed and bear the fruit of eternal Life.

"Common bread and wine" *do* "gain a fascination and emotional importance far beyond their practical function" because Jesus is them, or at least, in them—that's Spirit in bread and wine that He called His Body and His Blood.

So, Scripture tells us that if a person eats the bread and drinks the cup of the Lord in an unworthy manner, *"without discerning the body,"* the very thing meant to give us life . . . can kill them (1 Cor. 11:27-32). Not because it's bad, but because their discernment of something very good is bad. Their perception is bad—they don't perceive Jesus, the Lord their Helper; they only see bread and wine to consume and possess.[10]

It's like having sex in an unworthy manner, without discerning your groom or your bride. If you perceive them as your covenant partner, you manifest the

---

[10] It's like coming to Jesus on the tree in the garden. If you discern that He gives you His life and makes you in God's image, you have eternal life. If you think you take his life, or knowledge of His life (He is the Good), to make yourself in God's image—you just crucified "the Life" and everything dies. At the cross we confess—we die. And at the cross we receive God's Grace—we live: expire and inspire.

love of God. But if you perceive them as an object to consume, just body and blood—but not Spirit in body and blood . . . well, I think you worship Baal the possessor.

You inspire and don't expire. You only take and never give.

Perhaps we have an unbiblical view of sex, for we have an unbiblical view of communion. The modern problem is not that we've made too much of sex. Our problem is that we've made far too little of sex. I mean we don't discern the sacrament. Modern society has *not* turned sex into a sacrament, for it was made a sacrament from the beginning—not a sacrament of our covenant with God, but a sacrament of the covenant of marriage, which is the image of, and reference to, our covenant with God.

Because the marriage covenant is an image of God's covenant, the sacrament of the marriage covenant is to be a picture of the sacrament of God's covenant. In other words, God made us male and female and gave us these urges and longings—all so that we'd understand how God feels, what He wants, and what life in the paradise of the Kingdom is all about.

Sex is an education.

> A little girl was talking to her grandmother. She asked, "Grandma, how old are you?" The grandmother replied, "Now dear, you shouldn't ask people that question. Most grown-ups don't like to tell their age."
>
> The following day, the girl had another question. "Grandma, how much do you weigh?" Once again the grandmother replied, "Oh, honey, you shouldn't ask grown-ups how much they weigh. It isn't polite."
>
> The next day the little girl was back with a big smile on her face. She said, "Grandma, I know how old you are, you're sixty-two. And you weigh 140 pounds." The grandmother was a bit surprised and said, "My goodness, how do you know?" The girl smiled and said, "You left your driver's license on the table, and I read it."

Grandmother said, "Oh, so that's how you found out." The girl said, "That's right, and I also saw on your driver's license that you flunked sex."[11]

That's pretty bad: she got an "F" in sex.

I think the modern church gets an "F" in sex.

We haven't discerned "the Body." We haven't discerned Christ's Body, and so we haven't discerned our own bodies. And having not discerned our own bodies, we have not discerned Christ's Body. We have not discerned expiration and inspiration, *perichoresis*, sacrificial Love, the dance of Love that is Life, a communion of delight, the paradise that is God.

Please pay attention: I'm certainly not saying that you have to have sex (as in sexual intercourse) to understand God. No one knew God better than Jesus, and He was single. Yet, maybe you do need sex (as in male and female—sexual feelings, in some capacity, at some point) to best know God. Maybe you need frustration, loneliness and longing for communion to best know God . . . or be known by God—*knowing* in the way that He wants to be known. There are different ways of knowing. Baal the possessor cannot know and does not want to know, the way God knows.

So, if you're frustrated with this topic, I hope you realize that almost everybody is frustrated with this topic. I think that's part of the design, part of coming to know the way God knows and wants to be known:

- Some have been very hurt, and now they're terrified at their own desires.
- Some long for sexual relations, but can't have them and shouldn't have them for at least a time.
- Some long for the desire and mourn the fact that it's gone.
- Some feel torn to pieces because their desires are confused.

[11] James S. Hewett, *Illustrations Unlimited* (Wheaton: Tyndale House Publishers, Inc, 1988) p. 101

For all of us, it's so difficult to talk about because it taps into desires and long-ings that we can hardly bear and can barely control. But do you see? In all these things, in fulfillment and in longing—even longing for the longing—God is telling us something about Himself and making us long for Him.

Our sexuality is a sign. It's a message built into our very bodies. The problem isn't that we make too much of the sign. The problem is that we make too little of that to which it points. And if we think it points to nothing, we think the sign is nothing—just some broken bread and wine, just biology. But a sacra-ment is far more than bread or biology. It points to our Creator.

> Sex is the sacrament of the covenant of marriage.
> And this refers to Christ and the Church.

Denominations argue incessantly over the details of what is technically a sacra-ment and what is not a sacrament.[12] In seminary, I was taught that a sacrament is "a sign and a seal." A sacrament seals things. It takes two and makes them one. It consummates a covenant and seals it. Sex "seals" the covenant of marriage as baptism and communion seal the covenant of Grace. In other words, most Christians believe that something "supernatural" happens when you take the bread and the wine and place it in your mouth—you commune with God in Spirit!

You know, if you bump arms with another person nothing happens. Hearts are not fused and hearts are not broken That's because we don't really wear our hearts on our sleeves. Actually, we wear our hearts somewhere else, a place that we cover and call private.[13] When two people join private parts, they fuse pri-

---

[12] Some traditions (i.e. Roman Catholic) refer to marriage as a sacrament others (i.e. most protestant denominations) do not. "Sacrament" is a word that religious people made up, so it makes little difference to me. The point is that sex is a "sign and seal" of the covenant of marriage and sexuality is a sign (but not a seal) pointing to our rela-tionship with Christ.

[13] A good friend commented, "Peter, I don't get this word picture. It conjures up literal hearts on sleeves." Well, I think that may be what sex organs literally are. Sorry to be graphic, but at least on the male, doesn't the sex organ look like something on the outside that belongs on the inside? And indeed it is. It is the way that two become one body. "This refers to Christ and the church."

vate hearts as well. Two become one. So, to sleep around is to make a covenant and break a covenant over and over again. It's to fuse two hearts, then tear them apart—fuse and tear, fuse and tear until hearts are callous, hard and broken, until we lose faith in love. Or maybe we never really "knew" love. God is Love.

When people sleep around, they think, "We're just making love," but they end up *breaking* love and don't know love. God is Love. We all broke His heart and hung it on a tree.

> Actually we can't "make love."
> But this is the Gospel: Love makes us.
> And at that tree, He knows us and creates faith in us, and we know Him.
> He is Love, and there He makes us in His image.

When Israel worshiped other gods, God didn't call it "bad theology." He called it adultery. Do you understand? Do you know? Can you feel? They didn't just disobey God's law; they broke God's heart. "Jesus Christ and Him crucified" is God's broken heart.[14]

So, the broken heart of every lover in this world tells us about the broken heart of God—how God feels and what God wants. Sacraments help us know things deeper than words. They put flesh on words . . . or *the* Word. We all are beginning to know something for which our words fail. I think that's why there are so many words, songs and poems about love—romantic love. It's people trying to express things greater than our words; they're trying to express God's Word.

As a man, I can't fully describe that passionate longing for a woman— for a beauty that you can't describe; that feeling that nothing else matters; that yearning to be with her, to be one with her, to be buried in the soil of her body, to be in her. It's easy to think, "No one understands. No one knows." But God knows. That's how He feels about you!

> *As the bridegroom rejoices over the bride, so shall your God rejoice over you.*
>
> —Isaiah 61:5

---

[14] "No one has ever seen God; the only Son who is in the bosom of the Father, he has made him known" (John 1:18 RSV).

And women, you know that longing to be covered. I'm not sure that I feel it in the same way as you, but I learn of it from my bride: that desire to be covered, nurtured, cherished and filled; that feeling that nothing else matters but to receive him, to be filled with him and become one with him, to have him planted inside you like seed in the womb of this broken, rent and dirty earth. It's easy to think, "No words can describe..." Well, your body describes. And God knows. That's how He longs for you to feel about Him.

> *"I, Jesus... I am the root and the descendant of David, the bright*
> *morning star." The Spirit and the Bride say, "Come."*
> —Revelation 22:16–17

God wants you to know: He made you for Himself. Men know it in one way, and women know it in another way, but ultimately it is the same Way—the same thing. Perhaps women can sometimes feel it as men, and men can feel it as women because two become one and it is the same thing. Women know the Man, Christ, because they are His Body. Men know the Woman, the Bride, for that is who they are. All believers know the same thing from a unique and individual perspective. It is communion in the image of Love. God is Love.

The sacrament of the marriage covenant helps us understand what God wants in His covenant. He wants us. Even more, He wants the incomplete and imperfect us! He wants the naked us. He wants our weakness.

This is counter-intuitive. This flies in the face of conventional religion and the "survival of the fittest." This is shocking, rather insulting, and a bit weird: He wants the part of us that we're tempted to cover in shame.

> But Love has pitched his mansion in the place of excrement;
> For nothing can be sole or whole that has not been rent.
> —William Butler Yeats[15]

When a bride and groom make love, they are attracted to that very place of which they are normally most embarrassed and feel the most shame; that place

---

[15] W. B. Yeats, "Crazy Jane Talks with the Bishop" from *The Poems of W. B. Yeats: A New Edition*, edited by Richard J. Finneran (New York: Macmillan, 1933)

where their difference, incompleteness and desperate need is revealed and exposed; that place they each need the help of the other, their helper.

Do you know that you are incomplete without God?
Do you know that you need God?
Do you know it in your gut, or do you just know *about* it in your head?

You will feel it in your gut,
   Like an empty stomach ... or a womb.
You're empty without God,
   And the emptiness expresses itself as sin ... or worship.
You're naked without God,
   And the nakedness expresses itself as shame ... or surrender.

God longs to cover you with the righteousness of Christ.
God sends His Word in flesh to fill your emptiness with His very self.
Jesus is the Helper made fit for you—His Bride.

I believe that He is aroused by the confession of your sin; aroused by your surrendered shame; aroused by His Bride, no longer hiding in fig leaves and trees, attempting to justify herself—but now, surrendering herself, naked, broken and exposed, yearning for Grace.

He longs to meet your need with Himself. He is God freely given. He is Love poured out. He is Grace in the flesh. He is the Helper made fit for us, come to fill us. He is the Promised Seed planted in the broken and dirty soil of our hearts. For "*where sin increased* (in us), *Grace* (Jesus) *abounded all the more*" (Rom. 5:20).

Do you see what we're saying? God built the Gospel of Jesus the Christ into our very bodies from the foundation of the world. He built Eden into our flesh even before the fall, in order that we'd long for home even in the midst of our exile.

Great sex is a momentary taste of Eden. [16]

---

[16] That first Adam and Eve, were not satisfied with Eden, because they did not yet have the capacity to *know* Eden. Eden is "delight."

It's a picture of life in the Kingdom.

Think about it:

- In this world, obeying God is usually not all that fun.
- Dying to myself is a drag. Losing my life is painful.
- Another person's pleasure is often my sorrow. Their gain is my loss. Their need is my problem.
- So, I want control.
- In this world, being humiliated, exposed and naked is not a joy.
- Obedience to another's wishes is a heavy burden.

In this fallen world, God's command is a huge burden, except for a few moments—a few moments in the sanctuary of my covenant, celebrating the sacrament of my covenant with Susan, my bride.

- In those moments, obedience is ecstasy (*ek-stasis* "out of myself")
- I die to myself, but live. I expire and inspire.
- Susan's pleasure is actually my pleasure. Her gain is my gain. Her need is my deepest desire.
- I surrender control and experience joy—I gain her pleasure, a communion of pleasure (*Eden* means "pleasure").
- Being naked, exposed and vulnerable is a communion of delight.
- Obedience to her wishes is paradise; it's work that's rest; it's expiration that's inspiration, the dance of life—two persons and one substance— One Will—both wills joyfully obedient to the One (Good and Free) Will.

Like C.S. Lewis wrote, "...obedience—humility—is an erotic necessity." [17]

And then, the most amazing thing of all: this is where babies come from!

You see? In those moments of sexual ecstasy, I fulfill the entire law: I love God, I love my neighbor, and fruit happens.

---

[17] C. S. Lewis *That Hideous Strength* (New York: Macmillan, 1948) 148

The sacrament of my covenant with Susan fills me with hope for life in the Kingdom of God. It helps me trust my Helper. It produces faith in Love. God is Love.

> *Therefore, a man shall leave his father and mother and hold fast to his wife, and the two shall become one flesh. This mystery (mysterion in Greek, sacramentum in Latin) is a profound one, and I am saying it refers to Christ and the Church*
>
> —Ephesians 5:31

Sex refers to Christ and the Church.

And that means every love song ever written was somehow written about Jesus and us.

So, does "Burning Love" belong in Church?

Does "Burning Love" belong in the Sanctuary of the Covenant?

Yes! God is One "hunk, a hunk, of burning love."

Stop hiding in the trees and invite Him to come and fill His Temple.

*   *   *

Do you hesitate?

> Fire can keep you warm.
> Fire can bring you life, but fire can also burn.
> *"Our God is a consuming fire"* (Heb. 12:29).
> And *"God is Love"* (1 John 4:8,16).
> Love is a fire isn't it?[18] What does it burn?
> Does Love burn Life or death, Truth or lies?
> Maybe you've believed a lie about yourself.
> Maybe you've believed a lie about God.
> We all have.

---

[18] "...for love is strong as death... Its flashes are flashes of fire, the very flame of the Lord." – Song of Solomon 8:6

Maybe this chapter didn't feel like "love . . . " but more like sorrow. Perhaps you were never married but you want to be and don't know if you will be. Perhaps you've lost your partner and hope for deeper communion. You feel that hope as sorrow. Perhaps you're sick, or getting older (like Susan and me), so the communion is less physical and must become more spiritual—I think that's probably by design.

Well, if this chapter is experienced as sorrow, I suspect that testifies to hope, and like Paul writes, "...*Hope does not disappoint us...*" (Rom. 5:5 RSV). The communion you long for, you will more than receive. The lie is that you're finished, and the truth is that you've barely begun.

Maybe this chapter didn't feel like "love . . . " but more like shame. Don't cover your shame. That's what Adam and Eve do in the next chapter of Genesis. We'll discuss it in our next book on Genesis chapter three, and in three chapters of this book we'll address it again. But for now would you consider that the Lord is attracted to that which you cover in shame?

He doesn't want you to sin. But having sinned, it's there in that place of shame that He plants His seed. It's there that He'll build His mansion, and you are His mansion. Where sin increased Grace abounded all the more. Yes, His Light and Life will burn away the darkness and death—and sometimes that hurts. But that pain turns into the ecstasy of relentless and Amazing Grace.

> For some this chapter feels like sorrow. Have hope!
> For some this chapter feels like shame. Confess and believe!
> For some this chapter feels like rape. PLEASE keep reading.

> Someone or some thing has been lying to you about God—
> Could've been a snake. Could've been Baal the possessor. Keep reading.

> Jesus will not rape you, but He does arrange all things to romance you.

True masculinity and femininity emerge and develop only in the midst of other-centered relating. The more a man understands a woman and is controlled by a Spirit-prompted other-centered commitment to bless her, the more "masculine" he becomes. And he will become more masculine in an unselfconscious fashion. Ask this man to define masculinity, and he will need to think awhile before answering. In exactly the same way, the more a woman understands a man and is preoccupied with doing all she can for him, the more "feminine" she naturally becomes. We will neither understand nor enjoy our sexual natures until we take seriously our responsibility to use our distinct natures to serve others.

—*Larry Crabb, <u>Men and Women</u>*

Maybe the problem is not that people are getting naked, but that they aren't getting naked enough: we stop at the skin instead of going deeper, into the soul.

—*Philip Yancey, <u>Finding God in Unexpected Places</u>*

As the poet Yeats expressed this paradox, "Love has pitched his mansion in the place of excrement." . . . Like prayer, sex is a thing of exertion, of sweat and of groaning, and like death it is intimately acquainted with surrender, with excretion, and with the mournful frailty and heart-rending glory of flesh. And these are all things that God has made. He made the woman with an open wound in her body, such that it can only be staunched by a man; and the man He made with a tumor, the maddening pressure of which is only alleviated when it is allowed to grow inside the woman's womb. He made the man to root and to flower in the aching earth of a woman.

—*Mike Mason, <u>The Mystery of Marriage</u>*

Life is sexually transmitted. —*Anonymous*

CHAPTER 10

The Desecration of the Sacrament

Genesis 2:24–25

Many years ago, when Susan and I were newly married and living in L.A. in a rather dangerous part of town, I came home unexpectedly from a great distance, at an hour Susan did not expect. It was three in the morning, and she was sound asleep. I had been driving all night with my best friend, from a camp in northern California. That night, his new bride had called him and told him she wanted a divorce. He was in absolute agony. I dropped him off and couldn't wait to see Susan. I desperately wanted to hold her, to commune with her, to be lost in her.

I tried not to startle her. But trying not to startle a person at three in the morning makes a person all the more like a thief in the night. I remember thinking, "If only I could enter her dreams and somehow communicate to her, 'Honey, it's me. I'm coming home, and I'm coming in like a thief in the night. Now I feel like a thin whisper in a dream—your dream (your world)—but in a moment, in the twinkling of an eye, you will awaken. When you do, you must know it's me, and that I love you with everything I am.'"

I worked at the lock. The key in the door made a sound. And then I heard a voice of absolute terror coming from the other room: "Is somebody there? Who is it!? Oh my God who is it? Oh my God!" I knew in that moment that my bride believed that whoever had opened that door was about to rape her.

I called out, as quickly as I could, "It's me! It's me! It's me! I love you!"

When she saw me, she clung to me more tightly than she ever had before. She kissed me like she never kissed me before.

After a time, I undressed her and covered her with myself. I entered her and she received me with great delight. We communed in the sanctuary of our covenant. Hell turned into heaven and we "made love" like we never made love before—or maybe . . . Love was making us.

Our Lord told each of us to stay awake and keep our lamps burning, for He is coming like a "thief in the night." But He's not a thief in the night.

He can't steal what He already owns. Our house is His house, but He longs to fill us with delight.

So, He could be whispering to your soul right now:

> I love you. I long for you, but I will not rape you. Others may have done so, but I am not like the others. I am Holy. See my hands. See my feet. See my side. I give everything for you, that you would trust in me, that we might commune forever in my Father's sanctuary of endless Love. You are my Bride, and I am your Husband. You are my temple, and I am the Glory of God. I am Holy Fire!

> Now I feel like a thin whisper in a dream, your dream, your world. But in a moment, in the twinkling of an eye, you will awaken. When you do, you must know it's me and that I love you with everything I AM.

Has it ever occurred to you that the very same activity (sexual intercourse), the very same event is . . .

- Sometimes described as heaven and sometimes hell?
- Sometimes Love and sometimes hate?
- Sometimes ecstasy and sometimes rape?

The very same event . . . except for the intentions and perceptions of those involved, except for the faithfulness or faith of those involved, except for their faith in Love—not sex, Love. And God is Love.

Right now, some of you may perceive this message as good news, and some may perceive it as something closer to rape. If you perceive the message as rape, there's a good chance that you have been raped. *In some measure,* we've all been raped, and maybe we've done some raping.

I mean, perhaps someone has taken what you were unwilling to give. Or perhaps you gave, but now have come to see that they have only taken. So, now you feel raped and wish that you never had given. Perhaps someone abused your surrendered weakness and shame. You thought it was Love, but it wasn't Love and now you've lost faith in Love. You encountered the snake.

Jesus wants you to know: He's not the snake.

- God made Adam, male and female, and commanded them to be fruitful and multiply, and He called it "good." It is Life . . . and this way of knowing makes babies.
- The snake tempted Eve to take "knowledge of the good," to possess the good and make herself good. It is evil . . . and this way of knowing produces death.

There are two ways of knowing.

- God is revealing that He is our Helper. He completes us. He justifies us (makes us right). He creates us in His own image by Grace through Faith.
- The snake tempts us to complete ourselves and justify ourselves. He tempts us to create ourselves in the image of God, by flesh through fear, by works of the law—"the knowledge of good and evil."

There are two ways of knowing.

- God is "Good."[1] Jesus is the Good in flesh hanging on a tree in a garden.[2] When we receive Him as gift and know Him as Grace, we know "The Good," live His life, and become the image of God.[3]
- The snake tempts us to take the life of the Good in flesh hanging on a tree in a garden. When we take His Life, we know evil, crucify the Life and desecrate ourselves.[4]

---

[1] Mark 10:18, "No one is good except God alone."

[2] John 19:41, "Now in the place where he was crucified there was a garden." I Peter 2:24, "He himself bore our sins in his body on the tree."

[3] John 17:3 "And this is eternal life, that they know you the only true God, and Jesus Christ whom you have sent."

[4] This is a big idea, and I've been trying to save it for our next book in which we'll discuss these things in much greater detail. But since we're already in the garden talking

There are two ways of knowing.

- One looks like a book of laws and produces death.
- One looks like a honeymoon and creates babies.

God helps. Satan uses.
God gives. Satan takes.
God loves. Satan rapes.
God is Creator. Satan is the energy behind Baal the possessor.

God helps Adam and Eve in their weakness by creating faith through Grace. The snake exploits the weakness of Adam and Eve and causes them to hide their hearts, trapped in shame.

God knows us, that we would know Him.
Satan knows *about* us, to exploit us, that we would know nothing—the void.

God is our Helper.
Satan is our abuser.

Well, I hope you see that in the absence of faith in our Helper, we look for help in other places.[5] If we deny our need for God, if we repress our need for God, if we refuse to surrender our need to God, our need for God will drive us to other "gods." These other gods use sex to possess our hearts and shut them down.

That's why God cares so very much about your sex life, and that's why the evil one cares so much about desecrating the sacrament that is your sex life. He can plant a lie in your heart about the person of God by desecrating that sacrament—trapping you in a prison that is your own flesh.

---

about Adam, Eve, the snake, since we've already read about the tree and are discussing the two ways of "knowing," I need to introduce the idea here and now.

[5] "...the young man who rings the bell at the brothel is unconsciously looking for God."
—Bruce Marshall: *The World, The Flesh, and Father Smith* (Boston: Houghton Mifflin Company, 1945) , p. 108

The evil one and all his lesser "gods" use bad sex to possess our hearts and shut them down:

- So that, when the King of Glory appears, we will confuse Him with Baal—the possessor,
- So that, when He kisses our cheeks it will feel like rape,
- So that, when our Lord gives us His body and blood—His surrendered weakness, like a baby in a manger—we'll shed that blood and nail that body to a tree because we don't understand.

. . . But then, we'll begin to know

Do you see? Even that is part of the plan. Actually, it's the very heart of the plan. On Palm Sunday, Jesus, the heart, said this:

> And I, when I am lifted up from the earth will draw all people to myself." He said this to show by what kind of death he would die.
> —John 12:32–33

"Will draw" is the Greek verb, *helkuo*. It means to draw by an inward power, to impel, to romance. He does not rape us. He romances us.

And what is our sin? Isn't it a form of rape? Isn't it taking life, and He is "the Life?" Isn't it taking knowledge of the Good, and He is "the Good" in flesh?

> When tempted by the tempter, we seek to possess the life.
> When tempted by the tempter, we seek to inspire and never expire.
> When tempted by the tempter, we seek to possess the Good.
> When tempted by the tempter, we seek to rape . . .

But, the Great Bridegroom, the *Eschatos* Man, romances . . .
What we seek to take, He gives—He forgives.

And then we begin to know "the Good."
We expire ourselves and inspire Him. We begin to Live—eternal Life.

> He does not rape.
> He will only romance.

The romance creates faith.

It's with faith that we discern the body and blood and come to know our Helper.

We've all been raped by evil and done some raping. The Bible calls it sin.[6] I'm sorry that this sounds so harsh, but what else is it when we claim that "the Life" is our own possession, and we use "Love" for our own ends as if we created Him and judged Him? Jesus is "the Life" and "God is Love."

We've all sinned against Life and Love, but *"where sin increased, Grace abounded all the more"* (Rom. 5:20b). Grace creates faith. Faith is a good free will. Faith in Jesus is the will to commune with the One who wills to commune with you. Faith is trust and the trust is won at the expense of His Life and the sacrifice of Love. If you're proud of that faith, it's not Faith in the One that created it with body broken and blood shed. If you're proud of "your" faith, then it's not Faith, but just more sin; it's more taking the Life and using the Love. Faith is a gift of the Spirit of Jesus and God the Father.

He does not rape. He will only romance. But nothing is more powerful than the Romance of God. He is the Word of God through whom all things are created.

The evil one seeks to possess, consume, and rape; he seeks to know you against your will; to know you—not as a person, but as a thing—as only an earthen vessel. He seeks to trap you in your earthen vessel—holding your breath in fear and shame, so that you would never again risk communion.

In some measure, we've all been raped. But I have some friends that have been physically raped by men, women, and even demons. One was tied to a bed, raped, and left alone. In a vision, as we prayed for her, Jesus revealed that He had stopped this man from taking her life. She had always wondered why he had dropped the knife—even as he lunged at her—dropped the knife, and ran in terror. Jesus had held out His hand and stopped the knife. But that still left a terrible question: why hadn't He stopped the whole thing? I don't know exactly,

---

[6] When we come to the communion table we confess our sin: We "take" the body and blood of the great Bridegroom. AND when we come to the communion table we confess our faith in His Grace: He gives us His body and blood, transforming sin into the gift of Grace in the Sacrament of the eternal covenant.

but I do know that it was a page in the story of a great romance—a very painful page, but an even greater romance.

One night—perhaps it was that night—she had a vivid dream. Jesus came to her while she was alone and tied up on the bed. He untied her, covered her in His robes, placed her in the corner, tied Himself to the bed, and then she watched as everything done to her was done to Him. And then she knew: He knew her.

In that place, He revealed His glory to her. In that place she surrendered to Love, and God is Love. She knows Him in a way no one else ever has or will. She knows His pain—He was raped first—and He knows hers. They commune in a great romance.

Another friend sent me a letter after hearing something in a sermon about rape and romance. She describes a vision she received while praying with members of our prayer team. As they prayed through this horrid memory of abuse, when she was just two years of age, Jesus appeared. He removed the abuser from her. Then she writes, "Jesus lied down and took the rape and abuse for me." She then describes how He picked her up and held her to Himself. He wiped away her tears and took her outside, clothed in a little white dress, to play in the sunshine. At one point, He held out His hand to stop her abuser from entering the scene. My friend watched as the abuser turned from a monster into a little blonde boy who turned around and walked away. Then she writes:

> My Jesus further spoke to me in your sermon. He said He will ask permission. He will not rape me. HE WILL RO-MANCE MY HEART! This following week, Jesus revealed many names and thoughts He has for me: Princess, beloved daughter, beautiful, child of God, ...healed, redeemed, loved, forgiven, pretty, feminine, attractive, special, woman, BRIDE OF CHRIST!

In the "very place" that she believed that she was "not his people,"—to borrow the words of Hosea and Saint Paul—in that "very place" she learned that she was His people; in the very place she thought she was not beloved, she learned that she could not be more beloved (Hos. 1:10, 2:23, Rom. 9:25–26).

If you've been raped, I hope you can begin to hope: "Your sorrow will turn into joy."[7] And then you'll see that none of it has been wasted. All of it is being transformed into joy.

> Now his word is that our sorrow shall be turned into joy. Surely, if I knew for certain that all my stones should be changed into gold, the more and the larger stones I had, the better I should be pleased.[8]

Those are the words of the medieval philosopher and mystic Meister Eckhart. If you've been raped, they are extremely hard to believe, and yet he was quoting Jesus—who is the Truth.

As I mentioned, we've all been raped (in some form) . . . and we've all done some raping. If you've been to the cross, you've begun to see—we are the harlot that is transformed into the Bride; we are the "Israel of God." We are the old Jerusalem, the harlot that takes His life. And we are the New Jerusalem, to whom Jesus gives His life—the New Jerusalem that comes down from Heaven as His living temple, His body.

When we see how He has known us in our place of dirt and shame, we begin to trust Grace and know God—our Helper. We begin to discern the body and the blood. We expire and are inspired. We ingest the body and blood. We have faith in Love. God is Love. He is *not* Baal the possessor.

His Story—all of history—is the story of the great romance: how Eve is romanced and redeemed by the *Eschatos* Adam, Jesus the Christ.

History is the romance of God, so that when the King of Glory—our Helper—appears we won't hide from His presence, but instead surrender to ecstasy. We won't be burned by the fire— we will drink the fire. We won't perceive His presence as rape—we will love the glory of "His appearing."[9]

---

[7] John 16:20, "Truly, truly, I say to you, you will weep and lament, but the world will rejoice. You will be sorrowful, but your sorrow will turn into joy."

[8] David O'Neal, *Meister Eckhart, from Whom God Hid Nothing: Sermons, Writings & Sayings* (Boston, Massachusetts: Shambhala Publications, Inc., 1996), p. 35

[9] 2 Timothy 4:8

God says it this way through the prophet Hosea:

> *"[She] ...went after her lovers and forgot me," declares the Lord.*
>
> *"Therefore, behold, I will allure her,*
>   *and bring her into the wilderness,*
>   *and speak tenderly to her.*
>
> *And there I will give her her vineyards*
>   *and make the Valley of Achor a door of hope.*
>
> *And there she shall answer as in the days of her youth,*
>   *as at the time when she came out of the land of Egypt.*
>
> *"And in that day," declares the Lord, "you will call me 'My Husband', and no longer will you call me 'My Baal'."*
>
> —Hosea 2:13–16

We think that God, our Husband, is like Baal, the possessor. Satan tries to wed us to Baal, the possessor, so we'll shut down our hearts, thinking Jesus, our Helper, is a possessor too. But Jesus will not rape us. He came to romance us. He descends into every "Hell" in which the children of Adam find themselves, and there, He romances us; He draws us to Himself.

He won't know us (in the biblical sense) until we choose to be known.

Choosing to be known by God is Faith in God.

And here in the Valley of Achor, God creates faith. "Achor" means "trouble."

I do not want to rape my wife or ever abuse my children, but I will take them to the Valley of Achor and make myself a door of hope.[10]

---

[10] The Lord will not "rape," but only "romance." Yet, He does seem to violate our will, doesn't He? By that, I mean that life does not always unfold the way you want it to. You suffer. Some say that God is non-violent. Yet, if God is sovereign, He controls all the events in your life and at times He does seem to make a whip and drive imposters from your temple. Well, I've come to believe that God violates our bad will—that's the imposter in your temple; that's the "old man" that desires autonomy, isolation, and control. Control is always violated when we suffer. He will violate our bad will, but He will not violate our good will. Indeed, He is our good will. He is Love manifesting in us. He will not, and cannot, violate love. He is Love. I think that's what it means to say, "He will not rape. He will only romance."

When my kids were little, and I wanted their hugs, I'd take them camping in the backyard in our big yellow tent. Along about midnight, the wind would blow, the neighbor's dog would bark, the tent flaps would flap and, to the kids, it felt like trouble. Then they'd snuggle and hug me tighter than they ever had before. I was a door of hope.

When I was dating Susan, I took her to scary movies. On our first date, I took her to *Close Encounters of the Third Kind*, hoping for a close encounter of "my own kind." Later, I took her to see *Alien*, hoping that she'd snuggle up to me, and I would be less "alien." I took her to the valley of trouble and made myself a door of hope, so that, no longer trusting in herself, she might put her faith in me, and discern me—that I adored her, and longed to be her helper.

I don't mean to belittle your suffering, but maybe this entire fallen world is like a night in the backyard in the big yellow tent. Maybe it's like a moment in a movie, and the trouble isn't as real as it seems—it's temporal, passing and basically a lie—but the One next to you is Reality, Eternity, Life and Love, and He's made Himself a door. The door is real. It is the Love of God poured out in the Valley of Achor. He is the Helper made fit for you.

Through Hosea God says:

> *"I will allure her...and speak tenderly to her...and make the valley of Achor* [trouble,] *a door of Hope...And you will call me 'my husband' and no longer will you call me 'my Baal'...And I will betroth you to me forever. I will betroth you to me in righteousness and in justice, in steadfast love and in mercy. I will betroth you to me in faithfulness. And you shall know the Lord.*
> —Hosea 2:14–20

That's what God wants. He wants to know you—*truly* know you.

This may mean very little to many of you, but for some of you it may mean the world. Many years ago my wife and I prayed with one friend who suffered the abuse of evil spirits. In prayer, Jesus would appear and hold up a mirror to show my friend who she truly is. In the mirror, she would see herself in a beautiful white wedding gown. She was single (at least in the eyes of this world), but felt led to buy a wedding gown. She was instructed to hang it on her door at night.

When she looked at the gown and believed the gospel—that she had been wed to Christ in the eternal covenant of Grace—the evil one could not enter.

The Lamb, who stands as if He's been slain on the very throne of God, is infinitely stronger than satan. Jesus will not rape you. He is always romancing you.

I'm a dude . . . and the sight of me in a wedding dress is truly apocalyptic. However, I have come to believe that I am to hang one, so to speak, on the door of my own heart. It helps me to resist the wanton desires that tempt my soul and wait for my Lord and His kingdom.

We were each made for wildly ecstatic, uninhibited communion. In this world we taste it through our own sexuality and in the covenant of marriage. Yet, it's still only a taste, and we all must wrestle with desire for that which we do not yet fully know. We're not home yet. And so, Baal the possessor and that old snake, that is the devil, tempt our desperation and legitimate wants so that we would seek to fulfill them in illegitimate ways, ways that don't lead to more intimate communion but desolate isolation.

In those moments, it helps me to remember that God is not leading me to some endless austere and joyless celibacy. God is leading me to the marriage supper of the Lamb, and I am His Bride. And that communion, which I so desperately desire, will be my eternal state. So, I can thank Him for the samples of communion that He gives me in this space and time and say, "no thanks" to Baal the possessor.

> I find strength to say "no" to wanton desire,
> When I remember that I am God's desire.

"This is the victory that has overcome the world—our faith" (1 John 5:4). That is Faith in God, who is Love, and His Word, who is our Husband.

> *Behold, the days are coming, declares the Lord, when I will make a new covenant with the house of Israel and the house of Judah, not like the covenant that I made with their fathers on the day when I took them by the hand to bring them out of the land of Egypt, my covenant that they broke, though I was their husband, declares the Lord. For this is the covenant that I will*

make with the house of Israel after those days, declares the Lord:
I will put my law within them, and I will write it on their hearts.
And I will be their God, and they shall be my people. And no
longer shall each one teach his neighbor and each his brother,
saying, 'Know the Lord,' for they shall all know me, from the
least of them to the greatest, declares the Lord. For I will forgive
their iniquity, and I will remember their sin no more.

—Jeremiah 31:31–34

There are two ways of knowing. The tragedy of the first will reveal the glory of the second. All of the empty "nothing" will be filled with the glory of the eternal "something."

Behold, is it not from the Lord of hosts
    that peoples labor merely for fire,
and nations weary themselves for nothing?
    For the earth will be filled
with the knowledge of the glory of the Lord
    as the waters cover the sea.

—Habakkuk 2:13–14

For I desire steadfast love and not sacrifice, the knowledge of God, rather than burnt offerings. But at Adam they transgressed the covenant; there they dealt faithlessly with me.

—Hosea 6:6–7 RSV

If anyone imagines that he knows something, he does not yet know as he ought to know. But if anyone loves God, he is known by God.

—1 Corithians 8:2-3

"My dear Father, you really are a perfect case of sublimation," Miss Agdala said. "Shades of Freud and ghosts of Jung! But what do you do about sex yourself? How do you manage to live without us?"

"That is perhaps the easiest part of the religious life," Father Smith answered. "To begin with, touching daily the hem of his garment, priests do not see these things as other men do; and to end with, women's bodies are rarely perfect; they soon grow old and sag, and always the contemplation of them at their best is a poor and boring substitute for walking with God in his house as a friend…"

"What you have said just proves what I have always maintained: that religion is only a substitute for sex, " Miss Agdala said.

"I still prefer to believe that sex is a substitute for religion and that the young man who rings the bell at the brothel is unconsciously looking for God," Father Smith said.

—Bruce Marshall, The World, The Flesh, and Father Smith

CHAPTER 11

The Sacrament . . . Everywhere?

Genesis 2:24–25

Years ago, I had a "Damascus Road" experience. You might remember that Saint Paul's Damascus Road experience burned him and almost killed him. I was in the valley of trouble. That morning, I had told God that I was leaving my ministry, for I didn't think He spoke to me. Later that morning, He revealed a deep wound in me, a deep lack of faith and love within me. The revelation wasn't condemnation, but Mercy. I wept for hours, but the tears weren't mine; they were His. He felt sorrow for me. I had been in the Valley of Achor.[1]

That night, He literally pinned me to the floor.[2] It started as a tingling feeling—like when your arm has been asleep, but then comes back to life as the blood begins to flow and the nerves begin to connect. Then the tingling feeling turned into something like a raging fire. It was the presence of burning Love. It was the Spirit. And in those moments (thirty minutes, an hour . . . I really don't know), I saw that God was everywhere loving me. He was constantly my Helper and nothing was stronger than His Love. He is Love. The sensation was so intense, I thought it might kill me, and yet part of me wanted to die, for it would be Life and "I" would be free. I thought I might die of joy—intense delight.

The power was so intense, it might easily have scared me to death, but I had some faith . . . and I had the distinct impression that, at any moment, I could say "stop" and it would stop.

Maybe with my fear I say, "stop" far more than I know?

---

[1] I suppose I'd been there a long time, and it's not like I don't spend time there now. Indeed this entire fallen world is the Valley of Achor.

[2] At one point, I thought He was going to break my arms—I had always prayed, "God if I'm out of your will, just break my arms." I felt this intense pressure on the bones in my wrists as my hands were lifted, and locked in place, in a position of praise. It was actually wonderful. I knew He'd stop if I asked Him to do so. It's brought me much peace: the knowledge that God can get me back on track if necessary. That day I had told Him I was leaving "the ministry" and that day He let me know that I was walking out of His will.

Well, it has given me hope for life in His Kingdom, as if He was saying, "Peter, this is where we're going, but it's not time yet. You're not ready yet." I don't know quite what to make of all of that, but I've thought long and hard about it.

I don't know if I'm saying this correctly, so please forgive me if I'm wrong, but I think my chief complaint against Jesus is that He won't "rape" me. He *insists* on romancing me. He might burn me. He might kill me. He has led me to the Valley of Achor. But He won't rape me—He won't simply overpower my will from without. He insists on romancing it from within. For unless I have faith in Love, I will be utterly destroyed by Love, and He longs for me to receive His Love and conduct His Love—to channel His Love back to Him and to everyone I meet.[3]

Copper conducts electricity so well because it offers little resistance. If it's impure, there's resistance and it is burnt up and destroyed. That night, I felt like a little impure copper wire.

Blood vessels conduct blood so very well because they're empty and pliable. I had been full of myself, my fear, my shame, my control. Blood vessels in a body conduct breath in blood. The life is in the blood. A life is a communion of spirit; it's a body circulating blood.

> We are Christ's Body, the Body of the *Eschatos* Adam. Remember?
> We are His Bride and Body:
>
> *"... and they shall become one flesh"*
> —Genesis 2:24
>
> *"... a plan for the fullness of time, to unite (anakephalaiomai –* bring together under one wounded head) *all things in him...* *There is one body and one Spirit."*
> —Ephesians 1:10, 4:4
>
> *"... it is written, 'The two will become one flesh.' But he who is joined to the Lord becomes one spirit with him."*
> —1 Corinthians 6:16–17

---

[3] As I mentioned earlier, perhaps He does burn up my bad will and is Himself my new will (Faith, Hope and Love).

We are His Body, being animated, coordinated, filled and enlivened by His Spirit ... Christ is the Groom, and we are His Bride ... and Body.

"We are His Bride" ... Is that polygamy?[4] Well, if we are all one body coordinated by one Spirit, perhaps it's not polygamy, but monogamy. Whatever the case, it is happy. The Bride, who is that Body, *is* happy.

I once read that there are nerve endings that register pain as well as heat, cold, and pressure, but there are no nerve endings that register pleasure.[5] So, an individual body part can feel pain, but pleasure is a sensation produced by many parts working together in coordination, cooperation, and mutual sacrifice— like a dance: *perichoresis*, communion, Life and Love.

I'm not a doctor or a biologist, so I don't know how true that is. But I do know that when Susan and I celebrate the sacrament of the covenant of our marriage, there is a moment where I don't feel pain, and I don't feel my pleasure alone. I feel *our* pleasure together. I expire and inspire. (The French call it *la petite mort*—"the little death," and it's life.) I lose "my life and find it" ... not my life; I find *our* life. The earthen vessel is penetrated and we commune—no longer two, but one. I know her, and she knows me.

---

[4] I find it interesting that bigamy or polygamy is never explicitly condemned in the New Testament or the Old. It's never condemned, yet elders and deacons are to be the "*husband of one wife* (1 Tim. 3: 2,12, Titus 1:6)" as if no mortal man, stuck in the confines of space and time, can truly love and give his all to more than one wife. Old Adam can only give his all to one Eve. However, Jesus does truly love and give His all to each one of us—correct? But then again, we are not many, but one in Him. I do know that throughout the Scripture, the thing that seems to make sexual immorality immoral is not the joining, but the separating after the joining. In other words, the thing that makes sexuality immoral is the lack of a covenant bond, the lack of faithfulness.

[5] "There are nerves for pain and cold and heat and touch, but no nerve gives a sensation of pleasure. Pleasure appears to be a by-product of cooperation by many cells... Erogenous zones have no specialized pleasure nerves; the cells concentrated there also sense touch and pain.... All these factors [visual delight, memories, music, psychology, sociology, spirituality] work together to produce sexual pleasure."
Dr. Paul brand and Philip Yancey, *Fearfully and Wonderfully Made* (Grand Rapids: Zondervan, 1980) 24

One could know everything about her, possess her, dissect her, even crucify her and still not *know* her. But in that moment, I *know* her—the *breath* in the clay. I-contact.

In Luke 20, religious leaders tried to trap Jesus in error. They were Sadducees, and they will make you "sad you see?" Sorry, I can't help it. But it's true! We religious leaders are constantly tempted to *possess* God, and we end up crucifying God. If we do that with God, why wouldn't we do that with people, and especially our wives? The Sadducees tell Jesus about a man who died, leaving a widow, who was then, in turn, married to his six younger brothers who each, in turn, also died. Then the woman died. They say to Jesus:

> *"In the resurrection, therefore, whose wife will the woman be? For the seven had her [possessed her] as wife." And Jesus said to them, "The sons of this age marry and are given in marriage, but those who are considered worthy to attain to that age and to the resurrection from the dead neither marry nor are given in marriage, for they cannot die anymore, because they are equal to angels and are sons of God, being sons of the resurrection. But that the dead are raised, even Moses showed, in the passage about the bush, where he calls the Lord the God of Abraham and the God of Isaac and the God of Jacob. Now he is not God of the dead, but of the living, for all live to him."*
> —Luke 20:33–38

Taking their cue from these verses, people will say, "There's no marriage in heaven." But Jesus didn't say that, He said there would be no marrying or giving in marriage in the resurrection. Well, is that because no one is married or because everyone is married? He says it's because the resurrected "cannot die anymore," as if people get married because they're dead or afraid to die, as if death is separation and life is communion in a covenant.

There is no getting married in Heaven, but Heaven is eternal Life and Heaven is a marriage. Remember? It appears as the "marriage supper of the Lamb" (Rev. 19:9). And we appear as a *"bride adorned for her husband"* (Rev. 21:2). ... a bride that is also a city, described as the garden, that is also a temple, that is filled with God. And God will be our temple (v. 22)—mutual dynamic indwelling *perichoresis*.

We will be married to Jesus, and we will all be one body, with one Spirit. I think that means we will all be married and all freely will to be married. We will all love because love has become our nature. We will all expire and inspire one into another. We will all bleed one into another. We will all live to God.[6] We will all commune in the Covenant, the Eternal Covenant, made by the Head—our Head, in whom we are united. We will be one Body and we will be HAPPY!

> *You shall no more be termed Forsaken,*
>   *and your land shall no more be termed Desolate,*
> *but you shall be called My Delight Is in Her,*
>   *and your land Married;*
> *for the Lord delights in you,*
>   *and your land shall be married.*
> *For as a young man marries a young woman,*
>   *so shall your sons marry you,*
> *and as the bridegroom rejoices over the bride,*
>   *so shall your God rejoice over you.*
>
> —Isaiah 62:4–5

Far from being no marriage in Heaven, Heaven is one big marriage. And now I know what some of you are thinking: "That sounds like one big orgy. Is Heaven an orgy?"

NO! At least not in the way people think. People think like Baal the possessor. In this world, an orgy doesn't mean communion in a covenant, but communion that breaks covenant. In Scripture, it appears to me that the thing that makes sexual immorality immoral is not so much the joining, but the separating after the joining; not the communion, but ending the communion ... or

---

[6] "For none of us lives to himself, and none of us dies to himself. For if we live, we live to the Lord, and if we die, we die to the Lord. So then, whether we live or whether we die, we are the Lord's. For to this end Christ died and lived again, that he might be Lord both of the dead and of the living (Rom. 14:7–9)."

perhaps a false communion, that is a lie about true communion.[7] Whatever the case, Heaven is the deepest possible communion bound by a covenant that can't be broken, for none of us will desire it to be broken.

The covenant of marriage is a sanctuary to guard the holy act of physical communion from a fallen world. Yet, all of Heaven is a sanctuary, and the fallen world will be no more. We will be one body with our husband, Jesus, and one body with each other. Not a physical body, but a spiritual body. And pay attention: spiritual doesn't mean *less* real, but *more* real. So, if it's not sexual, it won't be because it's less than sexual, but more than sexual.[8]

Remember when Christ rose? He had a spiritual body, and He could pass through walls. We think the wall was solid, and Christ was not. But maybe Christ was solid, and the wall was not. Maybe one day we'll see that the spirit

---

[7] Some argue that homosexual communion is basically the same as heterosexual communion. I realize there is much legitimate debate surrounding this issue, but I think Scripture testifies that this union of two of the same (*homo*) is not the same as the union of two that are different (*hetero*); it doesn't work. Two men or two women can have communion, will have communion and should have communion, but not coitus—I don't believe that their earthen vessels are truly penetrated in this way, but that their hearts may be hardened in this way. Having said that, there is something in the *flesh* of all fallen people that deceives them, telling them that communion is taking and not giving; telling them the lies of Baal, the possessor; leading them to wantonness, fornication, divorce and rape. Praise God that "It is sown a natural body [and] raised a spiritual body...flesh and blood cannot inherit the kingdom...and we will all be changed" (1 Cor. 15:44, 50, 52). As for now, I have the greatest respect for those who struggle with desire and surrender it to Jesus—lesbian, gay, bisexual, transgender, "straight" or just plain old horney.

[8] "...a small boy who, on being told that the sexual act was the highest bodily pleasure should immediately ask whether you ate chocolates at the same time. On receiving the answer, "No," he might regard absence of chocolates as the chief characteristic of sexuality. In vain would you tell him that the reason why lovers in their carnal raptures don't bother about chocolates is that they have something better to think of. The boy knows chocolate: he does not know the positive thing that excludes it. We are in the same position. . . . Hence where fullness awaits us we anticipate fasting."

C.S. Lewis, *Miracles*.(New York, Macmillan, 1947) 160

It's a great quote, but you can eat chocolates and have sex. Whatever the case, no one will be disappointed.

contained in the earthen vessel was always more solid, real, and permanent than the earthen vessel, so the thing that's kept us apart, separate, and dead was not truly real, but more like an illusion . . . or a lie planted in our earthen vessel, that we needed to hide our shame, rather than surrender it in faith? Whatever the case, this much is true:

> *So is it with the resurrection of the dead. What is sown is perishable; what is raised is imperishable. It is sown in dishonor; it is raised in glory. It is sown in weakness; it is raised in power. It is sown a natural body; it is raised a spiritual body. If there is a natural body, there is also a spiritual body. Thus it is written, "The first man Adam became a living being"; the last Adam became a life-giving spirit. But it is not the spiritual that is first but the natural, and then the spiritual. The first man was from the earth, a man of dust; the second man is from heaven. As was the man of dust, so also are those who are of the dust, and as is the man of heaven, so also are those who are of heaven. Just as we have borne the image of the man of dust, we shall also bear the image of the man of heaven.*
>
> —1 Corinthians 15:42–50

We don't know what we will be, but we know *"we shall be like him"* (1 John 3:2). And we know we will commune in Spirit.

I don't have a perfect marriage or a perfect sex life. And the older we get, the more we have to give up the earthen vessels and the physical communion and relish the spiritual communion. And yet, that's always been the real communion. I am definitely grateful for attractive earthen vessels, but as I mentioned, there is a moment when the vessel fades and I commune in spirit—not covering my nakedness in shame but surrendering it in joy. And in those moments, I know Susan.

I've wondered if, in Heaven, in my spiritual body, I could know my dad in the same way. DON'T GET ME WRONG. I have no desire to have sex with my dad, but I do want to commune with my dad. I want to know my father, apart from my shame—my anxiety that I might not measure up, my embarrassment over things I thought he might find out.

I want to know my father apart from my shame and apart from his shame—that pressure he must have felt to make himself a good father with his knowledge of good "father-ness" and evil "father-ness," that pressure of being a pastor, that anxiety that he would fail and that shame that he might've failed. I want to commune with my dad, secure in the knowledge that he will never leave me nor forsake me, and I will never leave him nor forsake him.

Now he has a spiritual body (his physical one is a bag of ashes on the breakfront). My wife even saw him in his spiritual body in front of the church when he told me to not be afraid to drink the cup that the Lord had for me. He has a spiritual body, and I will have a spiritual body.

And I've wondered if, in Heaven, I could just lean into him or walk into him and commune with him. And that moment would be like that other moment with my bride. I wouldn't be ashamed of my inadequacies, incompleteness or even past sins, but together we'd delight in the Grace of God, the Spirit of God, the life that is God in us, flowing between us.[9]

I've wondered if I could just lean into Jesus or He into me and that moment would be like that other moment with my bride. I wouldn't hide my failures in shame . . . but delight in the wonders of His Mercy. I wouldn't cover my emptiness . . . but invite His fullness. I wouldn't cover my unrighteousness . . . but delight in His righteousness—like I delight in a warm robe covering my naked body on a cold day. I wouldn't hide my sins . . . but rejoice in the realization that where they had increased Grace abounded all the more. I wouldn't hide my need for help . . . but delight in my Helper. Lewis puts it this way:

> All times are eternally present to God. Is it not at least possible that along some one line of His multi-dimensional eternity He sees you forever in the nursery pulling the wings off a fly, forever in toadying, lying, and lusting as a schoolboy, forever in that moment of cowardice or insolence as a subaltern? It may be that salvation consists not in the canceling of these eternal moments but in the perfected humility that bears the shame forever, rejoicing in the occasion which

---

[9] Knowing that I'll commune with everyone in Heaven helps me resist the temptation to sexual communion with women other than my bride, right now.

it furnished to God's compassion and glad that it should be
common knowledge to the universe. Perhaps in that eternal
moment St. Peter—he will forgive me if I am wrong—forever
denies his Master. If so, it would indeed be true that the joys
of Heaven are, for most of us in our present condition, "an
acquired taste"—and certain ways of life may render the taste
impossible of acquisition. Perhaps the lost are those who dare
not go to such a public place.[10]

Humankind invented the private place and became a private part after listening to the snake—Baal the possessor. We build huge walls and fences. We
enact reams of legislation. With our knowledge of good and evil we claim our
"rights," employ police and even armies—all to protect our private places and
insure that each one of us is private... and apart—a "private part."

But Heaven is a very public place with few, if any, "private parts," full of body
parts all in perfect communion and animated by Love.

And so, our Lord doesn't rape us. But He does lead us into the Valley of Achor,
and there He makes Himself a door... a door out of the dark prisons in which
we trap ourselves. He romances us, eager for the day of communion, the consummation of the covenant, the wedding supper of the Lamb.

   Several years ago, I shared these thoughts in a sermon, including my specu-
lation that, one day, I may be able to just "walk into my Dad" and experience
some sort of ecstatic communion similar to, and even surpassing, that which I
had experienced with my bride. I was extremely nervous about the e-mails that
I would receive the following day.

   I only received one... that I can remember. It came from a woman I didn't
know at the time, but who has become a great friend and part of my church. In
it, she described an incredible encounter with Jesus, where he appeared to her in
a dorm room at a retreat center. He reminded her of several wounds and places
of shame from her past. Then, she shared how the Holy Spirit filled each place
with health and purity. She writes:

---

[10] C.S. Lewis, *The Problem of Pain* (New York: Macmillan Paperbacks Edition,
1962) 61

When we were done, Jesus was sitting by my side on the little twin bed. He had the sweetest smile, though the distinct features of His face were a little fuzzy. He leaned toward me and I kind-of froze. I thought, "What the heck is He doing? Am I going mad or is He about to kiss me?" Which is kind-of funny when you realize He knew what I was thinking.

Anyway, He leaned toward me and went into me. Just like you described it yesterday. He went right into me and I was filled with a joy and glory so overwhelming I pulled away in shock. He just chuckled at me while I cried and apologized for freaking out and He said, "That's okay, we have time." It was the most beautiful experience... there are no words to describe it. Then I just said that I thought I needed to sleep now and He said okay and [lay] down next to me and I fell asleep weeping with joy.

If you're freaking out: "That's okay, we have time."
I think that's why God made time.

He does not rape.
He will only romance.
The Romance creates faith.
It's with faith that we discern the body and blood

> ...and come to know our Helper.

But the day of the Lord will come like a thief, and then the heavens will pass away with a roar, and the heavenly bodies will be burned up and dissolved, and the earth and the works that are done on it will be exposed... But according to his promise we are waiting for new heavens and a new earth in which righteousness dwells.

—2 Peter 3:10

For the earth will be filled with the knowledge of the glory of the
Lord as the waters cover the sea.

—Habakkuk 2:14

As I mentioned in Chapter 9, "He is One hunk a hunk of burning Love."
And He doesn't just belong in church.

He belongs everywhere.

Genesis 2:24 *Therefore a man shall leave his father and his*
mother and hold fast to his wife, and they shall become one flesh.

Are you aware that in the fourth century A.D., the Christian community borrowed and assimilated the spring fertility symbol of the Roman Empire and put it into our Easter liturgy? At the baptismal rite of the Easter vigil, a lighted candle is inserted into a vase of holy water to symbolize that when Jesus Christ rose from the dead He consummated His union with His bride the church. . . .

Have you ever been sexually aroused to an intense degree? Really stimulated in a sensuous way? Passionately turned on? Both the Scripture and the liturgy of the Christian community say that human sexual arousal is but a pale imitation of God's passion for His people. That is why human love, though it's the best image we have, is still an inadequate image of God's love. Not because it overdoes it, but because human desire with all its emotion cannot compare with the passionate yearning of Jesus Christ. That is why saints can only stutter and stammer about the reality, why Blaise Pascal on his famous night of fire, November 21, 1654, could not speak a word, why Bede Griffiths wrote, "The love of Jesus Christ is not a mild benevolence; it is a consuming fire."

—*Brennan Manning, Lion and Lamb - The Relentless Tenderness of Jesus*

CHAPTER 12

The Closed Garden

And the City Whose Gates are Never Shut
Genesis 2:24–3:1

*But at Adam they transgressed the covenant; there they dealt
faithlessly with me.*

—Hosea 6:7 RSV

In 1979 Susan and I were both seniors at Heritage High School in Littleton
Colorado, dating and very much in love. That same year, Michael and Lisamarie
were also both seniors in a high school only a few miles from our high school.
And like Susan and I, Michael and Lisamarie, were dating and were very much
in love. They had been friends since childhood. It was like paradise.

One day in Michael's basement, Michael's brother Joe pretended to be the
minister and they had a wedding ceremony—Michael and Lisamarie. Michael
sent love notes to her, which she has kept her entire life.

In the spring of 1979, as they were preparing to graduate and dreaming of
marriage, Lisamarie chose to participate in her school's annual senior spring
trip to Mexico, and Michael couldn't go. For some reason, the fact that Lisamarie would go, and he would not, made Michael very nervous. But Lisamarie
made a promise to Michael: "Nothing will happen."

On the trip, late one night, the kids had a party on the beach. A group of local boys showed up and there was alcohol. Lisamarie had never had a drink, but
this night she did. That group of boys deceived her, took her to a shack . . . and
there, they beat her and sexually assaulted her. She almost died. In a way, she
did. She buried her heart. In her mind, she had broken her promise, their covenant, and now she would hide her shame.

Michael was waiting for Lisamarie at the bus station. He could barely con-
tain himself. He was hiding a $69 ring, and he was rehearsing a question:
"Lisamarie, will you marry me?" When she got off the bus, he said, "Lisamarie,
I have something to say to you." She responded, "Michael, I have something to
say to you as well." Michael said, "You first." Lisamarie took a breath and said,
"Michael, I want to break up." In shock he asked, "Why?" She couldn't tell him.

She was distant and cold. Michael knew he couldn't propose marriage, yet he did manage to say, "Lisamarie, I bought you a ring. I'd like you to have it."

She refused. It was the end of paradise for a very long time.

In the coming months, Michael pursued her. His every statement was like a question, "Where are you?" But she hid her heart. And she tried to hurt Michael's heart so he'd leave her alone. She even gave herself to some of Michael's friends and let him know, hoping that his love for her would turn to hate . . . because now his love, which had once been her hope, comfort, and joy burned. His presence convicted her and made her hide in shame. She felt she didn't deserve Michael—that she didn't deserve love. And because of that, Michael felt he didn't deserve love and didn't deserve Lisamarie.

Well, nobody "deserves" love.
>God is Love. So, real Love is God.
>>Love is a gift. It's Grace.

They both believed a lie. And they both wrapped fig leaves around their hearts and hid their nakedness in shame. Lisamarie actually forgot the shack. She repressed it, and Michael never knew. Animated by a wound locked deep in her soul, Lisamarie went on to marry another man. That marriage fell apart after three years and two children. Then she married an abusive alcoholic and that marriage crumbled as well.

Michael was suicidal for a time, and he acted out of his pain. Eventually he married and that marriage collapsed as well. For Michael and Lisamarie, paradise was a distant memory . . . like a ring on a shelf, in a box . . .

Michael had finally convinced Lisamarie to at least keep the ring. She did, and she wasn't sure why. Michael wasn't sure why she did either. It was like a seed of faith, hope, or love waiting to be planted in the broken dirty soil of what had once been a garden—a paradise.

"Paradise" is a Persian word describing a walled garden—well watered, full of pleasure, and a constant delight[1]. When God made Adam, He put him in a paradise—the Garden of Eden, the walled garden of delight. And then God said, "It's not good that the man should be alone." So, Adam was in paradise, in the presence of God, who is Love . . . yet Adam was alone. Adam didn't realize that God completes him, that God is his Helper and that knowing God—and being known by God—is the real substance of paradise.

I don't think Adam understood. Maybe Adam—who is us—does not understand that we are created. In other words, he doesn't have faith in grace. We don't have faith in grace. Grace means "gift." Adam doesn't understand that everything, and I mean everything, is a gift. It's all grace. What else could it all be? For, we didn't create ourselves. We can't *deserve* a thing, *merit* a thing or *earn* a thing, particularly Love who created all things including us! What an absolutely absurd notion to think we ever could.

Everything is gift from God who is GRACE and who is our Helper.

Well, in order to see Grace, and know Grace, it makes some sense that we would need to be created . . .

    and in some sense uncreated . . .

        and then re-created . . .

            in order that we could witness our own creation.

In other words, we'd need to be created, somehow desecrated, and then redeemed.

In other words, we'd all need to be *"consigned to disobedience"* and then watch God *"have mercy on all"* (Rom. 11:32).

In other words, we'd need to be forgiven by our Helper to truly know—and be known—by our Helper, who is Grace.

---

[1] Jesus uses this word, as He hangs on the tree, speaking to a thief hanging on the tree next to Him, in the garden on the side of the temple mount, where His body was placed in the tomb like a seed. He said, "This day you will be with me in Paradise" (Luke 23:43).

That's a lot to ponder, and we will continue to ponder. But for now, just note that at the beginning of the sixth day, in paradise, Adam didn't realize that God creates him, so God completes him. God is his Helper . . . our Helper.

So, God begins the great lesson: He puts Adam to sleep. Then He fashions his bride from his bleeding side. He brings the woman to the man, and the man says, *"Bone of my bones and flesh of my flesh."* That is— "She completes me." We know that she doesn't really complete him, and he doesn't really complete her. Yet their union is a picture of the great union that completes us all. Sex is the sacrament of the covenant of marriage.

> *"Therefore a man shall leave his father and his mother and hold fast (cleave to, be united with, joined to) his wife, and the two shall become one flesh,"* writes Paul, quoting Genesis.
>
> *This mystery is profound, and I am saying that it refers to Christ and the church."*
>
> —Eph.5:31–32

Well, Adam and Eve cleave, but they do not (and maybe we do not) yet understand that it refers to Christ and the Church. They do not yet understand that God is their Helper, that He completes them in His own image, that He covers them.

> **Genesis 2:25** *"And the man and his wife were both naked and were not ashamed."*

I don't believe that they should have been "ashamed" of their nakedness. Yet, it's clear that they did not understand how naked, and incomplete, they actually were . . . or are—how incomplete we actually are.

It's fascinating that by the end of Scripture, when we see Eden again, no one seems to be naked. The children of Adam are clothed with some outrageous clothing. Eden is a city, and the city is a bride. " *'It was granted to her to clothe herself with fine linen, bright and pure'—for the fine linen is the righteous deeds of the saints"* (Rev.19:3). *"It was granted to her."* The clothing is a gift. It's like the righteousness is a robe that's been given to her—a living robe.

Paul writes that God made Christ our *"righteousness, sanctification, and re-demption"*(1 Cor.1:30 RSV). He also writes, *"While in this tent...we yearn not that we would be unclothed, but that we would be further clothed, so that what is mortal may be swallowed up by life"* (2 Cor. 5:4).

You know, in the Sacrament of the covenant of marriage, the groom clothes his bride with his very self . . . his body and blood.

He is her covering

Jesus is our Groom, and we are His Bride.

They were both naked, but didn't understand. Next verse:

> **Genesis 3:1** *"Now the serpent was more crafty than any other beast of the field that the Lord God had made."*

They meet evil (the presence of the void). Now remember, this is the sixth day. God is still making humankind in His image. He is still making us in His image. The evil one tempts Eve to create herself in God's image, to complete herself, to cover herself, to sanctify herself, to redeem herself—to create herself with knowledge of good taken from a tree . . . BECAUSE, argues the snake, God cannot be trusted. You can't rely on Grace.

So, Eve takes from "the tree of the knowledge of good and evil." She gives some to Adam, who is with her, and immediately they know they're naked. They cover those very parts where they are to be completed through the sacrament of the covenant of marriage. And they cover themselves—those very selves that are to be completed through the sacrament of the covenant of grace.

They cover their private parts with fig leaf underwear.

They cover themselves by hiding in the trees from God, who calls out to them,

"Where are you?"

They shut down their souls and close their hearts.

Then God closes the Paradise of Eden, placing the flaming sword and the Cherubim at the eastern gate.

That brings up an interesting question that we've touched on in previous chapters: Where is Eden?

- Orthodox Jews believe it is on the Temple Mount in Jerusalem where the Cherubim would guard the way to the Mercy seat, on the Ark of the Covenant, in the Holy of Holies.
- In the Revelation, it shows up as the New Jerusalem, which is a city, temple, Bride . . . and us.
- In the Song of Songs 4:12 we read, *"A garden locked (enclosed, shut up) is my sister, my bride, a spring locked, a fountain sealed."*

Now I'm not saying Eden wasn't a physical garden on the temple mount. I'm saying that in some amazing way, our soul is like a garden, and perhaps Eden is within us. For we actually are God's temple, and the New Jerusalem. And Jesus said, *"The Kingdom of God is within you"* (Luke 17:21 NKJV), and that He would make us a spring of water and cause us to bear fruit like a garden.

If that's the case, then when we fell, we were exiled from the deepest part of ourselves . . . the place where God goes walking. We were exiled from the breath, the Spirit of God, within us. I-contact was broken. To get it back, it appears that something—like our flesh—must be cut. At the edge of the Holy Land, the children of Israel all had to be circumcised. And as they entered the land they encountered a God-man with sword drawn and ready to cut.

I don't know exactly how to say it, but I do know that satan wants us to be separated from God, who is Love. He wants us to close our souls so we won't commune with God in the sanctuary of our own deepest being—there, in Paradise. Maybe we don't shut God out so much as we cast ourselves out, terrified of Love. It does seem that the more we violate the sacrament of the covenant, the more difficult it becomes to surrender to Love.

In the previous chapters, we argued that sex is the sacrament of the covenant of marriage, which refers to communion with Christ in the Covenant of Grace. Satan attempts to desecrate the sacrament of the covenant of marriage, so he can destroy its witness to the ecstatic, penetrating, impregnating, life-giving presence of God. Satan works constantly to destroy your understanding of sex in order to destroy faith in Love.

When two people have sex, it's not only bodies that are joined; heart and soul are joined, and a covenant is sealed. When two people have sex outside that covenant, hearts are fused, and then . . . torn. Hearts are raped and then closed in shame. A person might become promiscuous with their body, but only do so by hiding their heart in calluses, scabs, and pain. They close the garden.

Years ago, at a Hollywood dinner party, Hugh Hefner turned to my old friend and pastor Don Moomaw, and he said, "Don, what do you have against my magazine?" Don had a brilliant response. He said, "It's not sexy enough."

Great sex is a communion of two hearts as two bodies become one. When the sacrament is desecrated, we associate intimate communion with rape. Then, when God goes walking in the garden, we hide. His Presence frightens us, and His Love—His very nature—burns our shame. So, at His coming, we run from His Glory and hide our nakedness with leaves from the tree; we justify ourselves with our knowledge of good and evil, the law. We hide in outer darkness . . . or maybe we hide from our true selves in outer darkness. Whatever the case, we no longer live in the Garden of Delight. We hide from Heaven and indeed "all things."

Well, Lisamarie hid her heart from Michael.
    Hid her heart from herself.
        . . . and hid her heart from God.

So, you see, sex is not a bad thing to simply be denied or repressed. Sex is a sacrament to be bound in a covenant.

When Israel worshiped other gods, our Lord didn't refer to it as bad religion, but adultery. You are made for the most intimate communion in the Sanctuary of the Eternal Covenant of Grace. *"For it is written, 'the two shall become one flesh.' But he who is joined to the Lord becomes one spirit with Him"* (1 Cor. 6:16-17). Wow. Sex refers to that.

So, may I digress for just a moment and make a few obvious points that I could've made in chapter 9, but it was already too long?

1. WE NEED TO HELP "KIDS" GET MARRIED:
    "It's better to marry than to burn with lust." (1 Corinthians 7:9)

    I think that may be the most ignored scripture in modern day America. In biblical times, youth were often married at age twelve, thirteen or fourteen, often before they went through puberty. So, puberty would hit, and someone might say, "Hey, you ought to have sex with your wife."

In modern cultures, due to better nutrition, puberty comes earlier, but marriage comes much later. It was just 150 years ago that modern society invented a new class of people: teenagers—people that society viewed as children, but with bodies that screamed: "adult, adult, adult!"[2]

I used to be confused as to why there really wasn't a biblical term for "pre-marital sex" in Scripture. Then, one day, it hit me: In Scripture, there is no such thing as "pre-marital sex" because to have sex is to get married. The sacrament seals the covenant. In Scripture, the "punishment" for pre-marital sex is marriage. It's no wonder teenagers are depressed. It's no wonder so many feel like they have been violated and divorced, for in reality, they have.

2. WE NEED TO HELP THEM STAY MARRIED.

I understand your objections to point #1. I really think I do.

"Kids aren't mature enough to be married." Who is? And according to God, if they have sex, it appears that they already are.

Maybe we need to drop the idea that anybody's "ready" to be married.

---

[2] Ronald L. Kotesky, *Understanding Adolescence* (Victor Books, Wheaton IL) 1987. Page 15 of Kotesky's book has a remarkable little chart that explains all the insane frustration of trying to be a good Christian teenager, as well as the heartbreak of being indulgent. On page 15, Kotesky has a chart plotting the average age of puberty (taken from medical records) over the last thousand years, against the average legal age of marriage over that same time. In the last century, the lines crossed for the first time and simultaneously our culture invented "the teenager." In the 1960's, almost every state made it illegal to "marry rather than burn with lust" before the age of 18. I think I started "burning" around 14, and didn't get married until I was 21. Oy veh.

Maybe we need to drop the notion that people should be "in-dependent" before they're married.

Maybe I'm terribly naïve, but maybe our society is rigged against marriage and we could change our social norms to help our kids get married and stay married.

3. WE NEED TO IGNORE WHAT THE GOVERNMENT SAYS ABOUT MARRIAGE.

Since when did a secular government define marriage? Since when did they define divorce? Why is it that people get married in churches . . . but go to courthouses to get divorced? The government can't tell you *when* you're married; the government can't tell you *when* you're divorced.

4. IF YOU'RE MARRIED, DON'T IGNORE THE SACRAMENT.

For the wife does not have authority over her own body, but the husband does. Likewise the husband does not have authority over his own body, but the wife does. Do not deprive one another, except perhaps by agreement for a limited time, that you may devote yourselves to prayer; but then come together again, so that Satan may not tempt you because of your lack of self-control.
—1 Corinthians 7:4–5

Need I say more? Sex matters.

The sacrament strengthens the covenant and testifies to the Gospel.

5. FLEE FROM THINGS THAT STEAL YOUR DESIRE FROM YOUR GROOM OR FROM YOUR BRIDE.

Don't commit adultery in your heart.[3]

---

[3] I know that many would like me to define this more precisely, but I'm afraid I can't. The Lord knows I've tried, but you see the issue is in your heart. You and the Lord must discuss this in your heart. Obviously, imagining sex with someone other than your spouse is "adultery in your heart," but for unmarried fifteen-year-old boys this can be-

6. HONOR THE DEEP BEAUTY OF GENDER DIFFERENCES, AND
SHOW COMPASSION FOR THOSE THAT STRUGGLE WITH
WHAT THOSE DIFFERENCES MEAN.

You see? Gender is so much more than penises and vaginas,
and it makes sense that the differences would be reflected in
all sorts of social norms. Norms change. God seems some-
what committed to some "norms" and not to others, which
leads to all sorts of lively debate, but I don't think we can debate with much meaning until we get in touch with the story
that God is telling. He made Adam, male and female, in His
own image, for a reason.

Gender is more than sex organs, and sexual attraction is so
much more than hormones. Homosexuality, bisexuality,
transgender identity issues . . . you see they're each so challenging and can be so painful because they not only intersect
the deepest parts of our being, they also intersect the story of
Adam and His Bride. You are not simply your apparent sexual
identity. You are the Body of the Bridegroom (that's male),
and you are His Bride (that's female). And you are infinitely
loved, even in—especially in—the place of your shame.

What this means in each situation, what exactly Scripture
says in this regard, and what the Spirit is saying to you in this
particular moment is something far greater than the scope
of this book or any book. But I want you to know, you are
not defined by your desires; you are defined by God's desire.
You are not gay, lesbian, transgender or straight. You are the
"beloved." Yes, you are a sinner. Yes, we all are sinners. Sin is
bad or broken desire—we learn it, and it's latent in our flesh.

---

come quite complex. And if we leave the heart and start talking externals, we will find
ourselves drawing an infinite number of lines somewhere between hard core pornog-
raphy and mandatory full body burqas for all women. And believe me, even if all the
women wore burqas, men would still find a way to "commit adultery in their hearts."
No, that won't do. You must invite Jesus to be a constant companion in your heart.
Laws may help, but only Love, living in your heart, can set you free and heal our society.

It's biologically-based and also the product of environment. All sin is bad desire. God is giving us all new desire. Trust Him with your desires, and He will reveal His desire in you. I believe that He implants that new desire in your place of shame . . . don't hide it in fig leaves. You, just you—naked you—are His desire!

You see, it's not that God is uptight about meaningless biology. He's using it all to show you: You are His desire.

7. WE NEED TO HONOR SINGLENESS.

To go without the sign is not to go without the substance. To go without the sign is not to go without communion and intimacy. Christ was single on this earth for the most profound and intimate of reasons: He is to be wed to His spotless Bride—the Church. Some men are called to walk with Him in that place. Some women are called to be the image of His virgin Bride.

PS It's never too late to be a virgin. "*I betrothed you to one husband*," writes Paul to the Corinthians, who had been notoriously unchaste, "*to present you as a pure virgin to Christ*" (2 Cor.11:2).

I have wondered if there are those in our sexually indulgent, and sexually ignorant, society that are lacking in sexual desire, but feel the need to identify with a particular sexual orientation due to peer pressure and our incessant social dialogue. Perhaps, this is you.

According to Saint Paul and to Jesus, there are people who are apparently born with low sexual desire and this is not a curse, but a blessing—not a shortcoming, but in fact, a gift from God. In Matt. 19:11-12, Jesus states that there are "*eunuchs who have been so from birth*" and that this is for the "*sake of the Kingdom of Heaven.*" In 1 Cor. 7:1-7, Saint Paul, who writes so eloquently about Adam and His Bride, states that his singleness is a gift and that he wishes that all could be as he, "*but each has his own gift from God.*"

Perhaps you lack the sign or much desire for the sign. If so, please hear me when I say, you may be highly favored and deeply gifted. And even though you lack desire for the sign, I know that you desire the substance. Perhaps you are called to be like Christ, or Saint Paul or any number of female disciples called into this unique and blessed service. I'm sure I don't understand all the reasons for such a calling, but like Paul and Christ Himself, perhaps the lack of physical union with one other person allows you to more deeply commune with God and many others.

Saint Paul warns us against those who "forbid marriage" (1 Tim. 4:3), yet he also makes it very clear that, to those, so called celibacy is a sacred gift. It's a gift to you, to those around you, and to Jesus. And, you will not be "single" indefinitely. You will be wed "*as a pure virgin to Christ.*"

8. WE NEED TO SEEK THE SUBSTANCE MORE THAN THE SIGN.

We are all dying. As we age, our ability to function sexually fades, and that's by design. The sign fades so we'll seek the substance . . . deeper nakedness and more intimate communion. Don't worry. Have courage. Heaven will leave you lacking for nothing.

Well, I thought I should mention those things. I used to think it was my job to teach on all those things so you wouldn't do any bad things; I used to think it was my job to keep you from desecrating the sacrament. Now, I realize that most of you already have. I bet all of you already have. Jesus said, "*I say to you that everyone who looks at a woman with lustful intent has already committed adultery with her in his heart*" (Matt. 5:28). What exactly that means, I'm not sure, but I'm really sure that I've already done it.

And whether or not you've committed adultery against your spouse or someone else's spouse, we've all committed adultery against God—we've worshipped another "god." That's my point.

We've listened to the snake . . .
 surrendered our hearts to other helpers . . .
  and shut down our gardens in shame.

Genesis 2:17 *"In the day you eat of it, you shall surely die."*

- Death is a lack of respiration, circulation—*perichoresis*. It's the refusal to love and be loved.
- On the sixth day of creation we all die.
- At the end of the sixth day of creation, on the sixth day of the week, at the sixth hour of the day the body of the great Bridegroom is broken on the tree in a garden; the life spills out and His Bride, from His side, is created saved and redeemed.
- On the Seventh Day of creation *"everything"* is *"very good."* *"It is finished."* All is filled with God, and God is Love, and Love is the dance of Life. "In Him was life." On the Seventh Day, everything is eternal ever-flowing, ever-circulating I-contact.

Genesis 2:17 *"In the day you eat of it, you shall surely die."*

I hope you see that the "original sin" was NOT sex. However, the "original sin" was adultery; by that I mean, a lack of faith in the Word of God, the Truth. It was our trust in a liar and a lie—yet a lie is ultimately nothing, and as we learned in the last book, the devil is full of nothing. So, our lack of faith in the Word of God may be our faith in ourselves, and so, our punishment is to be stuck with ourselves for a time. We hold our breath; we save our own life; we refuse to love and be loved; . . . we sin and die.

Death is the result of a lack of faith in the Good. *"God alone is good."* And God is Love. And Love is respiration and respiration is life.

But how are we to know that God is Good, that His Word is Good, that Love is Good, that we must expire to inspire?

If we try to *take* knowledge of the Good, don't we kill that Good and that knowledge of the Good, because we took it as our own possession?

To take knowledge of Love is rape.

To pay for Love, to think you've earned Love, is harlotry.

To take the Life of Love is *death*.

But what if in the very place we took, God *gave*—forgave?

To receive knowledge of undeserved Love is grace.

To receive the Life of Love is salvation.

To receive Grace is to *know the Good* and to *live*.

Grace is the Word of Love, who is the Good, given on the tree.

Jesus Christ, crucified and risen from the dead, is the revelation of the Good and the gift of eternal life.

It's in the place that we took the Life that God reveals He gives the Life.

It's in the place that we took "the knowledge of the good" that God reveals He is the Good, and His Word is Life.

It's there at the tree in the middle of the garden that Christ creates faith within His Bride: "*Where sin increased, Grace abounded all the more*" (Rom. 5:20).

If you were raped, I'm certainly NOT saying it was your fault. I'm saying it was *our* fault—long before the incident occurred. It was humanity's fault. Yet, I don't think God blames us, as if we could've known better. We didn't know "the Good" when we tried to take "knowledge of the Good." It was our failure, yet He expected our failure, and He uses our failure so that we would be known by "the Good," that we would surrender to Love.

I'm saying that all sin is rape. It's taking the Life of Love as if you owned the Life of Love. We've all sinned and been sinned against. It's resulted in a closed garden. In every sinner, there is a closed garden.

When we surrender that garden, in the very place that we encountered the horror of sin, God reveals the wonders of Grace and creates Faith . . . in Love. In that garden we die, and in that garden we rise, for it's in that garden that God reveals, "I am your Helper."

Twenty-four years, three marriages, three children, and a world of pain later, Michael and Lisamarie reconnected at her father's funeral and began to see each other once again. For twenty-four years, Lisamarie hadn't told a soul about the night in the shack. Not even herself. The gate to the garden was locked, and she couldn't even go there herself. In the intervening years, and because of all the questions that invariably rise from a locked garden in the depths of one's soul, she once again went looking for her Helper.

When her children were born, she was surprised by Life born from the very place that once meant shame. She recommitted her life to Christ. But still, people would ask her, "Where does all this shame come from?"

Where does your shame come from?

Lisamarie didn't know. In 2006, she had an argument with Michael and, all at once, the memories came flooding back. She was in agony. Yet, Michael loved her in the midst of all her shame.

In fact, the very thing she had kept from him for twenty-four years—that very nakedness that she had hidden in shame—became the greatest attraction for Michael. Her shame explained his shame. And her naked heart drew him to her in a flood of mercy. He longed to cover her nakedness. It was a nakedness far deeper than Lisamarie's skin. She was more than physically "sexy" to Michael. He was attracted to Lisamarie's empty soul.

But it wasn't just Michael. It was Someone else in Michael. It was the Second Adam, the *Eschatos* Adam, returning to His garden. Or, maybe we should say, that the closed garden was surrendering to Him. I would argue that He had always been in the garden. He's the meaning (the *Logos*) of the garden. And now He was rising from the dead.

Lisamarie entered counseling. One day, the counselor walked her back into the memory. She had a vision. She saw Jesus there in the shack.[4]

In Christ's day, the Jews believed that when the Messiah came He would open the doors of the Garden of Eden.

- Remember that He was crucified in a garden on a tree (John 19:41).
- Remember that He said, "When I am lifted up" (and He was speaking of being lifted up on the tree), "*I will draw all people to myself*" (John 12:32).
- Remember that He was buried in the garden like a seed and when He rose from the dead, Mary—a prostitute, or maybe a bride—saw Him first. She thought He was the gardener . . . and He is (John 20:15).
- Remember that we meet the Bride in the garden on a mountain— that's where the New Jerusalem comes down (Rev. 21:1-22:5).
- The closed garden becomes a City whose gates are never shut by day— and in that City there is no night.

Well, Jesus descended into Lisamarie's shack, or better yet, He revealed that He had been there all along. And there, He covered her nakedness with His righteousness. He is the Helper fit for Lisamarie.

I wasn't Lisamarie's counselor, and I don't know the details of what Jesus revealed to her that day. However, along with my wife, I have prayed for others that have been abused. Over and over, Jesus has taken them back in visions to the shack, or the closet, the garage, the basement or the garden in which they were abused. And then, there in that place, He has shown them that their shame is His shame. And there in that place, He takes their shame and gives them His righteousness. It's a righteousness fit for their individual shame. He covers them and completes them, revealing their unique beauty in all creation.

---

[4] It was just about the time that Lisamarie told me her story that William Paul Young published The Shack. In the Shack a man named Mack is led back to the Shack where his daughter had been raped and murdered. Father, Son and Holy Spirit meet him at the Shack and even repair his "garden." What I'm trying to say, my new friend, Paul Young, says more beautifully in The Shack.

He is the Helper "fit for them." He is the Helper fit for you and fit for me. We are all Lisamarie. We have all been deceived and have all done some deceiving. We have all been violated and have all done some violating. We have all sinned, and where "sin increased, grace abounded all the more." Where sin increased, there we meet our Helper. And what has been the curse becomes the blessing.

Let me put it this way: The absolute worst thing becomes the best thing. The place we witnessed the Life die becomes the place Love captures our heart and we begin to live: the cross, that miraculous tree.

Romans 11:32 *"God has consigned all to disobedience that He may have mercy on all"*—cover all, clothe all, fill all, complete all with faith in Love—Grace. The Bride of Christ is covered in the righteousness of her Groom.

- That Righteousness is not a stone wall around a dead garden, like a set of laws keeping others out.
- That Righteousness is more like an open gate in a great city, inviting others in (Rev. 21:5).
- That Righteousness isn't dead law, but living love.
- That Righteousness is like a fire burning in a heart and encircling a soul: *"Jerusalem shall be inhabited as villages without walls, because of the multitude of people and livestock in it. And I will be to her a wall of fire all around, declares the LORD, and I will be the glory in her midst"* (Zech. 2:4-5).
- That Righteousness is Grace.

People clothed in Grace don't cling to the false security of "rights," regulations, and law; the righteous don't demand their "rights." Their soul is an open city protected by the Grace of God. And you've seen it, haven't you? It's true beauty. It's the Glory of the Groom that covers His Bride (Rev. 21:11). Lisamarie forgave her abusers, and Lisamarie saw that she is forgiven. Michael forgave and saw that he is forgiven.[5] It's the Glory of God that delivers us from evil and unites us with all that's good—and on the Seventh Day all creation is good.

---

[5] Michael had an amazing encounter with Jesus during worship recently. He forgave his enemies and Jesus allowed him to experience the ecstatic thrill of pulling them through the cross and into the Kingdom—*perichoresis*.

People of Grace are an outpost of Seventh-Day life in this sixth-day world, and they are beautiful. They are good because they've been known by the Good and now they know the Good.[6]

Lisamarie and Michael are beautiful—they are Christ's Bride and two of the most beautiful people I know. Seven years ago, I officiated at their wedding. Like a mustard seed buried in a dry garden, Lisamarie had kept that $69 ring in a box in a closet on a shelf. And with that ring, they were wed. Last year, they moved to Hawaii.

Now, if you're thinking, "I wish that was my story; it sounds like Sleeping Beauty, Snow White or Cinderella . . . and Prince Charming; it sounds like a fairy tale, where the curse turns into an endless blessing . . . I wish that was my story."

Well, I'm telling you it is!
Your name is Eve, and your Bridegroom is the Ultimate Adam.

And let me remind you. Even Michael and Lisamarie's story isn't their real story. I mean it's only a shadow of the story, like a sign pointing to the substance. Michael and Lisamarie still live in the sixth day . . . and it turns out that Hawaii is nice, but it's not paradise. And Lisamarie has some very challenging health problems. They're both getting older, and one day their bodies will die. And then, they'll find themselves in Paradise, but Paradise won't be entirely unfamiliar because they've already tasted it here in the garden of their surrendered soul.

So, would you surrender your garden?

Would you just pray: "Lord Jesus I surrender my soul. I surrender my shame. I surrender my wounds, and I surrender my guilt—for how I have wounded *you*. I surrender my anger and my confusion. I surrender myself to you, my Helper."

I think I so love Michael and Lisamarie's story because it seems the covenant was made long before the sacrament was desecrated. I mean Michael and Lisa-

---

[6] *Tobe*, The Hebrew word translated "good" in Genesis chapter two, does not first imply good as in "ethically good," but good as in "beautiful."

marie were kind of like married in Michael's basement by his brother Joe, when they barely had a clue as to what it meant. And now, Michael and Lisamarie can be naked and unashamed in a way they could barely have begun to understand in 1967 as children, or 1979 as teenagers. They can experience *perichoresis*; they can commune as they never could have before; they can experience what, in some way, they always had but could not "know." They can be naked souls in the presence of Grace.

Did you know that our covenant with Christ is eternal[7] (Hebrews 13:20)? Do you remember that the Lamb was slain (Christ was crucified) *"from the foundation of the world"* (Rev. 13:8)? See, I think that means God formed the covenant long before we broke the covenant . . . and He knew we would break the covenant. Actually, He arranged things so that we would break the covenant (Rom. 11:32), that He might show us the depths of His Love. It makes my head spin. The Covenant of Grace is eternal, but God made us male and female, subjected us to futility, and redeemed us on a tree in a garden, in time. Perhaps in some way, it's so that we might know what the angels cannot know as we know: We are created by Grace. We know Grace, for Grace has known us. We have faith in Grace, so we can be naked souls in the presence of God who is absolute Love: That's Grace.

He's always been our Helper, but we don't truly *know* our Helper, until we see that we need help and know we've been helped; we don't know until we are known. He's always been our Creator, and we have always been His creation, but believing that we create ourselves, we can't be naked before the Truth, which is His Word, with which He creates us; we do not truly know our Creator until we are known by our Creator in our place of shame.

So, would you surrender your garden?

> *"A garden locked is my sister, my bride,*
> *a spring locked, a fountain sealed...*
> *Awake, O north wind,*
> *and come, O south wind!*
> *Blow upon my garden,*
> *let its spices flow.*

---

[7] By "eternal," I think the Scripture means, outside of the linear flow of time.

Let my beloved come to his garden,
*   and eat its choicest fruits...*
Eat, friends, drink,
*   and be drunk with love (or by Love)."*
                                    —Song of Solomon 4:12, 16–17; 5:1b

I don't know exactly what that means to you. I'll tell you one thing it means to me. Actually, I already did in chapter one. It was seven years ago that I began to preach *once again*, having stopped for almost a year. And I was preaching once again on these verses in Genesis chapter two. I knew that preaching on sex, and particularly the desecration of sex, would push everyone's buttons and I was tired of being hurt. The year before I had been publicly tried, defrocked, and removed from my large and "successful" church for hoping that God could really "make all things new" (Rev. 21:5) and hoping that a day was still coming when "everything" would be "very good" (Gen. 1:31).

At the time, I felt so very much shame—I had exposed the deepest longings in my heart, then, felt thoroughly violated and abused. I couldn't decipher what I'd done wrong from where I'd been wronged. For about two weeks, every morning I woke up with the same image in my mind—an image I'd never seen before. It was graphic, and I won't describe it here. I saw that I had been, or was being, raped.

I don't think it referred to any particular person or people. I think it referred to principalities and powers, to a religious spirit—maybe the snake that tempted Eve in the Garden, the one that tempts me even now. I'm fairly certain I didn't experience the depth of pain that Lisamarie experienced, but nonetheless, it was the worse pain I've ever felt, and I wanted to shut down my heart. I wanted to close down the garden.

Well, seven years ago, as I sat in our now little church downtown and began to preach on these verses (having not preached for a year) I began to experience what I described in chapter one: puffing. It was so bizarre. At one point, I saw my notes move. It was that strong. I couldn't explain it away. I was a bit encouraged, rather frustrated, and a lot confused. I thought, "Thanks Jesus. But rather than puffing, how about some money or some vengeance!"

Then as I prepared my message on the "Desecration of the Sacrament and the Closed Garden," I read this from Scripture:

A garden locked is my sister, my bride...

Awake, O north wind,
and come O south wind!
Blow upon my garden...

Song of Solomon 4:12,16

I looked up the Hebrew word *puach*, which is translated "blow."

It means "puff."

I think the Lord was saying, and is still saying, "Peter, open your garden. Receive my Spirit. Preach my Word: not for an institution, not for approval, not to justify yourself or make yourself in my image, but for me. I AM your Helper."

The month before at a retreat for wounded pastors, my wife heard the Lord say this to me:

> Peter, you are my heart.
> They cannot take away from you who I have made you to be.
> Totally stripped of all, God has been allowed to clothe you.
> I will show you the way to go, my heart.

I have Susan's note, recording that word, framed and displayed on my shelf. I am utterly unworthy of what it says, but it's worth being stripped of all, just to hear it said. And I don't think that "stripping" part is just for me. We are all being stripped of our pride that we might be clothed in Grace and forever know His delight.

We have each suffered a closed garden, that we all might become a city whose *"gates are never shut by day—and there will be no night there."* That city is already descending on the face of this earth. It began on Pentecost in the first century and will grow until the earth is *"filled with the knowledge of the glory of the Lord as the waters cover the sea"* (Hab. 2:14). And it won't stop even then or there. *"Of the increase of his government and peace there will be no end"* (Isa.9:7). There can be no end because He is "the end" (Rev. 22:13). There is no end to Jesus, *Yeshua*—"God is Salvation." There is no end because He is the End, and we are His City, His Bride and His Body.

Then I heard what seemed to be the voice of a great multitude, like the roar of many waters and like the sound of mighty peals of thunder, crying out,

"Hallelujah!
For the Lord our God
*   the Almighty reigns.*
Let us rejoice and exult
*   and give him the glory,*
for the marriage of the Lamb has come,
*   and his Bride has made herself ready;*
it was granted her to clothe herself
*   with fine linen, bright and pure"—*

for the fine linen is the righteous deeds of the saints...

Then I saw a new heaven and a new earth, for the first heaven and the first earth had passed away, and the sea was no more. And I saw the holy city, new Jerusalem, coming down out of heaven from God, prepared as a bride adorned for her husband...

Then came one of the seven angels who had the seven bowls full of the seven last plagues and spoke to me, saying, "Come, I will show you the Bride, the wife of the Lamb." And he carried me away in the Spirit to a great, high mountain, and showed me the holy city Jerusalem coming down out of heaven from God, having the glory of God, its radiance like a most rare jewel ...

And I saw no temple in the city, for its temple is the Lord God the Almighty and the Lamb. And the city has no need of sun or moon to shine on it, for the glory of God gives it light, and its lamp is the Lamb. By its light will the nations walk, and the kings of the earth will bring their glory into it, and its gates will never be shut by day—and there will be no night there...

Then the angel showed me the river of the water of life, bright as crystal, flowing from the throne of God and of the Lamb through

*the middle of the street of the city; also, on either side of the river,
the tree of life with its twelve kinds of fruit, yielding its fruit each
month. The leaves of the tree were for the healing of the nations.*
—Revelation 19:6–7, 21:1–2, 9–11, 22–24

Genesis 2:24 *Therefore a man shall leave his father and his
mother and hold fast to his wife, and they shall become one flesh.*

When we become aware that we do not have to escape our pains, but that we can
mobilize them into a common search for life, those very pains are transformed from
expressions of despair into signs of hope.....A Christian community is therefore
a healing community not because wounds are cured and pains are alleviated, but
because wounds and pains become openings or occasions for a new vision. Mutual
confession then becomes a mutual deepening of hope and sharing weakness becomes
a reminder to one and all of the coming strength...Thus ministry can indeed be a witness to the living truth that the wound, which causes us to suffer now, will be revealed
to us later as the place where God intimated his new creation.
—*Henri Nouwen, The Wounded Healer*

All times are eternally present to God. Is it not at least possible that along some one
line of His multi-dimensional eternity He sees you forever in the nursery pulling the
wings off a fly, forever in toadying, lying, and lusting as a schoolboy, forever in that
moment of cowardice or insolence as a subaltern? It may be that salvation consists not
in the canceling of these eternal moments but in the perfected humility that bears
the shame forever, rejoicing in the occasion which it furnished to God's compassion
and glad that it should be common knowledge to the universe. Perhaps in that eternal
moment St. Peter—he will forgive me if I am wrong—forever denies his Master. If so,
it would indeed be true that the joys of Heaven are, for most of us in our present condition, "an acquired taste"—and certain ways of life may render the taste impossible
of acquisition. Perhaps the lost are those who dare not go to such a public place.
—*C.S. Lewis, The Problem of Pain*

With this word 'sin' our Lord brought to my mind the whole extent of all that is not
good: the shameful scorn and the utter humiliation that he bore for us in this life and
in his dying, and all the pains and sufferings of all his creatures, both in body and
spirit -- for we are all to some extent brought to nothing and should be brought to
nothing as our master Jesus was, until we are fully purged: that is to say until our own

mortal flesh is brought completely to nothing, and all those of our inward feelings which are not good. He gave me insight into these things, along with all pains that ever were and ever shall be; all this was shown in a flash, and quickly changed into comfort; for our good Lord did not want the soul to be afraid of this ugly sight.

But I did not see sin; for I believe it has no sort of substance nor portion of being, nor could it be recognized were it not for the suffering which it causes. And this suffering seems to me to be something transient, for it purges us and makes us know ourselves and pray for mercy; for the Passion of our Lord supports us against all this, and that is his blessed will for all who shall be saved. He supports us willingly and sweetly, by his words, and says, 'But all shall be well, and all manner of things shall be well.' . . .

And I wondered greatly at this revelation, and considered our faith, wondering as follows: our faith is grounded in God's word, and it is part of our faith that we should believe that God's word will be kept in all things; and one point of our faith is that many shall be damned--like the angels who fell out of heaven from pride, who are now fiends, and men on earth who die outside the faith of Holy Church, that is, those who are heathens, and also any man who has received Christianity and lives an unchristian life and so dies excluded from the love of God. Holy Church teaches me to believe that all these shall be condemned everlastingly to hell. And given all this, I thought it impossible that all manner of things should be well, as our Lord revealed at this time. And I received no other answer in showing from our Lord God but this: 'What is impossible to you is not impossible to me. I shall keep my word in all things and I shall make all things well.'

—*Julian of Norwich, Revelations of Divine Love (c. 1395)*

CHAPTER 13

The Fruit of the Sacrament

Genesis 2:24, 1:27–28

God made Adam, male and female, and bound them in a covenant in which they celebrate a sacrament that produces fruit. Scripture informs us that this refers to Christ and the Church.

> **Genesis 2:24** *Therefore the man shall leave his father and mother and hold fast to his wife and they shall become one flesh.*

I once "held fast" to my wife, and we became one flesh. We named that flesh Jonathan. If scientists were to break down his DNA, they'd tell you (I hope), "Yep, he's literally two people that became one." Peter, Susan, and Jonathan—a trinity of flesh in the image of God.

> **Genesis 1:27–28** (On the 6th day of creation) *So God created man (Adam) in his own image in the image of God he created him; male and female he created them. And God blessed them, and God said to them, "be fruitful and multiply..."*

This is the very first commandment in all of Scripture. And it's a picture of Christ and the Church. It would seem that having some idea as to how we go about "being fruitful" would be utterly foundational, not only to Christian life but also human life. Yet, we "Christians" really do seem to struggle with the concept. We live in a sexually indulgent and promiscuous society that distorts the picture—a promiscuous, yet sanitized society, which leaves us shockingly ignorant as to what it all means.

In the poor agrarian society of Jesus' day, where private rooms were a luxury and every child was involved in farming and animal husbandry, any six-year-old would know about seeds, and sowing, and where baby lambs come from. But we, modern and enlightened people, struggle to make the Biblical connections: *"Be fruitful and multiply."*

On May 28, 1983, I entered a covenant. And in the sanctuary of the covenant, I celebrated the sacrament. In obedience to God, Susan and I strove to *be fruitful*. I remember the night so well. We went right up to our hotel room and got to work. How to make fruit was rather confusing and perplexing at first. After some brainstorming, and hard work, this was the best we could do:

In the morning, rather frustrated and exhausted, we realized that we needed help. We needed more knowledge of fruit, and fruit manufacturing; we needed an expert. We went into town and found a professional fruit maker, and he helped us make a few of these.

It's rather disappointing. They turned out to be fake. It looks like fruit, but it's not fruit. You know, when you're hungry, fake fruit is worse than no fruit. Fake fruit is a lie about fruit—a mockery of real fruit.

The Bible says that the fruit of the Spirit is "*love, joy, peace, patience, kindness, goodness, gentleness, faith and temperance.*" When you're hungry, fake fruit is worse than no fruit.

Do you realize that with all of our knowledge and all of our skill, the world's greatest experts are entirely incapable of making one piece of fruit, one scrap of organic matter, one molecule of food? We cannot make life. Yet God says, "*Be fruitful...*"

"*Be fruitful and multiply...*" "yourselves," I would suppose, perhaps the fruit in Genesis 1 is a reference to more persons. So, obviously I'm just teasing about my honeymoon night.

We didn't manufacture fake apples. We went up to the hotel room and immediately went to work with the serious business of making a person. Once, I shared with my congregation that I had captured actual video footage of our first attempt to create a living person. I shared that the footage was disturbing in some regard, but if we were to take seriously the first commandment, perhaps we needed to get serious about our studies. "It's *that* important. Susan basically looks the same," I said, "but my hair was a little different." We dimmed the lights and rolled the film:

> A man with crazy hair stands in a laboratory in what looks like an ancient castle. He's wearing a white lab coat and a stethoscope:
>
> He says: *This is the moment. Well dear, are you ready?*
>
> She replies: *Yes, Dear.*
>
> The man: *Elevate me!*
>
> The woman: *Now? Right Here?*
>
> The man: *Yes! Yes, raise the platform!*
>
> The woman: *Oh! The Platform! Oh that, yes.*
>
> Hoisted by chains and pulleys the platform begins to ascend toward an opening in the roof under a dark and stormy sky. On a table on the platform a sheet covers the form of what

appears to be a person. The man, Dr, Frankenstein played by Gene Wilder, calls to the woman:

The Man: *Tonight we shall ascend into the heavens. We shall mock the earthquake. We shall command the thunders and penetrate into the very womb of impervious nature herself. Get ready! Get set! Go!*

Dr. Frankenstein slides his goggles down over his eyes and watches his "creation" with great anticipation. His assistant, played by Terry Gar, who does look remarkably similar to my wife, pulls a large lever:

Dr. Frankenstein: *Throw the second switch! Throw the third switch!*

Assistant: *Not the third switch!*

Dr. Frankenstein: *Throw it, I say! Throw it!*

The third switch is thrown. There is Lightning. Thunder. Shattering glass.

Dr. Frankenstein Screams: *Life! Life, do you hear me? Give my creation life!*

As the lights came on in the sanctuary, I began screaming at the congregation, "Life! Life, do you hear me? Give my creation life! Live, live, live I tell you!"

Does that remind you of church: a pastor yelling at a bunch of lifeless zombies, "Live, live, live! Bear fruit! Be fruitful and multiply! Try harder"? Then the monsters walk out and pretend to have love, joy, peace, patience, kindness, goodness, gentleness, faith and self control, when inside they're filled with anxiety, doubt, anger and death, secretly longing to feed on the living.

Do you see my point? With all of our biology, psychology, theology and ecclesiology, with all of our knowledge of good and evil, we can, at best, make fake fruit and hang it on monsters. Creepy! Do you ever find church to be a bit creepy?

Well, the greatest experts—the most brilliant scientists and most insightful theologians—cannot make one piece of fruit. However, farmers (even little children) can "grow" fruit or, at least, "multiply" fruit. But the way they do it is entirely counter-intuitive.

First, you must have a seed.

It's what you do with the seed that's so counter-intuitive. You see a seed is an absolute marvel. It's so small, yet it contains an entire new creation. It looks dead, yet it's an author of life. Scientists can't make one seed or even comprehend one seed, but they know a seed is a treasure. In the Millennium building in London, and in the Svalbard Global Seed Vault in Norway, scientists keep seeds in vaults designed to survive nuclear war. They keep the seeds in vaults safe from dust and decay.

Yet to grow fruit, you must place the seed in dust and decay. I sold (tried to sell) vacuum cleaners to protect people from dust and decay, but unless you put a seed in dirt, you will grow no fruit and fruit is food. Human life is dependent on the death of a seed.

In the 60's, the Peace Corp was discouraged to find that vast shipments of kernels of corn never made it to the fields, but were eaten instead. That makes sense because the seed is fruit, and the fruit is food. It would take some faith in the seed to put your dinner in the ground. What you do with seed is entirely counter-intuitive.

To preserve the seed you keep it from dirt. Dirt is dust and decay.

Hey . . . you're made of dirt, and I bet you've experienced some decay. Do you ever feel like dirt—maybe even full of crap? Then your wife says, "Honey, it's time to go to church." And what do you do? You hide the dirt and bury the crap; then you fake a bunch of love, joy, peace, and patience at church; when it's time for communion, the pastor issues a warning, so you sit in your seat and don't partake because you're too full of crap. You protect the seed from the dirt and the crap—the garden.

But to grow fruit, you have to put the seed in the soil—the dirt and the crap—and not just any soil, broken soil. It would be easy to think that, in order to grow fruit, you'd have to get your "crap" together, but in reality it's best if you're broken apart. To grow fruit, the seed must fall into broken, crappy, dirt—fertile soil . . . and then be left alone. You must let it be: "Let it be. Let it be."

Remember in Sunday school when you buried your bean in the Styrofoam cup or maybe planted that seed in your father's garden? . . . You'd worry about it, then, dig it up to check on its growth.

> Do you hate that you don't love *Love?*
> Are you sad that you don't feel more *Joy?*
> Do you worry that you don't experience more *Peace?*
> Are you impatient with the growth of your *Patience?*
> The more you worry about your fruit and try to manufacture that fruit, the less it will grow.

A farmer needs faith, not in himself, but faith in the seed. If he doesn't have faith, he'll never sow the seed. He'll eat it, or maybe just put it in a vault or a barn. And if he does by chance sow the seed, he'll dig it up in fear because he doesn't have faith in the seed.

But if the farmer just buries the seed in the soil and walks away, the seed turns into a plant (like a tree). And the plant (or tree) takes the dirt and crap in the soil and mixes it with light and turns it into fruit, bearing even more seed.

Well, to be fruitful and to multiply is to lose control and exercise faith. Where does a farmer get faith? Jesus compared faith to a seed (Luke 17:6), and we are constructed of soil. We are "*God's field*" (1 Corinthians 3:9), maybe even his garden. Whatever the case, being fruitful must involve a death and a resurrection. So, the psalmist writes:

> *Those who sow in tears shall reap with shouts of joy! He who goes out weeping, bearing the seed for sowing, shall come home with shouts of joy, bringing his sheaves with him*
> —Psalm 126: 4–5

In this world, the sowing and the reaping, the sorrow and the joy don't normally happen at once, but Amos prophecies another day:

> *"Behold, the days are coming,"* declares the Lord, *"when the plowman shall overtake the reaper and the treader of grapes him who sows the seed; the mountains shall drip sweet wine and all the hills shall flow with it."*
> —Amos 9:13

So, in that day:
   The sowing will be reaping, and the reaping will be sowing.
   The giving will be receiving, and the receiving will be giving.
   The losing will be finding, and the finding will be losing.
   The humbling will be exalting, and the exalting will be humbling.
   The emptying will be filling, and the filling will be emptying

Like a river of life flowing through all things, even the hills will flow with red wine—like a great dance of love, like *perichoresis*, like sowing seed in a garden of delight. And that reminds me of how human fruit is made in the sacrament of the covenant of marriage.

Adam and Eve were cast out of the garden to till cursed ground. But Eve was not cursed ground, and though she would experience pain in childbirth, the sacrament of their covenant is a vestige of life in the Garden of Delight.

And that reminds me of communion. From one side of the table we see body broken, blood shed, and an entire world of suffering and pain. From the other side, Jesus sees the marriage supper of the Lamb, where the covenant is consummated in eternal ecstasy.

THE SOIL

Well, I was just saying that being fruitful and multiplying is a rather counter intuitive activity for the dirt, the farmer, and the seed: that is the bride, the groom, and the seed.

I think this is why we find Jesus' parables, particularly the seed parables so frustrating. In the Synoptic Gospels, Jesus tells seed parables, and, in all three, He tells the parable of the four soils or fields (Matthew 13, Mark 4, and Luke 8). People always want to know, "What's the practical application point? What do I have to do?" Well, I've preached these parables several times . . . and there is no "practical application point." It seems there is nothing that *you* can do.

You're the dirt, not the seed. The dust is dead. The seed contains the life. Jesus compares His words to the seed, and He's speaking to the dust. Maybe the seed does something to the dust? Maybe the Word is doing something to the dirt. (You know, tree roots can break rock.) Maybe He's doing something to the dirt like a seed, or a root, or even a sword, or a plow.

In the midst of explaining the parable, and the purpose of parables, Jesus quotes Isaiah: "...so that 'seeing they may not see and hearing they may not understand'" (Luke 8:9, Isa. 6:9). Isaiah is told to prophecy about a field that is a vineyard that is unproductive and filled with thorns but is burned with fire down to a root that is a stump. "The Holy seed is its stump" (Isa. 6:13). Through Isaiah the Lord declares,

> ...My word...
> > shall not return to me empty,
> but it shall accomplish that which I purpose,
> > and shall succeed in the thing for which I sent it.
>
> "For you shall go out in joy
> > and be led forth in peace;
> the mountains and the hills before you
> > shall break forth into singing,
> > and all the trees of the field shall clap their hands.
> Instead of the thorn shall come up the cypress;
> > instead of the brier shall come up the myrtle;
> and it shall make a name for the Lord,
> > an everlasting sign that shall not be cut off."
>
> —Isaiah 55:11–13

Nothing is more powerful than the word of God, and Jesus calls it "seed." Even if a bird (like a devil) eats the seed, it excretes the seed back into the dust coated in fertilizer. The seed takes root and breaks up the hard ground. Even if the seed sprouts on shallow ground then withers and dies, it turns the dust into dirt (fertile dirt is dust and death or decay). Even if thorns spring up, that's not the end of the story.

You may remember that when Eve and that first Adam took the fruit from the tree, God cursed the ground with thorns "until" Adam returns to the ground; for out of the ground he was taken—"*you are dust, and to dust you shall return*" (Gen. 3:19). But that's not the end of the story, for God just declared that the "seed" of the woman would crush the head of the snake (Gen. 3:15). And of course it would, for the word had already gone forth, "*Let us make man in our image...*" (Gen. 1:26)."

Well, I'm just saying that the Seed does the work, and we are the dirt (*adamah*: "the ground"). Jesus is talking to dirt—kind of like God breathed into the dust of the ground. So, Jesus tells His parable and says to His disciples, "*Blessed are your eyes, for they see and your ears for they hear*" (Matt. 13:16). In other words, "Blessed are you dirt bags—dirty and broken, surrendered to the Seed." Surrender your broken crappy dirt to the Seed. That's counter-intuitive.

"Surrender." Is that a practical application point? Well, I suppose that depends on whether or not you consider it something *you* can do, of which you then feel proud *or* something the *Word of God* does in you, for which you then feel grateful.

In Luke 9, Mark 9, and Matthew 17 Jesus is asked to cast a demon out of an afflicted boy, and He compares faith to a mustard seed that can move mountains. He asks the boy's father if he has faith, and the boy's father says, "*I believe; help my unbelief*" (Mark 9:24). And Jesus casts out the demon. I think the father had a seed of faith, and that faith was a gift—if it's not a gift, I don't think its faith. He used the faith, or maybe the faith used him, to surrender his field. It seems the faith grew.

Jesus had just said, "*All things are possible for the one who believes* (has faith)." He believed, and Jesus helped his unbelief. So, use the faith you've got, or may *it* use *you*. And the next time you're in prayer, or the next time you're at church, don't hide from communion, but surrender your dirty broken heart to the Seed. Surrender the garden. Confess your sins, believe the Gospel, and thank God for the Seed. It's counter-intuitive, but that's how we become "fruitful and multiply."

Actually, Susan and I didn't attempt to create fruit in a laboratory like Dr. Frankenstein and his assistant. However, Susan and I tried like crazy to have kids for a year[1]. Well, because she was desperate to bear fruit, she seized control. It was work, work, work and no longer play, but work (at least for Susan).

It was work, work, work and the garden seemed to lose some of its delight. I said to her, "Not that I'm complaining or anything, not that I'm not very happy to oblige, but sometimes it feels like . . . you're . . . using me, just to grow some fruit." She'd say, "Oh no, I'm just so attracted to you." And I'd say something like, "That's weird, 'cause until you wanted a baby, I can't ever remember sowing this much seed?"

Susan tried even harder. A friend who didn't want a baby, and in Susan's mind didn't "deserve" a baby, got pregnant at the time. Susan's heart began to grow some thorns. With resentment and anger, it grew hard and the devil stole her joy, until . . . one day, driving her car yelling at Jesus, her heart broke. She pulled over sobbing; she cried, "I give up, and I forgive." She surrendered the garden.

Then she made love to me, her groom, just because she loved me, and loving me was her delight. Then she got pregnant . . . four times! Then . . . she sent me to the doctor . . .!

Now listen very closely. If you want to have a baby and can't have a baby, I am ABSOLUTELY *NOT* saying it's your fault or that your heart is hard. Actually, in Scripture, it's barren women who seem to be God's favorites: Sarah, Rachel, the mother of Samson, Hannah, Elizabeth. And it's not their fault. And into their broken hearts, God speaks His word, even *the* Word, which He spoke into Mary. Through Isaiah the Lord speaks:

> Sing, O barren one, who did not bear; break forth into singing
> and cry aloud, you who have not been in labor! For the children
> of the desolate one will be more than the children of her who is
> married," says the Lord...For your Maker is your husband, the
> LORD of hosts is his name.
>
> —Isaiah 54:1,5a

---

[1] To be honest, I really enjoyed that year, but Susan did not. And I suppose that has some spiritual significance. Jesus may enjoy those times when you feel unfruitful and desperately call on Him for help. He likes to help.

If you *are* childless, you may be the most fertile of all. Surrender your broken heart to the Word and the "*children of the desolate one will be more that they children of her that is married,*" ... because you *are* married.

We can't bear fruit by *seizing* control. *We* can't create fruit. And if we act as if we do—if we pretend the love, joy, peace, patience, kindness, goodness, gentleness, faith and self control are our *own* doing—if we take credit for the fruit, it's fake fruit and we've made ourselves monsters, not human, but imitation human, false selves.

We can't make fruit, and we can't bear fruit by stealing fruit. If we do, the fruit dies. God said, "*be fruitful...*" and what did Eve do? She stole fruit and covered her shame. It's not until she surrenders her shame that she can bear fruit.

> "And here in dust and dirt, O here, the lilies of his love appear."
>
> —George Herbert[2]

That's counter-intuitive.

THE SOWER

The appearance of the lilies of Love in the dust and the dirt is counter-intuitive. It's counter-intuitive for the soil and counter-intuitive for a sower (but not for *the* Sower). It's counter-intuitive for the bride and counter-intuitive for the groom (at least us earthly grooms).

We are each the Bride, but a bride gives birth to seed—fruit—seed that is sometimes a groom producing more seed. Paul writes, "*The Jerusalem above... is our mother*" (Gal. 4:26). People of faith spoke words of faith that took root in you and became faith in you; that is the new you.

We are each the Bride, and we are each the Body of the Groom. I'm saying that Jesus uses you to sow His seed. And what the Sower does, what the farm-

---

[2] I pulled this quote from Anne Lammott's wonderful book *Traveling Mercies* (Anchor, NY) p. 51. She uses it to describe her "beautiful moment of conversion." She was a depressed alcoholic living alone who had just had an abortion and would rather die than call her self a "Christian." But, Jesus met her in that place and wouldn't leave her alone. Until, one night she hung her head and said, "Fuck it, I quit." Then out loud, "All right, you can come in."

er does, what the gardener does is counter-intuitive. He puts the seed in the ground and lets it *die*, so it can *live*.

Think about what God does. He creates space and time, breathes Spirit into dust (reminds me of a seed) and makes a person; then He allows the person to fail, then He speaks His Word of Grace (the Seed) into them and completes them in His own image. I just said more than I know, but isn't that how a father creates a son?

If you treat kids like machines and simply control them with rules and laws you may get some fake fruit, but you'll probably produce a monster. But, give your kids space to fail, then speak words of grace, like seed into broken soil, and I bet you'll grow a person in the image of God: someone who loves in freedom. *"The words I have spoken to you are spirit and life"* (John 6:63), said Jesus. And, He said:

> *The Kingdom of God is as if a man should scatter seed on the ground. He sleeps and rises night and day, and the seed sprouts and grows; he knows not how.*
>
> —Mark 4:26

If "he" says he "knows how," it's probably not real fruit that he's growing. There are a million of "how to" books written by experts on how to grow spiritual fruit, how to grow children, and how to grow the Kingdom of God. But if they "know how," it's probably not the fruit of the Spirit that they're growing. It's probably not people in God's image, or the Church of Jesus Christ, that they're growing. Those things, that we can comprehend and manipulate, may "grow" church attendance, bank accounts, and facilities, but that's not the Church.[3]

I've read lots of books and been to lots of conferences on church growth. One day, I realized that "ministry success" was being measured by one's ability to avoid being crucified by the people one intended to lead. All the principals, strategies, and techniques were designed to keep the seed out of the soil. By *that* standard, Jesus was the world's greatest failure. Yet, we know Jesus was God's

---

[3] If we think the Church is simply an institution manufactured by people, we need to stop referring to it as a Body or a Bride. Referring to a dead thing as a living thing creeps people out. It looks alive, but get close and you find its dead ... the walking dead. That's creepy!

greatest *success*. It's extremely rare to find a book that advocates the church growth method suggested in Scripture. It's entirely *counter*-intuitive.

On Palm Sunday Jesus said:

> *The hour has come for the Son of Man to be glorified. Truly, truly, I say to you, unless a grain of wheat falls into the earth and dies, it remains alone; but if it dies, it bears much fruit. Whoever loves his life (psuche) loses it, and whoever hates his life (psuche) in this world will keep it for (*literally: *"into") eternal life (zoe).*

—John 12:23–25

THE SEED

Is Jesus a seed? And did He die? What does it mean to die?

Jesus said, "*I am... the life*" (John 14:6). So, did "the life" die? Scripture claims that He "*became a priest*" for us, "*by the power of an indestructible life*" (Heb. 7:16). How could "eternal indestructible life" die?

Most English Bibles translate two different words with the one English word "life." In the two verses I just quoted, the Greek word translated as "life" is *zoe*. *Zoe* is almost always translated "life." The other word often translated as "life" is the Greek word *psuche*, which is also translated "soul" or "psyche" and sometimes "heart."

Jesus' words are "spirit and *zoe*" (John 6:63). And, "*In Him was zoe, and the zoe was the light of men*" (John 1:4). As we noted in chapter 2, and also in all four gospels, Jesus delivers up His Spirit as He dies. "*...The Spirit is zoe...*" writes Paul, in Romans 8:10.

Perhaps you could say that a *zoe* does not "die", but a *psuche*—psyche does die. And when the *psuche*–psyche dies it releases the spirit, the breath. It expires, and then it can be inspired. It can "enter into eternal *Zoe*." Perhaps it becomes a "vessel" of eternal *zoe*—a blood vessel in the eternal Body of Love channeling the river of life, *perichoresis*.

Or, maybe you could say, when a *zoe* dies, it truly begins to live. It was trapped in death, just as it was trapped in a *psuche*. So, eternal life is the death of death—Life! The second death is Life! You don't have to fear the second death if you've already lost your *psuche*. Jesus said in numerous places that if you lose your *psuche*, for His sake and the good news, you will find it! I suppose you'll find it full of *zoe* and flowing with a river of Eternal *zoe*.

> **Genesis 2:7** *Then the LORD God formed the man of dust from the ground and breathed into his nostrils the breath of life, and the man became a living creature (*Hebrew: *nephesh.* Greek: *psuche)*

Adam is an earthen vessel containing life. Adam is a seed. Unless a seed falls into the earth and dies, it remains alone. And what if a *psuche* falls into the earth and does not die? What if a body dies and the earthen vessel turns back into dust, but the *psuche* refuses to die? What if the *psuche* holds its breath? I think . . . that must be *Hades* (or as some translate the word, "Hell").

But *Hades* comes to an end in a lake of fire, called the second death (Rev. 20:14). Did you know that some seeds will only germinate through fire? Jesus taught that the Father can "destroy both soul *(psuche) and body in Gehenna*" (Matt. 10:28). That's the valley (Jer. 7:31) that's set ablaze by the "*the breath of the LORD*" (Isa. 30:33). Our God is a consuming fire. His Word is "*like fire*" (Jer. 23:29). He can force you to "lose your *psuche*" in Gehenna, after you have suffered isolation in *Hades*. Or you could simply trust that Jesus destroyed it on the cross: "*For if we have been united with him in a death like his, we will surely be united with him in a resurrection like his*" (Rom. 6:5). As we said in chapter 2, Jesus came to help us die so we could live.[4]

Jesus is the "*firstborn of all creation, ...firstborn from the dead* (Col. 1:15,18). He is "*the firstfruits*," (1 Cor. 15:20, 23) and we are "*firstfruits*" (2 Thess. 2:13). There will be more fruits! But the eternal *zoe* is already flowing through us that believe in Love and so constantly give life and receive life, like blood vessels of mercy in the Body of Christ.

---

[4] Obviously, the details of final judgment, the atonement, and the boundary between this age and God's age (eternity), are hard concepts for the human mind to comprehend, but this much is clear: It is the greatest gift to die and rise with Christ NOW. For more on the nature of *Hades*, *Gehenna* and the Eternal Fire, please see the appendix to my last book, *The History of Time and the genesis of you.*

See? Jesus is the Promised Seed, the Holy Seed, whose body was placed in the ground in the garden, immediately after He delivered up His Spirit on the tree. That's the Spirit that falls on the Church at Pentecost, producing more seed. That's the Church that preaches the Word that will not return void! And so, you're reading this book because you think it might be good news and you might tell someone that news. *You* are seed.

When you have faith in Love—the faith *of* Love—and so give your life, you lose your old *psuche* and find your new *psuche*, filled with the Spirit of God. That new *psuche* is part of one *psuche* (Acts 4:32), the *psuche* of the Body of Christ!

Unless a seed dies it remains alone. You must lose your life to find it. It sounds awful, but maybe not. In this age we sow with tears, and we reap later—with joy! But a day is coming when the reaper will overtake the sower. The giving will be receiving, the losing will be finding, the humbling will be the exalting.

It's counter-intuitive.

When Susan and I finally were fruitful and multiplied, it wasn't because she seized control and held on to her life. And it wasn't because I seized control and held on to my life. We lost control and held on to *each other*. We both *lost* our psyches and became *one* psyche, and I sowed seed in the garden of delight.[5]

The Sacrament of Communion
    In the Sanctuary of the Covenant
        Producing the Fruit of Life.
            Work, work, work in the Garden of Delight!

It's counter-intuitive because your intuition is your *psuche*.
You see this world is not the Garden of Delight.
But one day it will be *filled* with delight.

---

[5] The normative Greek word translated "seed" is *sperma*. (Jesus is "the *sperma* of Abraham.") In both Greek and Hebrew, "seed" and "sperm" are one word. The word *sperma*, in some form, appears in the New Testament ninety-seven times. In the Greek version of the Old Testament it appears 269 times (366 total). That's one for every day of the year, even on a leap year. And yet these verses have been so sanitized by translators, that we seem to have forgotten where biblical "fruit" comes from.

THE FRUIT OF THE SACRAMENT

Genesis 1:27–28 *So God created Adam in his own image, in the image of God he created him; male and female he created them. And God blessed them. And God said to them, "Be fruitful and multiply and fill the earth and subdue it..."*

THE EARTH FILLED

How will Adam "fill the earth?"

I have a geology degree. The earth is rock. The rock turns to dust, and the dust turns into dirt. To make great dirt, it takes time, and roots and plants that grow, die and decay. Sometimes it takes fire that reduces everything to ash. And it takes bird poop and worms to make the very best dirt—fertile soil.

When I sold Kirby vacuum cleaners, we advertised that they could get rid of the dirt, but they didn't really get rid of the dirt. They just sucked it into a bag, hid it, and then we moved it around. When we clean up our homes or "clean up our acts," we don't get rid of the dirt. We just suck it up, hide it, and push it around.

As I mentioned earlier, seeds are kept "safe" from dirt in the Global Seed Vault in Norway. It's easy to think dirt destroys the seed (that's what we thought on Good Friday), but it's the Seed that destroys the dirt! It doesn't just hide the dirt or push it around; it takes root, eats the dirt and turns it into a tree. A tree takes dirt, mixes it with light, and produces life, even fruit, which is more seed.

In the middle of the garden there is a tree.

Genesis 2:7–9 *Then the Lord God formed the man of dust from the ground and breathed into his nostrils the breath of life, and the man became a living creature. And the Lord God planted a garden in Eden, in the east, and there he put the man whom he had formed... The tree of life was in the midst of the garden, and the tree of the knowledge of good and evil.*

Both trees are in the middle, so some ancient rabbis thought they were one tree. In the middle of the Garden City, who is the Bride and the New Jerusalem, there is one tree—the tree of life.

The cross is a tree (*'ets* in Hebrew and *xulon* in Greek. Both can be translated "timber," "cross," or "tree"). It's what our next book is all about, but for now just see this: The cross is a tree, and we are made of dirt. God is Light, and Jesus is the Light of the World. A tree mixes dirt with light and makes life—life producing more fruit and more seed, which makes more trees..

- On the tree, we *took* our Lord's life, and on the tree He *gave* His life.
- We *took* knowledge of the Good and killed the Good.
- But there He *gives* the Good, and we are known by the Good—alive and risen from the dead, the *Eschatos* Adam, our Helper.
- The Tree of Knowledge becomes the Tree of Life.
- The fruit of the tree is Body Broken and Blood Shed. The life is in the blood.
- The Body Broken and Blood Shed is placed within your broken heart and transforms your dirt into life—more fruit, more seed, that's sown in more dirt.
- The Seed is placed within the womb of our soul, and we give birth to the Body of Christ (Matt. 12:49).
- We are known by the Good and that knowledge is not death, but Life.
- That's how the Ultimate Adam fills us, and *"fills the earth and subdues it."*

There will be death and destruction, dirt and decay, and fire that burns everything right down to the stump that is the Holy Seed (Isa. 6:13), but Isaiah had already heard the Seraphim sing, *"Holy, holy, holy is the LORD of hosts; the whole earth is filled with his glory."* In Chapter 11, he continues to prophecy saying, *"the earth shall be filled with the knowledge of the Lord as the waters cover the sea"* (v.9).

In Ephesians, Paul writes that we, *"the Church, which is his body,"* are the *"fullness of him who fills all in all"* (1:23). And he prays that we would *"know the love of Christ which surpasses knowledge, that [we] may be filled with all the fullness of God"* (3:19). Then he proclaims that Christ *"descended into the lower parts of the earth"* (4:9) and *"ascended far above the heavens that he might fill all things"* (4:10).

This is a picture of what I call my "life plant." It's a tree that grew from a seed, which was given to me by my grandpa when I was in junior high. I think my wife is sick of it, but I've cared for it for forty-eight years. Several times, I've had to prune it because we didn't have space for all the life. And, several times, I've had to add more dirt to that clay pot in which it's planted because the seed destroys the dirt, by turning it into life.

Well, imagine if that tree bore the fruit of eternal life—I mean, life that never died—eventually, there'd be no dirt and only life: Love, Joy, Peace, Patience, Kindness, Goodness, Gentleness, Faith, Self Control and Delight. This whole earth is an earthen vessel.... And one day the earth will be filled with Delight.

Through Christ, the Ultimate Adam, God our Helper was *"pleased... to reconcile all things to himself... making peace by the blood of his cross* (Col. 1:20)" ... which is a tree.

When I catch a glimpse of My Lord and His wondrous tree, I forget myself, and I begin to worship.

- And that's how a bride gets pregnant; she is an earthen vessel, who surrenders to the seed.
- And that's how we become fruitful and multiply; we are broken dirty ground transformed by seed.
- And that's how the *Eschatos* Adam fills the earth and subdues it; He transforms all things by the power of His Love... even in us, especially in us—and through us, His Body. He fills us and through us fills the earth.

When we expire, that another may inspire, when we forgive as we've been forgiven, when we love even though it hurts like hell, we are His body broken and His blood shed on the tree. That can be terrifying in space and time and yet it transforms all space and time into eternity. It transforms dust into the sexy body of the living God.

Jesus is the Door, and the Door is opened upon the tree, and everything that's anything passes through that Door... And every*where* that's any*where* is on the other side of that door. Even every-*when* that's any-*when* is on the other side of that door.

- On the other side of that Door the perishable has put on the imperishable and the mortal has put on immortality (1 Cor. 15:53).
- On the other side of that Door, all things have been subjected to God, who is Love, through Christ Jesus our Lord, the *Eschatos* Adam (1 Cor. 15:27).
- On the other side of that Door, all things are united under one sacred head now wounded—*anakephalaio*.
- On the other side of that Door, all persons are joined in a sacred dance of mutually indwelling and relentless Love—*perichoresis*.
- On the other side of that Door, you and I are made in God's image and likeness, and filled with his very substance—what the Church Fathers called *theosis*.

- On the other side of the Door we are no longer "*naked and ashamed*," but entirely vulnerable to God, filled with God, covered by God and reconciled to God and all creation—*apokatastasis*.
- On the other side of the Door God is "*all in all*" (1 Cor. 15:28).

Jesus is the Door opened on the tree—the tree of death that becomes the tree of Life. Jesus is the Good hanging on the cross. Jesus is your Bridegroom naked and exposed, broken for the love of you. Do you see that He is Good? The Good you have tried to take is the Good that God has freely given. God is Good. God is Love. Jesus is Love in flesh broken for you. Would you surrender to love?

> Pray: "To you, Jesus my Lord, I confess my empty self. Come fill me with yourself. Cover me with your life. *'It's not good that I am alone.'*"

That's right.

You are the Sexy Body of the Living God.

> "*Sing, O barren one, who did not bear;*
> *break forth into singing and cry aloud,*
> *you who have not been in labor!*
> *For the children of the desolate one will be more*
> *than the children of her who is married,*" says the Lord.
>
> "*Enlarge the place of your tent,*
> *and let the curtains of your habitations be stretched out;*
> *do not hold back; lengthen your cords*
> *and strengthen your stakes.*
> *For you will spread abroad to the right and to the left,*
> *and your offspring will possess the nations*
> *and will people the desolate cities.*
>
> "*Fear not, for you will not be ashamed;*
> *be not confounded, for you will not be disgraced;*
> *for you will forget the shame of your youth,*
> *and the reproach of your widowhood*
> *you will remember no more.*

> *For your Maker is your husband,*
> *the Lord of hosts is his name;*
> *and the Holy One of Israel is your Redeemer,*
> *the God of the whole earth he is called.*
>
> —Isaiah 54:1–5

That's right.

You are the sexy Body of the Living God.

And the fruit of the Sacrament is an entire new creation.

> *Therefore, if anyone is in Christ, he is a new creation; old things*
> *have passed away; behold all things have become new.*
>
> —2 Corinthians 5:17 NKJV

Another Note to the Reader

Humanity is predestined to be (and in eternal reality, already is) the Temple of the living God, His City, His Bride.
Humanity is God's Sexy Body.

But He will not rape us. Instead, He has arranged all things to romance us.
　　He is romancing us,
　　　　through His Word in creation,
　　　　　　and His Word sacrificed on the tree.

He is romancing us, that we would surrender to His intimate and passionate advances, and invite Him to fill His Temple, His Body, His Bride with Himself.

He is romancing us that we might freely and willingly participate in the ecstatic communion that is His very nature.

He is romancing us that He might create within us a good free will—His Will.

We become His Bride in this world of space and time when we surrender to His covenant of Grace, receive His Word of Life, and invite Him to fill us with His Spirit.

We become His Bride, and participate in His work of redemption, by giving birth to His New Creation, in which He is *"all in all."*

We are the Bride of Love, and we give birth to Love by receiving His Word of Love, and bearing His Fruit of Love, which is our true selves, and an entirely new creation—filled with Love.

In this world, giving birth to the Will of God can be very confusing, painful, and messy—like giving birth to a baby or being crucified on a cross—painful, but Good.

Believe Him; receive Him; be known by Him, and you will give birth to Him—the Will of God: Jesus

"Who is my mother, and who are my brothers?" And stretching out his hand toward his disciples, he said, "Here are my mother and my brothers! For whoever does the will of my Father in heaven is my brother and sister and mother"

—Matt. 12:48–50

We will talk about that more in our next book, but for now:

You are the Woman on the cover of this book.

You are the Body of the Man with the wound in His side,

Created at His side, in a garden, as He hangs on a tree.

You are the sexy Body of God,

And He could not love you more than He does.

Peter Hiett

Peter is the pastor of The Sanctuary, a non-denominational church meeting in downtown Denver and Evergreen, Colorado. He is a graduate of the University of Colorado with a degree in Geology and a graduate of Fuller Seminary where he obtained a "Masters of Divinity" degree—as if anyone could master Divinity. The son of a Presbyterian pastor, Peter has been ordained in both the Presbyterian Church USA and the Evangelical Presbyterian Church. He has been married to his high school sweetheart for thirty-three years. They have four wonderful children, whom he really likes almost all the time.

Peter has published three other books prior to *God and His Sexy Body: The Story of Adam and His Bride.*

- *Eternity Now! Encountering the Jesus of Revelation,* (Nashville, TN: Integrity Publishers, 2003)
- *Dance Lessons for Zombies,* (Nashville, TN: Integrity Publishers, 2005)
- *The History of Time and the Genesis of You,* (Denver, CO: Relentless Love Publishing, 2015)

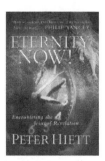  

Peter is also producing short films with DownsideUp productions.

To learn more, visit www.PeterHiett.com.

Made in the USA
San Bernardino, CA
29 July 2016